JUST AROUND THE CORNER

JUST AROUND THE CORNER

YVONNE RUMBOLT-JONES

BREAKWATER
P.O. Box 2188, St. John's, NL Canada A1C 6E6
WWW.BREAKWATERBOOKS.COM

COPYRIGHT	© 2025 Yvonne Rumbolt-Jones
ISBN	978-1-77853-035-7
	a CIP catalogue record for this book is available from Library and Archives Canada

COVER & AUTHOR PHOTOS:	Becken Photography, Labrador
PAINTING BY:	Linda Coles
PAGE LAYOUT:	Nadine Hodder

We acknowledge the support of the Canada Council for the Arts.

We acknowledge the financial support of the Government of Canada through the Department of Heritage and the Government of Newfoundland and Labrador through the Department of Tourism, Culture, Arts and Recreation for our publishing activities.

PRINTED AND BOUND IN CANADA.

Breakwater Books is committed to choosing papers and materials for our books that help to protect our environment. To this end, this book is printed on recycled paper and other sources that are certified by the Forest Stewardship Council®.

Wherever you go, no matter the weather,
bring your own sunshine.

— Diane Poole,
employment counselor

CONTENTS

PROLOGUE

The phone wouldn't stop ringing.

I had spent the night tossing in an ocean of disappointment and betrayal. All I wanted to do was pull the covers over my head and go back to sleep.

It was 1996, and I had just lost my first bid for the provincial Liberal nomination in the district of Cartwright-L'Anse au Clair. I hadn't lost fair and square. I had done everything I could to win, only to see victory snatched away from me, not by a better campaign or a clear decision of the people, but by a dirty trick pulled by backroom boys at Liberal headquarters in St. John's. In one of the strongest Liberal seats in all of Newfoundland and Labrador, I'd gone up against incumbent Danny Dumaresque. But with two strong challengers—myself and Lawrence O'Brien—Dumaresque and his party loyalists decided that desperate times called for desperate measures. A pointed deadline set at headquarters made sure no new face would secure the Liberal nomination in Cartwright-L'Anse au Clair.

Well, who was I anyway? A twenty-seven-year-old woman from Mary's Harbour, Labrador. What made me think I could defeat a seasoned politician like Dumaresque, touted by some as a shoo-in for a Cabinet post in the next government? There was no doubt that Brian Tobin, one of the most charismatic and effective politicians I'd ever met, was going to lead the Liberal Party to victory in the 1996 election. But I would not be part of his team.

I had not entered the race because I thought I was better than anyone else. Quite the contrary; I had always had a battle within myself. I knew there were things I could do to make life better for people, but I couldn't help feeling inadequate. That was, and is, a common struggle for many young women, but maybe I felt it more intensely than most, growing up in a small, isolated community with rigidly defined roles for men and women.

But unlike many women in rural communities across Newfoundland and Labrador, I hadn't grown up in a traditional household. My mother had a job outside the home. Moreover, she never gave up, going from one job to another—an aide at the local clinic, a worker at the fish plant, a clerk at my uncle's small grocery store, and later a cook in the only local hotel. As well, she volunteered with whatever organization needed her efforts and skills, whether it was to support her four kids at school or in the Brownies and Cubs, or to organize events for the community. When elections came around, she was always active there as well, organizing meetings and knocking on doors.

When Bill Rompkey, the Member of Parliament representing Labrador, and later a Senator, came to town, he often visited our home. Politics and service went hand in hand in our house; my mother eventually ran for council and became the mayor of Mary's Harbour, a position I occupied myself many years later. Mom took real joy in the service she gave to people, and I found the same joy in helping people, and in politics.

From under the covers, I could hear that the phone was ringing again, but whether it was a journalist's bold questions or a friend's thoughtful commiseration, I wasn't ready to hear it. It was much more pleasant to imagine what might have been.

As a teenager and later as a college student in Stephenville, I ran for everything going. My mother had taught me the valuable skill of multi-tasking by example. Working, community service, politics, raising a family—she juggled her responsibilities with consummate skill. I came to see that way of life as normal. In high school, I was elected to student council and sat on various non-profit and Indigenous committees. I taught Sunday school at the local church and trailed my mother to many public meetings.

When I went away to study journalism, I was elected to the campus student council, the NL Federation of Students, and served on the Board of Governors for the College. I was on the editorial committee for the school newspaper, served as editor of the yearbook, and found time to volunteer and record shows for the local cable station. All of this was fun; it also taught me a lot about working with others and about listening to what was really important to people.

Right after I finished my Applied Arts Program in Journalism, I got a tremendous opportunity to see politics up close, reporting for community newspapers in Lewisporte, Grand Falls, and at home in Labrador. I was still finding my feet professionally and after my first year, I took a student position at the *Northern Pen* in St. Anthony for a few weeks. Afterwards, I went home to Mary's Harbour to visit my family before heading back to college.

MP Bill Rompkey invited me to travel with him to some of the small fishing communities in his Labrador riding. I suppose he thought it was a good way for me to expand my journalistic horizons and understand what the job of a politician really was. Of course—being young—what really excited me was that we were going to make the tour by helicopter!

Young or not, that trip opened my eyes to the importance of democracy and representation of the people. We went into Cape St. Charles, a very small, vibrant fishing community located at the easternmost point of continental North America. Everyone came out to see their Member of Parliament, and they all had something to give to him, whether it was a basket of berries, salt cod, or some other bounty of the land and sea. There would be a feast, with piles of delicious food laid out on the best tablecloth they could find. I remember thinking this was what you would do if a Christian bishop had come to call.

Rompkey accepted it all graciously. Then he sat down and talked with them about the fishery, which was both their livelihood and their way of life. Even though they lived in a small community far from the rest of the world, they talked to him about current events they had heard about over the radio—things that would impact their lives, even at a distance. He listened, and every issue they raised was written down.

We made stops in many communities, visiting Henley Harbour, Murray's Harbour Square Islands, William's Harbour, and George's Cove, the home of my Grandmother Burden. And we kept on going. At Punch Bowl we met many fishing families from the island of Newfoundland, who resided there over the summer in small cabins, trying to earn a living on the harsh shorelines. They were a match for our Labrador pioneers and many would make Labrador their home.

That trip informed my idea of what politics should be: listening to people's concerns, building relationships with them, and then doing everything in your power to help make their lives better. There was nothing complicated about it.

I returned to Mary's Harbour and took up serving on the community council as mayor—the same position my mother had held before me. This was in the wake of the 1992 cod moratorium, which had opened my eyes to what politics *shouldn't* be. Neither the federal nor the provincial government seemed to understand what was needed, especially in small, rural communities. They offered solutions without first finding out what the problems were. Worst of all, they *told* people what was good for them, rather than *asking* them what they needed and wanted.

At a conference hosted by the Combined Councils of Labrador, an organization which brought together leaders from across Labrador, I found myself sitting at the table with some of the most prominent leaders of the region: Agnes Pike, Garfield Flowers, Ford Rumbolt, John Hickey, Joseph Roberts, Garfield Goudie, and many other strong community advocates.

They started to talk about resettling communities on the south coast of Labrador. My heart and soul belong to this coastline, and it pained me to hear people talk about resettlement. I stood and said it would never happen; we would stand and fight and stop it. At the end of the speech, I started to cry.

I still get teased about that speech and the crying at the end. But, to my amazement, they listened to me—a young woman with a dream. *Sometimes we all need the voice of hope just to get our bearings and keep going.*

Maybe it was my fighting spirit that caught people's attention. When Brian Tobin became Premier of Newfoundland and Labrador, he wanted a fresh start. Clyde Wells had left the job under a cloud—at least as far as the people of Labrador were concerned. The proposed privatization of the electric power corporation, NL Hydro, and the closure of government offices in many communities had led to huge demonstrations. People were angry, too, about the reduction in the marine ferry service. Money that was supposed to have been spent in Labrador had all gone to the island; meanwhile, most of the roads in Labrador—where they existed at all—were little more than gravel paths.

Danny Dumaresque had been part of that Wells government and had defended it, putting him at odds and out of touch with many of his constituents. With an election approaching, I got a call from officials in Tobin's office suggesting I might take a run at the nomination. On the other end of the line were Ed Roberts and Harold Marshall. Both had strong connections to Labrador and distinguished careers in public service; Marshall had even closer ties to the Premier. He was his brother-in-law.

Perhaps they only wanted to give Dumaresque a wake-up call, but the people I talked to seemed sincere and sure that I had a chance at winning the nomination. Certainly, if it hadn't been for those conversations, I would never have taken the leap. Even if I didn't win, I figured I could raise the issues that mattered to people, make our concerns the province's problems, and force the new government to find solutions. But in order to win the nomination, I had to sign up hundreds of new Liberal Party members—people who would be willing to support me against the status quo.

One of my biggest supporters was Agnes Pike. Agnes was a pioneer woman in politics; having her behind me was a great help, not only because she was well known and respected, but because she had already fought all those fights and could advise me on how to handle the inevitable criticism. There were a lot of others, too—Judy Pardy, Ina Jeffries, Phillip Earle, and Kevin Bird among them—who worked hard with me on that first campaign.

I signed up hundreds of members all over the district. Then came the big test: I had to go see Stelman Flynn. Flynn was a businessman in Forteau who had created a lot of small businesses and jobs in his community and was also closely involved with the Labrador Straits Development Corporation. *If Stelman supports you,* they said, *you have a good chance . . . but if he's against you, it's all over.* I went to meet him face to face, buying a plane ticket to fly down on Air Labrador's Twin Otter aircraft and landing on Forteau's snow-covered gravel runway for the meeting.

Flynn asked me tough questions. Most importantly, he wanted to know how I was going to make a difference for the district—how I would be different from Danny Dumaresque.

I answered him as honestly as I could and made it clear that I would put our people before the party. I was ready to put my words into action and fight to make the government do the right thing for our communities. I must have been convincing, because at the end of that meeting, he shook my hand and promised to help.

I had gathered all the new Liberal registrations and submitted them in readiness for the nomination meeting, but party rules said you had to be registered thirty days before the nomination meeting—and the date of that meeting was decided at headquarters in St. John's. It was now out of my control.

Dumaresque had a long history with the party and a lot of friends at headquarters.

The nomination meeting date was set for *twenty-five* days after I had submitted most of those registrations. Every one of them was stricken, so the people were unable to cast their vote in the nomination, as they had not been registered for thirty days. Lawrence O'Brien, the other candidate, was in the same boat.

It now looked like winning was out of reach, but I could still make people's concerns known and hope the powers that be would listen. At the very least, I could show them that no matter what, I wouldn't give up on the important things, on the issues that mattered.

At the nomination meeting, Dumaresque won handily; I finished third.

Now, the phone was ringing for the third time. Whoever wanted to talk to me wasn't going to give up. I pulled myself out of bed and, trying to sound more composed than I felt, picked up the receiver and said hello.

At the other end of the line was Stelman Flynn. Despite his support for my nomination, I had only known him for a few weeks, so I was surprised that he was the persistent caller. He said: *I'm here with Agnes Pike and Sheila Downer and Phillip Earle.* He listed off a few more names of people from communities around the riding.

I realized this was no ordinary call; it was a conference call, and included many of those who had helped in my campaign.

Flynn started by telling me not to feel too down about losing; it was my first time and I'd done everything I could to win. Agnes Pike immediately broke in, and I remember her words clearly: *It was the old boys' club, Yvonne. They always stick together, and they did this to you. It's not you; it's them.*

Those words struck me at the time and stick with me to this day. Things don't always go the way you want. You can't control events or what other people do. *You can only control what you do and what you make of the things that happen, what you learn from them.*

I was still devastated at losing, still mourning that experience. Now people were telling me that I wasn't the only one; that they were angry, and felt betrayed. This was not a sympathy call: they were mad at the system and they wanted to do something about it.

They wanted me to do something about it.

They wanted me to run as an Independent candidate.

It had only been three weeks since I had decided to seek the Liberal nomination. In that time I had visited a lot of communities, mostly by snow machine, and talked to a lot of people. I had raised the issues that mattered to people, from improved transportation, a renewed economy, and better schools, to essential municipal services—some communities had no access to clean drinking water or a decent place to gather. These were the things we needed to sustain our communities and to build a future for our people. In finding my voice, I had given voice to people across the nineteen communities that made up the district.

They didn't want me to shut up now.

You don't have a party, they said. *But you have people, people who are upset at what happened and feel betrayed, but who also feel their voices count and that you are the one to make sure they do. The people of this district want to vote for you, and we will help them do it.*

Independents sometimes ran in Newfoundland elections, but I later learned they seldom won. In fact, it had been more than twenty years since an Independent had been elected to the House of Assembly. Stephen Neary, a former Liberal Cabinet minister, lost the Liberal nomination but ran as an independent Liberal and won in 1975. Before that Tom Burgess had been a sitting MHA who had a falling out with his party; he ran and won as an Independent in 1971. The last Independent to win without having already served in the House was Charles Devine—in 1962.

I had put my heart and soul into the nomination process and I wasn't sure I had the energy or desire to do it again. Could I take another disappointment? Moreover, it cost money to run. Without a party behind me, fundraising would be tough.

I said I needed a day to think about it. Agnes piped up: "If you don't run, I will," she said. She added that Lynn Verge, the Progressive Conservative leader, had called her and asked her to run. Agnes said, "I won't run against you, but if you don't run I will. I won't see the Liberals grab this seat without having to earn it."

It didn't take all day to decide.

Sure, the defeat had been hard and disheartening, but in a way I had already succeeded. I had set out to raise awareness of the issues and needs of the district, and I had done that. People were fired up and they wanted me to keep fighting for them. If I couldn't stand up for them now, when they were asking me, how could I expect them to stand up for me at some future date?

The phone rang a few more times that day. The same people who had called to encourage me to run for the Liberal nomination, like Harold Marshall, were now on the line telling me not to run as an Independent. "You're young," he said. I was told I would have another chance in the next election—or the one after that. I was young and I wanted a future serving the people of coastal Labrador. However, I was being discouraged by the Liberal brass. They told me that running as an Independent in a Liberal stronghold was pointless; I'd be defeated and then I'd be forgotten. There would be no place in the Liberal Party for a failed Independent in the future. I had and still have tremendous respect for Harold Marshall. He was always good to me and the communities across Labrador, and he had given me good advice and direction in the past.

But I was not naive about how politics worked. It is nothing if not a team sport. Candidates win because of the people around them, the relationships they develop with volunteers and voters. Usually that team is based in the party, but I realized it didn't have to be. Maybe my team—the people who had called me first that morning, urging me to run—was strong enough. I decided that on this one, I would follow my own instinct.

The race was on.

Once the decision was made, the enormity of the challenge dawned on me. I was in Mary's Harbour, Labrador—a twenty-seven-year-old woman just starting my career, with no money for a campaign. True to form, my mother stepped in. She organized a bake sale and a community raffle to get me started. My new friend, Stelman Flynn, along with others, set about collecting donations. Now it was up to me to get out and meet even more people, to try and flip what was a Liberal stronghold into the Independent fold.

It was February, and that meant most of my travel from community to community was going to be by snow machine. There were twenty-three communities spread over 28,000 square kilometres; the journeys were frequent, and they were long. Luckily, I had great guides who did the driving while I perched on the seat behind them, bundled up in my warm hat and mitts, a down parka, and insulated snow pants.

Once, after a very long day of knocking on doors in Port Hope Simpson, I had Trent Parr drive me about forty kilometres to Charlottetown over the snow-beaten trails. We left around 10:30 at night. I was exhausted, and about halfway through the heavily wooded trail, which was lit by a full moon, I found myself lying in the middle of the path—I had fallen asleep and tumbled off the back of the snow machine! Fortunately, nothing was hurt—not even my pride. I was filled with determination.

I went town to town, knocking on doors, sitting at kitchen tables, stopping by wood sheds, listening to people tell me about their struggles, things people in other places could hardly understand. One fellow wanted to shingle his roof. If he lived in St. John's or Toronto, he could drive to the hardware store, throw supplies in the back of his truck, and get on with job. If he forgot something, he could go back for it. In Labrador's coastal communities, he had to make sure he ordered everything at once and then wait for it to be shipped to him in the short season when boats could arrive, paying a premium for every scrap. Once the supplies were landed on shore, he had to find a way to cart it all up to his house, often along footpaths. Finding a way to pay for it all up front, with the cod fishery closed and other work scarce, was almost impossible. Everyday living was a struggle; it was unaffordable and stressful for families.

I knew the communities of the Labrador coast were at a turning point. A lot of people had left, and more were just hanging on. I had gone away for my own education but now I was back. I could see that we were only going to survive if we had better transportation, a highway connection, and a more diverse economy. These are the things I said I would fight for. At almost every household, the response was the same: *I'll never live to see it.*

I knew deep down that our communities could not survive without change. We needed the government to step up to provide better transportation—roads, affordable airfares, improved marine services—and to build systems so that people could have safe drinking water and not have to fill buckets from ice holes cut in the river in the dead of winter and haul them home by snowmobile. We needed community centres where people could gather to celebrate their culture and the simple ceremonies of life. I also thought—perhaps a little naively—that I could help *because* I had no party or leader to answer to. My only responsibility would be to the people of my district.

House by house, voter by voter, I got the message across that change was possible. Day after day, mile after mile, I delivered little seeds of optimism, never knowing if they would take root.

When election day arrived, I thought the vote would be close. I thought maybe, *maybe* I could win. If not, at least I had brought focus to the hardships of the district, elevated their concerns; I'd gotten people riled up and interested again. Whoever won, the government would have to listen. They would have to act.

It wasn't close. I took almost fifty-seven per cent of the vote to Danny Dumaresque's forty-two per cent.

I was going to the House of Assembly.

CHAPTER 1

LEARNING FROM DEAD ENDS

I was born in 1968, during the time of resettlement on the south coast of Labrador. It was just a few years after the residents of Battle Harbour, Indian Cove, and other fishing villages had been moved into larger villages. For the first time, the population of Mary's Harbour was over 450 people. It was one of many communities that had been amalgamated by Joey Smallwood's resettlement program. Residents were given $1,000 or $2,000 to make the move, though many retained ties and even second homes in their former village—right up to the present day.

My mother, who had spent her teenage years living in the Grenfell Orphanage in St. Anthony—known today as residential schools as well as orphanages—was not an orphan. However, my grandmother had been very sick from tuberculosis and was hospitalized for nearly four years; after her release she was ill for much of her life. Mom was one of six children and they were dispersed to live with family members or to stay in orphanages. Mom and her brother, Denley, went to the St. Anthony orphanage, and her younger brother, Gordon, went to North West River.

When my parents met at Mary's Harbour in 1967, my mom was working as a serving girl at the local hospital and my father was fishing at Indian Cove with his father, Tom, and his older brothers, Wilfred and Paul. Young boys from the outports would often make their way to Mary's Harbour on Sunday afternoons to court the young nursing aides—the Grenfell Mission serving girls, as they were known locally. Dad could not take his eyes off the blonde-haired, blue-eyed young woman named Barbara Ann, and spent his time chasing after her until she finally said yes to dating him.

And so, at the age of 18, my mother found herself pregnant. She had a natural delivery at St. Anthony hospital, where south coast women were often sent to birth their first child. In those days the Grenfell Mission had tremendous control over families; many of the nurses were imported from Europe or the United States, and an unwed woman having a child was not what they wanted on their watch. My mother was pressured to place me for adoption. She was at a lonely spot in her life, filled with shame for having gotten pregnant out of wedlock. She was not ready for marriage or a child. Her older sister had just given birth out of wedlock and had moved back home to Henley Harbour to live with her parents. They had a nice home for those days, with four bedrooms on the second floor. My mother said she sent a telegram to her parents from St. Anthony asking if she and the baby could come home, as she had no place to go with a child. The telegram came back from my grandfather saying "NO. You made your bed, you have to lie in it," and suggesting she marry my father. At the time, my mother's mother was pregnant herself with her seventh child and their plates were full. Mom was on her own with a big decision to make.

The day we were released from St. Anthony hospital was like a scene from a movie. The nurses wanted Mom to leave me behind for adoption. My mother said she could not let me go; I was her baby girl. My father was adamant she would come home to Mary's

Harbour and they would be married. He was having none of this talk of adoption. So, my mom packed me up and off we went. It was late March when we landed on the harbour ice in a small Beaver aircraft used for transporting medical patients and essentials to communities. Mom said when the plane door opened, Dad was the first guy waiting there. He took me from her arms and said we were going home.

At first my parents and I lived in my paternal grandfather's house, which was perhaps fourteen by twenty-four feet, with two bedrooms. My grandfather was strict and demanding, and I think it was hard on my mother to live there. He was a very competitive man and always had to be first in everything he did. He would be up at 5:30 a.m. in the winter before the sun rose to be the first in the woods cutting firewood. If someone else was up fifteen minutes earlier, then the next day he got up at 5 a.m. His woodpile had to be the biggest and his catch of fish the largest. He was a hard worker and expected those around him to work just as hard. I suppose that drive was passed on to my father and then to me and my sisters and brothers, which may explain why we are all high achievers, ready to work twelve or more hours a day when others settle for eight. A competitive spirit can be a great thing, but it can also be hard to live with if you can't meet those sometimes-impossible standards.

My parents married a month later in April, at the community's Anglican church—the only church—in Mary's Harbour. It was a beautiful day and people attended the wedding from nearby communities by snowmobile and dog team. They held a community supper at the old schoolhouse, and after about four sittings everyone was fed and the dancing began.

Mom, Dad, and I occupied one room in Grandfather's little house. Soon, though, my mother became pregnant with my brother Keith. The living arrangement was becoming more difficult, but without money and after a bad year in the fishery, their options were limited. That fall my father left Mary's Harbour to work on the Upper Churchill Falls hydro project. He was one of many men who made the trip to Happy Valley-Goose Bay. He returned a few months later with enough money to build a small house of our own, where my two brothers and sister were born and where I lived until I went away to college at age seventeen. During those early years we had no electricity; it was available in the community, but we could not afford to have it installed. Dad said we had an electric cord that ran from the neighbour's house to ours to give us light at night.

Mary's Harbour had no roads connecting it to the outside world and there were only a few gravel streets within the community itself. The rest of it only had footpaths between the houses. The marine service, known as the coastal boat, brought in supplies in the summer and fall. In the mid-1980s we got an airstrip, with flights coming in from Goose Bay and St. Anthony, generally three times a week, which was how we got our mail. In the winter, a network of snowmobile trails connected us to nearby communities. Trips by snow machine were cold and rough and could take most of a day. Still, people would make trips for special occasions, such as weddings or funerals or to visit family and friends.

We had a small hospital and a school that offered up to grade eleven for those who wanted a high school certificate. A number of stores sold basic staples— the necessities of life—as well as a few small luxuries. There was a community hall built with free labour, where dances and other celebrations were held, especially around Christmas and Easter. The local Anglican church was the centre of the parish for Southern Labrador.

Most men worked in the fishery or the fish plant in season and repaired nets and boats in the other months, while the women mainly looked after the households. There were exceptions to that rule, of course—my mother being one of them. As a centre for the region, we also had professionals living in town, including nurses, teachers, members of the RCMP, and social workers.

There were tough times when the fishing was bad for a year or two, but generally people kept busy. If one family was having trouble getting by, someone would step up and make sure they had enough to eat. People always found time to be neighbourly, looking in on older folks or just dropping by for a chat and a cup of tea, or sometimes something stronger when the kids were in bed.

Communication with the outside world was limited, but we stayed informed by radio and a single television channel broadcast from St. John's, the CBC. Newspapers would often arrive with the mail and were avidly read. Of course, none of that compared to the communication network within the town. Whenever a boat came in, everyone would flock to the wharf to see what cargo was being unloaded and who was getting off the boat. If it was a stranger, not half an hour would pass before everyone in town knew about them, and questions were asked and answered before the person even had a chance to introduce themselves.

Despite its small size and isolation, Mary's Harbour was a wonderful place to grow up. The population was young and full of energy, with nearly half under the age of twenty. I had no shortage of friends and playmates.

For our family—like many others in town—Mary's Harbour was our winter home, where we lived from mid-September to mid-May. In the summer, we would "shift out," that is, move to our summer residence. For us, that meant going ten kilometres by boat to a small community called Indian Cove located on an island. My father would spend the summer fishing for cod, mackerel, herring, and salmon, which provided most of the family income. The trip was made in a motor boat no more than twenty-five feet in length, with an Acadian motor that ran very slowly and was steered with a tiller stick. My father would be in the back, working the engine and steering the boat. My brother, Keith, a year younger than me, would sit beside him, and from a young age would be given a turn with the tiller. He was always quick to learn things like that and soon became very good at it. Later, he and my youngest brother, Bradley, would learn all the skills necessary to be good fishermen from my father and grandfather.

My mother and Bradley, the baby of the family, would be in a sheltered area in the middle of the boat, while my sister Sherry and I were huddled in what was called "the cuddy," a triangular seating area at the front. We would be dressed in winter parkas Mom had sewn for us, and mitts, because the ocean air was cold. The boat would be loaded down with all the things we would need to stay for three months: beds and blankets, the stove, tables and chairs, and clothes. Each of the kids would have one garbage bag to carry their things, so there wasn't much room for anything but clothes and maybe one or two favourite toys.

The house at Indian Cove was tiny, maybe sixteen by twenty feet, with two bedrooms and no bathroom but a honey bucket for a toilet, and a wash pan. In the early years, we would have to bring a stove with us from Mary's Harbour, but later on when my father had a little extra money, he bought one that stayed there year-round. Heading for Indian Cove was always exciting for us; it was an adventure and a change from routine. As kids, we got to leave school early, and Indian Cove offered plenty of chances for fun. The days before the move were filled with excited chatter about what we would do when we arrived. Although it must have been a lot of work to move house and four children, my parents never seemed to mind. They were as excited as we were for the change, and optimistic about what the summer would bring.

We were a fishing family and, as such, everyone was expected to contribute to the household economy. As kids, we would be given small buckets and sent out to pick berries, which were abundant on the island. We would pick blackberries, red berries (also called partridgeberries), and bakeapples. Sometimes, when my father was fishing, we would all get in the boat and go to another island to pick berries. We would be dropped off in the morning and spend the day at it. Our mother would make us a good lunch of potted meat or jam sandwiches and juice (more often Tang or Kool-Aid). If it was cold, we might have a little fire to have toasted bread and hot tea. Most days it was warm by northern standards, with temperatures of 16° C or so, or even as high as 20° C. When the sun was shining, it was beautiful, with the blue arc of the sky overhead and the light dappling the waves like gemstones. We loved to lie in the berry patch and let the sun cover us like a blanket as we daydreamed and soaked up the scents of the land.

Most years, my father hired a shareman to help with the fishing—either someone local or brought in from Newfoundland—who was paid a wage for his work. He would sleep in a little shack called the bunkhouse but take his meals with the family. My mother, in addition to looking after us kids and preparing meals for us and the shareman, would also take on the work of preparing the fish after they had been caught, gutting and cleaning them, laying them out on the stages to dry, or salting them. When we were older, maybe nine or ten, Keith and I would help with this work. As he got older, my brother Bradley would also join in with the chores.

Other people lived at Indian Cove, most across the harbour on Great Caribou Island. A small tickle of water separated the two sides of the community, so you could only cross when the tides were very low. From the other side, you could walk as far as Battle Harbour Island. It was common to walk from Indian Cove, across Great Caribou Island to Trap Cove and Matthew's Cove, or take a boat to Battle Harbour on Sundays to visit family and friends. On our side of the harbour, my grandfather and grandmother had a place, as well as my father's brother, Paul, who ran a small store that he opened for a couple of hours a day between trips out fishing. It sold a few staples as well as lots of treats, like chocolate bars and chips.

Farther down the footpath was Bradley's general store which sold all kinds of food, like salt beef and salt pork and, on rare occasions, fresh fruit, like apples and oranges. Sometimes my parents would buy puffed wheat cereal and we would have it with skim milk made from powder; this was a big treat for us kids. The store also carried everything necessary for fishing: nets, ropes, rubber boots, oilskins, and so on. The two Bradley brothers—Doug, who ran the store and Paul, who was a fisherman—each had houses in Indian Cove with their families, not far from us. Their kids were older and would watch over us when our parents were busy, to make sure we didn't go down to the shoreline or get hurt.

My Uncle Paul and Aunt Ivy lived nearby, in both Indian Cove and Mary's Harbour, with four of their five sons; the oldest, Stanley, lived with Aunt Ivy's parents in Trap Cove. Our two families did everything together and I didn't think of the five boys as just cousins; they were like brothers, as well. To this day, I am close to all of those boys, but especially to Denley, who was almost my age and was one of my best friends when I was growing up. He was a great singer and I was a terrible one, but we would sing together and he would play guitar or some other instrument he would pick up. He was very talented.

Denley was also adventurous, like me, and we would walk along the shoreline and sail boats made of wood, which we towed over the water with a piece of string. Sometimes he would take me by the hand and we would wade through the water out to the tickle—the channel between the islands—and across to the other side, with my dress floating up around my armpits. It was a hard tickle to get across as a child, but it was proof of character, and I think it taught me a lot about taking chances. Being able to face my fears then is probably the reason why I have such instinctive survival skills today.

All my cousins hold a special place in my heart and in my life. Barry was the eldest cousin in the cove and, at twelve, he was already doing most of the work of a man—on the fishing boat and on shore. He was what we call an "old soul" and had a deep interest in history, both family lore and the history of the Labrador coast. He collected tales and artifacts from the past, and the stories he told both entertained and inspired us.

Todd was a year younger than me, the same age as my brother Keith, and they were the best of friends. They shared an intense curiosity and would take things apart to see how they worked and then put them back together again—which they attempted on my first new bike which I got at age eleven. They were inseparable; I would often see them together, laughing and carrying on, or fishing for eels or sculpins off the wharf. The youngest cousin, Craig, was a quiet, almost delicate child, though when he got older he was as rough and tumble as the rest. He was always a natural leader, but that only came to the forefront as he became a teenager. If there was a problem that needed a solution or a thing that needed fixing, it was Craig who generally came up with an interesting approach.

I consider myself lucky to have grown up surrounded by my brothers and sister and my cousins. They were all strong individuals, making their own place in the world, and I always had the sense that I could do the same. Throughout my life, each of them supported me in their own way, with advice or a kind word, or more substantially.

My mother always tried to make me into a "girly-girl," dressing me in pretty dresses and teaching me manners, only to see me preferring to hang out with the boys and go on adventures. My sister, Sherry, on the other hand, would happily spend time with my mother and the older girls. They would dress her up and go for walks and she was very much a little princess, pretty and gentle. Even now that we are all adults, most of us still think of her as a princess, delicate and sensitive. The irony is that she went on to spend over twenty years in the military, doing tours of service defending our country. When she retired from the Forces she went to work for the Department of National Defence, working in cybersecurity, and has been recognized as one of the top ten women in cybersecurity in Canada. Beneath her princess-like demeanour is one of the strongest, most determined women I have ever met.

My brother Bradley was five years my junior and the youngest of the family. I was very much the big sister to him, always wanting to protect him, and adoring him for being so cute. He used to follow my father or Keith and me like a puppy, wanting to be with us whatever we were doing. He was cautious and would sometimes hang on the edge of things, observing the action. Nothing ever escaped his sight and sometimes that got us in a little trouble if he reported it to our parents. We knew he meant no harm and always forgave him. I suppose those qualities of caution, curiosity, observation, and honesty are what made him such a great RCMP officer. The little boy I used to protect has become my greatest protector, always looking out for me and our family.

Keith and I were as close as a brother and sister could be as kids. We were only a year apart and shared the same rambunctious spirit and love of adventure. As we grew up, we continued to be close, and I could always count on him. When he was fifteen, Keith decided to quit school, which was a huge blow to my parents, especially my mother, who always emphasized the necessity of getting an education. They told him he either had to go back to school or get a job and move out of the house.

Despite my mother's tears and arguments, Keith neither returned to school nor left the house, though he did get a job and did very well. It turns out he had dyslexia and likely suffered from a lack of childhood confidence, but once he was in the working world he showed himself to be brilliant and was successful in everything he did—right up until the day he tragically died.

When I went away to school in St. John's, I had to rely on student loans and what little money I had saved working over the summer. My grandfather gave me $100 and my parents the same, and it was the most money I'd ever held in my hand in my life that was mine. Keith had spent the summer fishing and was collecting Employment Insurance in the winter. Every two weeks when his cheque arrived, he would put twenty dollars in an envelope and mail it to me at school. He did that the entire two years I was at college, even after his first daughter was born when he was only eighteen.

When we were on Indian Cove, once each summer we would go back to Mary's Harbour, which was exciting for us, as we got to visit all the stores. What really sticks in my memory is the smell of the land as we approached the town. Mary's Harbour was a little farther inland and, in our absence, all the shrubs and mosses would have grown up and the wildflowers were blooming, and the smell that came across the water was rich and alive.

However, the big excursion of the year was to the island community of Battle Harbour, which has since been resettled. For a long time, Battle Harbour was considered the unofficial capital of Labrador. The first hospital in the region had been built there by Dr. Wilfred Grenfell in 1892 and operated there until 1930, when a major fire destroyed it and many other buildings in the community. In 1904, the first radio tower on the Labrador coast was built in Battle Harbour, allowing the first transatlantic communication, an important attraction for the many European fishermen who came to the coast every year. It was from this station that American explorer Robert Peary broadcast his claim of having reached the North Pole in 1909.

Battle Harbour was also a key part of my own personal history. My grandmother, an Inuit woman from George's Cove, had been sent there by her family to work as a serving girl for one of the local merchant families at the age of thirteen. This was quite a common practice in those days—large families would send their young daughters or sons to work in other communities. Eventually she met and married my grandfather, and gave birth to my father and his siblings. Our yearly visit to Battle Harbour was like going home for my father; eventually, Battle Harbour became my second home, too, and an important part of my life when I worked to help restore the community and have it designated as the national historic site it is today.

The main purpose of the summer visit was to obtain salt from the three-storey salt house, which supplied the essential to fishers all along the coast. Salt, delivered in fifty-pound bags, was used to cure cod and prepare it for shipment abroad. My father would go two or three times a year to deliver fish and buy salt, sometimes as much a hundred bags at a time. He would take me and my sister and brothers with him on at least one of those trips, and when we pulled into the wharf we would scramble over the side of the boat and run as fast as our little legs could carry us, not only to visit the general store, but to explore the hills and visit the pond. This was where kids from the local communities went to play whenever their parents came to do their fishing business at the old general store that dated back to the late 1700s. Many of those playmates have remained friends my entire life, and we often reminisce about the great times we had at Battle Harbour.

One of my clearest memories of childhood comes from my visits to the general store. When you walked through the door, the first thing you smelled was the aroma of MacIntosh apples, which were kept in big barrels near the door. The heavenly scent permeated the building, mixing with the odour of wood smoke and pipe tobacco.

I still love those smells. For fifty cents, you could buy a whole bag of apples, a rare treat for families living in the isolated communities of the Labrador coast.

When I turned twelve, the pleasures of Indian Cove began to fade, and I wanted to stay in Mary's Harbour and finish the school year like everyone else, spending the summer with my friends who lived there all year. At that time, my mother decided she needed to work year-round to support the family, so I stopped going with my father and brothers and stayed in town, except for a short visit or two through the season.

Having a mother who worked outside the home wasn't that common in the 1970s in rural northern areas. Even as a child, I knew we couldn't get by on one income, not with four children and my father suffering from alcohol addiction due to his own childhood trauma. My father had watched his brother drown as he slipped off sea ice and into the ocean while hunting wild ducks one spring. In those days, bodies were laid out in the home for visitation until the funeral. He often talked about his brother—through heartache and tears—while he was drinking, reliving that dark day. He had also lost his mom to cancer as a young adolescent and pretty much had to fend for himself from then on. My father definitely suffered from post-traumatic stress disorder (PTSD), but in those days we would not have known of such a diagnosis.

Dad didn't drink every day, but when he could get a bottle or two of liquor, or had a batch of homebrew, he would binge drink for the time it lasted. Like everything else in coastal Labrador, alcohol was expensive—if you could find it—so it put a real burden on the household. When I was a little older, I used to look out for my dad when he was drinking, and I later learned he probably depended on that support to continue his binges. When I went away to college he stopped drinking for a few years, but started up again when I came home. Thankfully it was short-lived, and he began what would be a lifetime of sobriety. I wish I'd known what to do about that dependency at the time, but all I knew then was that he needed me to watch out for him.

I was the oldest, so it fell on me to take care of the others. When I was only nine or ten, I would arrive home from school for lunch and discover that neither of my parents was around. My mother was usually working at the nursing clinic and my father could be away fishing or hunting or working at some job or another. Keith would stoke the wood stove in the middle of the kitchen, and I would put together whatever Mom had left for us for lunch, feed the three younger ones, and make sure they got back to school afterward.

It would always be an empty feeling coming home after school when there was no one there. The fire would have burned low, and the house would be cold. Whenever I stopped at a friend's place, it was completely different. Her mother would have been home all day, except for popping out to run an errand or two. The house would be warm and filled with the smell of cooking. Still, we knew the efforts our parents were making, and we all supported each other.

On those days when we came home to a cold house, we'd often sit in the living room on a piece of carpet donated by a carpet company in St. John's. My mom used most of it to make a rug for the child-care centre, and from what was left she had made us a big colourful carpet of many pieces. We had a ten-inch black and white television that we would sometimes turn on, though there wasn't much on of interest to us at that time of day. We would watch it, I guess, out of fascination for the picture and sound, and for company. More often, we would sit and play together with our cousins or friends until one or both of our parents returned. It was hard, but knowing I could cope and look after the others was an important lesson for me at the time.

When my parents came home, they would stoke the fire, my mother would get started on supper, and once it was on she and my father would sit, drink tea, smoke together, and discuss the day, while my job was to get the table set. By then, some shows worth watching were on TV, and we would watch them until the beautiful smells of cooking filled the house and we knew it was time to come to the table.

The food in those days was pretty basic and quite different from what people are used to now. The coastal boat would arrive for the last time in December and drop off all the freight—including food—that had to last us until spring. The only things that would be flown in, at considerable expense, were things like fruits and vegetables that we couldn't keep in long-term storage or things we had used up that we needed to replace.

Mostly we had root vegetables such as turnips, potatoes, onions, and cabbage, things that would last quite a while in a cold room. I don't remember ever having lettuce or tomatoes when I was a little kid, though in later years we did. Things like green peppers, celery, and garlic were completely off the menu. As for fruit, apples were common, and we sometimes got oranges and bananas, too. Fruit mostly came in a can and was a luxury dessert reserved for Sundays. It was a treat, and certainly wasn't available or affordable all the time. It taught me to enjoy the good things of life when they came around and to make do when they didn't.

Fortunately, there was no shortage of berries, whether we picked them at Indian Cove or on the hills around Mary's Harbour, where you could find abundant crops of bakeapples, red berries, and blackberries. If we were lucky, we would find a patch of blueberries that hadn't been eaten by animals or picked by other able hands. We would harvest as much as we could and then dole it out all winter—fresh at first, then frozen or turned into preserves.

Another staple of our diet was potatoes. Mom cooked them in a variety of ways, but the family favourite was to have them fried in a big iron pot with onions. We had potatoes in one form or another at almost every meal to go along with soups or stews, and with fish and game my father had caught, shot, or trapped. If we were lucky it would be moose, which is a lot like venison but not as gamey. More often it would be rabbit or porcupine, eider ducks or geese, white partridge or ptarmigan, or a feed of the seabirds local people called "turrs."

The land wasn't our only supermarket, of course. We were a seagoing people and the water provided not only fish of all sorts—mackerel, herring, cod, capelin, and salmon when they were running—but also lots of seal meat. My mother would often make seal stew with chunks of meat cooked with vegetables. She would mix up a pastry—mostly flour and water with some lard or butter and a little salt, sugar, and baking powder—and spread it across our stew and bake it into a crust, which everyone called the "duff."

Despite being quite isolated and having to depend on our own efforts, we managed to have a fairly varied diet, and to this day, there are dishes made in mother's kitchen that I still think of as my comfort food. Relying on the land and participating in the traditional lifestyle and economy of the Southern Labrador Inuit and settlers gave me an identity and a foundation that continue to support me.

As we became teenagers, the burden of poverty began to weigh on us. We could see that our friends had newer clothes, nicer homes, and better snowmobiles. They could afford to do things that we couldn't. It was hard and it affected my confidence, and no doubt that of my brothers and sister, too. I'm sure it was a factor in Keith leaving school. He wanted to have his own snow machine—it was a dream to him. It forced me to toughen up and work harder to prove myself.

Still, it hurt to be told over and over that your family was dysfunctional—my parents had been through three separations during my childhood—or that my dad was a drunk, that I'd go nowhere and do nothing with my life. There were also many comments about my obesity, as I struggled with my weight. I often turned to humour as a defence against these attacks, something I continue to do to this day whenever I feel nervous or not as confident as I wish to be. *Humour is more than a defence; it forces you to see things in a positive light by turning away negative thoughts and feelings. I feel this is a technique that has guided me in many other uncomfortable stages of my life.*

Hard work fixes a lot of things, and I had my parents' example to guide me. Some years, the fishing was poor, and Dad would take whatever work he could find to support his family. Sometimes it was government make-work projects, such as cutting trails to access wood, or sawing logs for building materials when the community centre, school, or church needed an extension or a facelift. He had to use his own chainsaw and snowmobile, and these would often break down. I remember he would get home at dark from a job in winter, well after six o'clock in the evening, and he would eat, clear the dishes, and put a piece of cardboard on the kitchen table and take apart the motor of the snowmobile or chainsaw. He'd spend hours fixing it and putting it back together so that he could get up in the dark at 6 a.m. to start work again the next morning. If hard work was all it took, we'd have been the richest family around, but pride was always our driver, even as children.

No family should have to experience poverty. It wears you down physically and mentally. Nonetheless, I think my family's poverty— or, more importantly, our constant fight against its limitations— was the main reason we all became successful in our lives. While we may have been poor by some people's standards, we did not go hungry, unclothed, or homeless. I will always remember my father's willingness to work hard and long at whatever was offered him, despite his struggles with alcoholism and childhood trauma—which unfortunately was common among many Indigenous men of his generation, as they suffered from the effects of colonization and stereotyping.

My mom was equally hard-working, keeping a family going while working all day and often volunteering at night. Following her lead, I became very active in the community as I got a little older. Both Brownies and Cubs were offered in Mary's Harbour, and we were encouraged to take part, with Mom often volunteering to help with the activities. As I got older, I took part in a wide range of school-based events, eventually running for and serving on student council.

Of course, life is more than hard work. Like teenagers everywhere, we wanted to have fun and enjoy each other's company. Billy Smith was a local bachelor who, for forty years, ran a pool hall and games centre where we would all flock to have a snack or a soda, play games and hang out together. He was tremendously patient with all of us, providing us a place to go on a frigid winter's night where we could listen to a few songs on the jukebox and hone our pool skills. On weekends we'd meet kids from other communities when their families came in to shop or carry out their business. It was a great place to socialize, laugh, and sometimes cry, and a safe place for that first date where you could get to know one another and see if there was going to be a second date. No number of group homes or youth centres or counselling programs could ever fill the void in our lives and make us feel as safe and secure as we did at Billy Smith's. There was an old wood stove and an oil burner in the middle of the store, and the heat would warm your bones as we cobbled together enough quarters for a shop lunch—chips, candy, and pop. Billy Smith's was the best treatment program of my youth. With little or no education, he kept us in line, yet let us be ourselves.

Over the years, I would always see this photo of a young, beautiful, dark-haired girl in my father's wallet; he carried it with him every day. I would ask who it was, but no one ever answered me. But when I was twelve years old, I actually saw this girl on my aunt's veranda. I couldn't believe my eyes. I was curious, so I went to meet her. It was my aunt who told me the girl was my sister, Nancy, and that she lived with her mom in the Labrador Straits. I remember looking at her—she was fourteen and beautiful. I started to cry and ran home. I sobbed for the longest time and then became angry. Why had no one told us we had a big sister? Why had we never met? There were so many questions, and no answers to satisfy the feelings inside me.

Nancy was tall and kind. She was not shy and wanted to get to know us. Nancy had grown up with her mom, Myra, and her stepfather, Joe Fowler. She had a younger sister and brother at home and enjoyed a full and active life. She had come to Mary's Harbour to meet us—her other sisters and brothers and cousins. It took some time to get past the shock of discovering I had an older sister, but once I did, she became my idol. Over the rest of our teenage years and young adult lives, we got to know one another, and discovered how similar our personalities, humour, and work ethic really were. Now, she is one of my dearest friends as well as my sister. I am so proud of all that she has accomplished, and while we may have had a late start in life knowing each other, today we are very close.

In my last few years of school, I wanted to go farther afield— if forty or fifty kilometres counts as farther—and travel to a neighbouring community for a dance or some other weekend event. That feeling of wanting to branch out was probably inspired by meeting Nancy. The first time I went to Port Hope Simpson for the weekend, I had to throw quite a scene in the living room, crying and dancing around, before my parents relented and let me go. I got a ride with a guy called Irwin Kippenhuck on the back of his 3500 BRP snowmobile. I don't think it had any bottom gear at all, because every time we went over a bump—and there were thousands of them along the trails—we hit the ground with a bang. Bang-bang-bang-bang the whole way for hours; it seemed like the longest trip of my life by snowmobile, but I didn't care because it was my first time going away for a weekend. I stayed with my dad's cousin, Evelyn Kippenhuck, and her family, and it was so exciting. I had such a great time, I wanted to go every weekend. That wasn't possible, of course, but I did have other adventures, though none as memorable as that first one. When I was fifteen, my parents let me go to the Labrador Straits to spend some time with my sister Nancy and her family. That time meant so much to me; it was when we finally bonded as sisters.

As I've mentioned, Mom was always one for volunteering. She would often be out of the house in the evening at an event at the community hall, or at a town council meeting, or working with the Eagle River (later called Battle Harbour) Rural Development Association. While she was willing to let me take care of the house and my siblings at lunch time, she didn't like to leave us alone in the evening, and my father wasn't always available to watch over us. So sometimes, if she knew her meeting wouldn't run too late, she would leave us with our neighbours, Bruce and Linda Rumbolt, the parents of my lifelong friend Elaine, or she would arrange for a sitter to look after us. This went on until I was ten. I suppose it was a more innocent time, or maybe in a close-knit community we all felt safe with each other.

Feeling safe doesn't make you safe, though.

Strongest are those torn apart,
bruised & broken; then they conquer
the world with joy.

— Sandra Pye,
banker and financial adviser

CHAPTER 2

SECRETS WE CARRY

I guess when you write a book about yourself, there are a lot of things that you have to decide whether you will disclose—especially the secrets you carry.

There is something in my life that, even as I am writing this, I have never talked to anyone about. Except for myself—I've talked endlessly to myself about it. But to no one else—not my mother, not my husband, not my doctor, not to clergy or Elders. My brothers and sister knew it happened, but we never discussed it.

Now I'm going to tell you.

Beginning when I was six and continuing until I was ten, I was sexually abused. It was done in my own house, in my own bed, by two different boys who had been trusted on occasion to be my babysitter. I wasn't old enough to know at first that what they did was wrong, but I was old enough to know it felt wrong. I was ashamed and, perhaps, thought I was somehow to blame. I didn't tell anyone about it. For years I carried that trauma with me, and even after I dealt with it in my own way, I never told my mother.

These searing pains do not mar my memory of a mostly happy childhood. I worked hard to put them aside—compartmentalizing, we call it now. At the time, it seemed the only option for me.

My parents were young then; they liked to go out to community dances, darts, and card games, and to house parties with friends, where my mother could socialize, and my father could find buddies to drink with. They would hire babysitters to watch over us four young children; at six, I was the eldest. Most times it was one of these two boys who were eight or ten years older than me.

It was a small community with fewer than 500 people, and I am guessing no one thought such things could happen. If they did think it, they didn't speak of it. And if they did speak about it, there was never any action taken that I recall. I was only six, and feeling confused, hurt, and without understanding, only shame.

As an adult, it's hard to remember what happened when you were six, but I remember. It has played out over and over in my head my entire life. I can still see it, *as if I had floated away from my body*; feel it, *the cringing, the stopping of my heart and breath*; hear it, *the quiet footsteps, the ruffling of the bedclothes*; smell it, *tobacco, stale breath, sweat.*

My bedroom was just off the kitchen, and I was asleep. My brother Keith was sleeping in the same bed; he would always sleep near the wall, while I would be on the outside. It was cold; the only heat came from the kitchen stove and it was banked down for the night. The boy crept into my room and rolled the covers down and pulled off my pyjama bottoms. He began to touch me.

I didn't know what was happening, but I was scared and I knew it was wrong. And if it was wrong, it must somehow be my fault. But what did I do?

The boy pressed himself against me. His own pants were down, and he rubbed against me until something hot and sticky spilled on me. I was so terrified; it felt as if I were dying. I could not breathe, I was so scared. I actually thought I would die.

I know now that he was using me to masturbate, that he was rubbing against my child's body with his penis, but at six, I had no idea. All I knew is that it made me feel dirty, ashamed, and frightened, and I would pee the bed.

The next day, my parents asked me how I could have done that. I hadn't wet the bed in many years, since I was a tiny girl, but I couldn't tell them what really happened. I don't know why, but I couldn't. I said it had been too cold to get up. It was a reasonable excuse. Sometimes it got so cold in my room, frost would form, and the blankets would freeze to the outside wall along the baseboards.

It may have seemed reasonable to me, but it didn't stop my parents from yelling at me and, when it happened again, from spanking me. I took the beating because I was too frightened and ashamed to tell the truth. Fear and guilt are a powerful combination.

It did happen again. And again. And again. One boy or the other, when called on to babysit, would be there in the kitchen, waiting. I was in my bed, sometimes asleep, but—after the first time— mostly with my eyes wide open. I would stay in bed; I wouldn't get up and walk through the kitchen to go to the honey pot in the other bedroom. I thought if they didn't see me, they would forget about me, forget I was in the room and stay away. But no—soon I would feel the covers being turned back and my pyjamas being pulled down or my nightie rolled up and they would be rubbing themselves against me. And I would pee the bed from the fear.

I took to sleeping with my head under the covers. It somehow made me feel a little safer to be in the dark with the blankets over my face. To this day, I still sleep with the covers over my head, and when my husband asks me why, I just say I like it that way; but really it gives me a sense of comfort, like a protective barrier from the childhood abuse.

As time went by, the boys became bolder. They would take me out of my bed to the kitchen and make me watch while they rubbed themselves until they ejaculated. I learned to remove myself from the moment. I've since learned, by reading about childhood abuse, that reactions like mine are not uncommon.

There was never any penetration, but whether they took that final step doesn't matter. For five years, I was sexually violated on a regular basis by two boys in my town. For five years, I peed the bed and took a pounding from my parents when I couldn't stop doing it and couldn't explain. My mother took me to nurses about my bedwetting, and they determined I was too lazy to get up in the night—so untrue, and so unfair. When I was ten, the abuse stopped. Those guys were no longer around my house, as I was old enough not to need a babysitter anymore. In fact, that was when I became one myself for my younger siblings. A short while after, the bedwetting stopped, and my menstrual period started.

By then, the damage was done. From the day the abuse started, it changed my life. We didn't have much—our house was small and basic. There was no bathtub, just an aluminum tub for bathing and washing which only got pulled out on Saturdays. The water was heated by an electric donut you inserted in the tub of water. So, on many days I went to school smelling of urine. Other kids called me "pee girl" or "piss-ass." That was a very difficult time for me.

I had already had to take the nasty remarks about my father being an alcoholic. I was from a "drunk family"—but this new bullying was an extra level of hell. It was a small community, and I saw my abusers almost every day and suffered my humiliation in front of their uncaring eyes.

Perhaps learning to be absent during their nighttime intrusions helped me put them to one side during the day. Certainly by the time I was a teenager, I could put what they had done to me for all those years in a separate place where I didn't have to think about it or talk about it.

Not that it really helped. I remained the target of bullying for several years after. It only stopped when I learned to use humour. If I could tell someone a joke or make them laugh somehow, I could gain acceptance. I could think, for a moment, that they liked me, that I fit in.

For years, my life was driven by this desire for acceptance and the need to be liked. I joined every club, threw myself into every activity, volunteered to help others, to solve their problems. Even when I couldn't solve my own.

By the time I was fifteen, I continued gaining weight and was a plump teenager. No one else in my family, other than Mom—not my dad, my brothers, or my sisters—ever struggled with their weight, but I did. My reading tells me that it's a common response to childhood abuse. Some victims become anorexic; others, obese.

Whatever the cause of my overeating, for me, it was always because of what had been done to me. I could never—even when I was an adult and knew better—shed the feeling that I was somehow to blame for the abuse, that some flaw in my character had drawn them to me. The little girl who lives in my head is always willing to tell me: *You're not good enough.* She still pulls at me sometimes in a way that causes me to almost want to crumble because I need to hold her and tell her constantly that things are going to be okay. I know some of you will think that this analogy is crazy, but it isn't if you are the victim of child sexual abuse. If you are, you'll understand exactly why I use those words in telling my story.

For me, this is a little girl who's been hurt, who has struggled in pain, constantly needing reassurance. She needs to know that things will be okay, that life will be okay. I have carried her with me all of my life. She has been a big part of my journey. As I reassured her and told her things were going to be fine, I could accomplish more myself, because she was safe. I was reinforcing that message to me, the adult. Until now I was never ready to open myself up in this way, because doing so means I have a lot more work to do to look after that little girl inside me. My most difficult job in life has been taking care of her so that she didn't break, so that she could handle the suffering that she had endured without fear of judgment.

Victims of child sexual abuse often blame themselves, so they don't always just feel that they've been victimized by someone else or harmed at the hands of another; they feel they were a contributing factor. What would my contributing factor ever be from the age of six until ten? You're an innocent child; you are nothing but a victim, a victim without understanding. *Child sexual abuse is without comprehension. All you know is fear from that victimization; you know pain and hurt, you know that you're different, that something has transpired that has changed you forever.*

I look at my actions as a child growing up, and it wasn't just burying my head under the covers to look for safety and security; I was constantly seeking attention and love from my family—a family who loves me dearly and who could probably never have loved me more than they did. Their hearts were full of love for me and all my siblings, yet it seemed like I was always in need of love and acceptance. I got upset over not always getting my own way; I felt heartbreak over little things, little things that made no sense.

As a child I would run away and hide behind a big rock next to our house—which is not really a big rock anymore, but back then it was like a mountain to me. It was a mountain I could snuggle into, snuggle down into the soft moss that covered the hard rocks. I would hide there and wait for someone to come and look for me, hoping they would come soon because I wanted to go home. Even though I may have only been there thirty minutes, it seemed like three hours, because that is how things are as a child. I took a lot of solace in the crevice of those rocks in that little mossy spot.

Often I would sob my eyes out over something that I thought was huge—maybe Keith had stolen my toy and picked it apart, or painted his wooden boat with my first and only bottle of nail polish. Believe me, when you're seven years old, things that are very small seem very huge. I still remember the solace of that big rock. As time went on, it took longer and longer for my family to come and look for me, because they all knew where I was. They knew exactly where I would go because they knew I needed to cry it out. And I would go there and cry it out. When I was done, I knew someone would come get me, or I would get tired waiting and just go back home and be fine.

I believe that craving for attention and acceptance was a result of the child sexual abuse I had endured, because you feel a sense of loss and loneliness that is very difficult to explain at that age. Even at the age I am today it's difficult to explain, although my comprehension of it is very different.

I've had many years to reconcile within myself what all of that has meant for me, but the healing journey is forever. I understand that now. What pains me most is that I know there are kids out there who are still suffering through sexual abuse, and I hope and pray that they can escape it. I hope that in telling my story it will help them deal with the trauma of victimization.

I hope that kids today are more educated, more open. I hope parents talk to their children more freely and tell them to disclose activity that is inappropriate. Parents need to build an open relationship with their children around sexual touching and explain what's appropriate and what isn't. That's the only way they're going to know.

We teach our kids so many things. I grew up learning all kinds of great card games, how to skate over the harbour ice by pushing a five-gallon salt beef bucket, how to ski on strips of plastic taped or tied to our feet. I was taught how to chop wood and hunt for rabbits, how to cook, clean dishes, sew and knit. I was taught all of these things at a very young age: to speak, to be quiet, to listen, so I would have appreciated learning as a kid to identify signs of inappropriate behaviour and being taught to tell others when you felt something was wrong. Look for fear in your children and talk to them. I was too scared to disclose the information, afraid of repercussions. I have no idea what those repercussions would've been, but in my childish mind I was convinced I could never breathe a word of what was happening to me. Kids today should not have that fear.

We live in an open society of acceptance, and it's never too early to teach your children about what's right and wrong—even on difficult subjects like this one. To all those girls and boys who are victims of sexual abuse, talk to the little person inside you, help them through this, and be strong for them. That's most important.

In confronting my abuse and learning to understand its impact, I inspired that little girl inside of me to be strong, self-confident, and successful. My friend Sandra Pye sent me this quote many years ago: "You are worthy, and you are loved." I needed to hear that, and I remind myself of it on many occasions.

Will the impact of child sexual abuse always be with you? For me it has been fifty years, so yes, I believe so. I don't think I will ever wake up a day in my life and not feel some sense of insecurity. However, I have continued to keep myself strong through positive thinking and living, by focusing on success. Being strong is not about physical strength; it's about mental willpower.

When I first went into politics, I desperately wanted to serve. I wanted to fix everyone's problems. More often than not I succeeded, but when I didn't, I never thought it was because the problem was too big for a single MHA to solve or that others with more power had stopped me. I knew the truth. *You're not good enough.*

I suppose you could say it drove me to greater heights and to bigger efforts. Certainly in my eternal need to prove that little girl wrong, I threw myself into my work until it became everything to me. But at what cost? Lost relationships and missed opportunities with the ones I loved. Abuse is the gift that keeps giving.

When one of the men who assaulted me was sent to prison for molesting other children, the guilt hit me like a tidal wave. What if I had spoken out? Would those children have been spared? Every time I see that man—and, yes, he is back living in the area—I can't help but think I could have stopped him. Even though I know that my ten-year-old self could not have done it, I still wish I had or, at the very least, had tried.

It has taken a long time, but I have gotten better, though remembering this still hurts. As I wrote these words, I constantly had to stop to wipe the tears flowing down my face. *This was the challenge of my life: to feel worthy always. Today I know I am more than good enough; I am an incredible person and I love myself.*

I had not told this story to my loving husband, Joseph, who has supported me and loved me unconditionally through some of my greatest trials. Was I afraid he would stop loving me? I know, of course, that he would not; he admires my strength.

By the time you read this, I will have told him. He will have taken me in his arms and told me I am more than good enough, and we will have cried together. And yes, at some point, I will make him laugh as he makes me laugh, makes me feel safe.

Telling my mother will be harder. Even though she has shared with me her own stories of sexual abuse, I have never had the courage to tell her of mine. I know she won't blame me, but I am terrified she will blame herself, though she was no more to blame than I was. Still, it is a conversation I must have, and no matter what else she says, she will tell me—as she has told me all my life—that I am good enough, that I am loved, that I am her little princess, and that she is proud of me.

Healing is hard, but it can be done. By fighting for what I believe in, while also learning there are some battles you can never win, I have gotten stronger. By helping others I've realized that sometimes help is beyond my power; I have grown wiser. By pursuing my Inuit heritage and my connection to the land, I have become more complete.

Telling my story now may be another step in my healing process. But more importantly, it may help protect other girls and boys from experiencing what I did, keep them from carrying the hurt for their whole lives and from having to think: "I'm not good enough."

There is an expression that whatever doesn't break you makes you stronger, but I often wonder why we must suffer so much to be strong.

People also say one step at a time, so when one of my abusers tried to friend me on Facebook—imagine the nerve!—I blocked him so hard and fast, I may have fried his computer. *Some things are not only unspeakable, they are also unforgiveable.*

But I'm truly not a vengeful person. Recently, I was walking down the wharf in Mary's Harbour and there was the man who had abused me, and who had gone to prison for child sexual assault against other children, standing on the edge of the pier. I've never wanted anything more in my life than to push him into the water, to make him feel what it was like to stop breathing from fear. Instead, I looked straight ahead, relegating him to the small, cramped box I've set aside for the unpleasant things in my life, and got on the boat and left him behind.

It almost—almost—felt as good as pushing him into the ocean.

CHAPTER 3

GAINING RESILIENCE

College gave me many of the tools I needed for my career in politics. First and foremost, it was my first experience living in a "big town." While 7,500 people—Stephenville's population in 1986—might not seem like much compared to other Canadian communities, coming from Mary's Harbour it was like moving to another world. While I'd made a few small excursions outside my home community to visit relatives and had taken a few school trips to Goose Bay, living in Stephenville and later in the city of St. John's, was an entirely new experience.

Fortunately, there were other students there from Labrador, and I was soon involved in the Newfoundland and Labrador Federation of Students, which gave me a steady connection to home. My habit of volunteering for whatever could make a positive contribution to people's lives served me well, and I was soon involved in a number of organizations and projects, mostly centring around student government and communications—not surprising since I was studying journalism.

Journalism was a natural fit for me. I've always loved telling stories and getting to know the people behind the stories. As soon as I graduated, I took a job with the *Lewisporte Pilot* in central Newfoundland. It was a summer position only, but in any case I wanted to get back to Labrador. Robinson Blackmore, who owned the *Pilot*, had just bought *The Labradorian* weekly newspaper from the Kelland family, and they offered me a job. That August of 1988, I took the ferry from Lewisporte to Goose Bay to start my new job back in Labrador.

I had booked a bunk on board the *Sir Robert Bond* and wound up sharing a stateroom with another woman, Jane McGillivray. She was a doctor, heading to take up her position in Happy Valley-Goose Bay, and I got to know her a little during the trip. Through her subsequent career, she made a great contribution to Labrador and continues to make her home in North West River, where she has earned great respect from the Indigenous people who live in the area. I am always proud to say that I met her as she was embarking on her remarkable vocation. I could understand her excitement and energy, as I felt the same.

I spent a year working for *The Labradorian*, enjoying the work and the opportunity it gave me to get to know another part of Labrador. My sister Nancy was living in Goose Bay as well, working on the military base, and we got to spend time together, getting to know each other at this new phase in our lives.

I was young and eager for a more exciting life. When a job came up with the *Evening Telegram*, a daily provincial paper out of St. John's, I applied and was soon making my way to the big city. I'm not sure if I worked more or partied more in the following year, but I certainly had a lot more fun than when I was going to college, all while earning a few dollars. I must have impressed the bosses, because they asked me to become a staffer at the new *Gander Free Press* for three months, to get the paper up and running. They then hired an editor out of Nova Scotia; she was already there when I arrived.

The *Gander Free Press* only lasted a short time. Before I knew it, I was heading back home to Labrador, and while I had no idea where I would go from there, I did know Labrador was where I wanted to be.

At 21, I was going home to live with my parents after five years away. It was a bitter pill to swallow, but I took my medicine and headed back to Mary's Harbour. Like every downturn in life, it was followed by an upturn: it was then that I met my future husband. In fact, I had known Jim Jones all my life—he was fourteen years older than me. That had seemed like a huge difference when I was a teenager, but now that I had been out in the world and was an adult, it didn't seem like so much. We soon began dating, and enjoyed spending time together. .

Not long after, I got a job with Memorial University as a researcher at the Labrador Institute in Happy Valley-Goose Bay. I moved in November and Jim followed, and we rented an apartment from the Feldsbergs, a lovely immigrant couple from Germany who had a welding and machine shop in the same yard. It was a busy place and we enjoyed it, and we lived there through the winter before returning to Mary's Harbour in the spring. Jim's mother, a widow, was living alone in a trailer, and it had been a hard winter for her with him away. Fortunately, the university transferred me to start a research project on the history of Battle Harbour. I had come full circle and was moving back home.

Much of my work consisted of interviewing people and recording their oral histories of places and people, as well as reading diaries that had been kept by families. I also had to track down the journals kept by pioneers like Dr. Wilfred Grenfell and the many explorers who had passed through the town over the years. These were gathered from libraries all over North America, and as I read them, I became truly aware of how important Battle Harbour had been in the history of Newfoundland and Labrador.

Jim was a great help to me in this work, as he had deep roots in the community: his mother had been born there. His father had come from Heart's Content to work in the general store, and they had married and had purchased and lived in the restored parsonage to the Anglican church. Jim's maternal grandparents had also grown up there, so he had stories passed down from his parents, grandparents, and great-grandparents, which gave us both tremendous insights into the early life of people in the community. Sometimes it seemed he was doing as much work on the project as I was. In any case, we both became deeply immersed in the community and involved in the restoration project that was getting underway.

When Jim and I decided to get married, I was determined to do it in the old Anglican church at Battle Harbour that had fallen into disrepair. Jim and I, with the help of the local development association and others, worked on getting government funding to pay for the restoration of the church and other buildings in the town. Gordon Slade, who was head of the Atlantic Canada Opportunities Agency (ACOA), took a risk on investing ACOA dollars in Battle Harbour—a risk that paid off. After he retired from the federal public service, he took over as the head of the Battle Harbour Historic Trust, and I enjoyed working with him for many years. He had the drive to turn the old resettled community into one of the most important historic sites in Newfoundland and Labrador, if not in all of Canada—a monument to the Labrador coastal fishery.

When Jim and I took our vows in the restored church, it was the first wedding there in over twenty-seven years—the last being that of my father's cousin, Harvey Rumbolt, and Doretha Pye. So it was a symbol of optimism for our future together and for the community. Over the years, many others have used the church to celebrate marriages, baptize their children, or mourn the loss of a loved one at a funeral. It was so good to see the rebirth of a place that had largely been abandoned during resettlement, with the exception of the presence of local seasonal fishing families.

It was through my marriage to Jim that my love for Battle Harbour really grew, and the pleasant memories of my childhood became an integral part of my existence as we worked hard to secure funding, establish the Battle Harbour Historic Trust, and restore one beautiful building after another over the next decade. In 1992, we took over the operations of the general store until it was ready to be turned over to the Trust. Removing ourselves from the work of the Trust to become contractors, we wanted to continue to have a connection to the site and see it succeed. It was a fascinating, but not a particularly profitable, experience. Working alongside Gordon Slade and the manager at the time, Tom Paddon of North West River, and others in the community, we didn't worry about the investment we were making—we were living the dream.

In 1992, however, some dreams turned into nightmares.

Cod stocks in the North Atlantic had been failing for a number of years. In 1987, the Newfoundland Inshore Fisheries Association commissioned a study of the Department of Fisheries and Oceans' estimates of the remaining cod stock, which found their numbers were twice what they should be. It took a lawsuit to get DFO to do an internal review. In 1990, scientists recommended quotas be cut by fifty per cent, but the Minister of Fisheries, John Crosbie, didn't listen. Two years later, on July 2, 1992, just before the summer fishery was about to start, a moratorium on cod fishing was declared. "Two years," the minister said, "for the cod stocks to recover." I still remember the images of angry fishers trying to break down the doors to the press conference at a St. John's hotel while nervous aides hustled John Crosbie down the back stairs.

The history of our province is very much the history of fishing. Long before Europeans arrived, Indigenous people who had lived in the area since time immemorial harvested rich bounties of fish and marine mammals from rivers and coastal waters. Many of the settlements that dot the coast of Newfoundland and Labrador began as temporary stations where fish could be dried and salted. Temporary soon became permanent, and for generation upon generation, people relied on the riches of the sea to sustain them and their communities, including my own hometown of Mary's Harbour and the whole Labrador coastline.

Of all the species that lived in our offshore waters, none was more important than cod. "King Cod" it was sometimes called, and, no doubt, the cod harvest formed the backbone of the entire industry. The cod stocks had always gone up and down, delivering good years and bad to local fishers. Still, even a bad year produced enough to keep a family fed and sheltered in the hopes that next year would be better—and it often was.

Many of the people along the Labrador coast worked the "inshore" fishery, going out in small boats—most of them thirty-five feet long or less—into the shallow waters of the continental shelf, fishing with nets and lines. They would return the same day to unload their catch for processing at local plants, to be sold to local merchants for processing, or else they'd clean and salt them on their own stages. As in many small, isolated communities elsewhere in Canada, many people living along the coast in Newfoundland and Labrador relied on a single industry for the majority of jobs and business opportunities. If there were no jobs in fishing, where would jobs be found? Ultimately, they could only be found in the resilience and ingenuity of the people.

Imagine, for a moment, the situation many people found themselves in. Most had left high school without graduating, often at the age of sixteen or younger, to go to work on boats often owned by their fathers or uncles, or in the fish plants. In a good year, a fisher could make a solid living, enough to settle down, get married, build a house, and raise a family. In a bad year, they could at least hang on to what they had, relying on government EI, temporary work projects, or the help of family.

The work was hard. When you weren't hauling fish out of the sea, you were repairing boats or mending gear, getting ready for the next season. It was also rewarding, and it gave people a purpose. They were not only feeding their families, they were feeding the world. The fishery also gave people a sense of place and history. Their fathers and mothers and grandparents and great-grandparents had done the same work, shared the same burdens, survived and thrived in the same harsh environment, and built communities based on shared experience and culture. Even the stories they told and the music they made were rooted in the fishing experience. It wasn't just a job; it was a way of life and of living.

People did everything they could to keep their communities strong and viable during the difficult years that followed the cod moratorium, and I did everything I could to help them. One advantage we had was the strong presence in our district of the Labrador Fishermen's Union Shrimp Company Ltd. and the Labrador Community College, which eventually became College of the North Atlantic. Their approach to training was significantly different and much more suited to the needs of small communities.

It was thinking about serving community that led to the creation of the Labrador Fishermen's Union Shrimp Company (LFUSC), headquartered in L'Anse au Loup. Throughout the difficult decades that followed, LFUSC was always ready to seize an opportunity to expand the fishery (as they had with the opening of the crab processing plant in 1987) or to reinvest in the fleet or fish plants along the Labrador coast, whenever finances and feasibility allowed. Founded in 1978 to take advantage of two shrimp licences reserved for Labrador, "the mandate of the Company was to provide one share to each fish harvester and to reinvest all profits back into Company operations, for the creation and development of sustainable employment for coastal communities." To this day, the company continues to build a place for Labrador fishers in the global market for seafood. It has become a model for the world of how a corporate social enterprise can sustain people.

At this time, I had finished the contract with Memorial University and was working as an employment counsellor and community outreach worker for the Canada Employment Centre. My job as an employment counsellor was directly focused on the cod moratorium after the closure of 1992. Those were tumultuous times in small rural communities all around Newfoundland and Labrador, as so many people had been displaced from their livelihood in the fishing industry.

Because of this work, the business was a nights and weekends job for me, but it was Jim's full-time occupation. Jim was operating a small longliner when we met, moving freight around the south coast of Labrador between isolated communities, mostly for fish processing companies. After we married, we saw an opportunity to expand the business into freight transport between Newfoundland's Northern Peninsula and Labrador, and purchased an eighty-five-foot freight vessel. We ran the freight business along with the general store, and between the two we were kept pretty busy. We were also able to create a few jobs for my old high-school friends, and for new friends who loved the place we had made in Battle Harbour. It was a great feeling to be able to provide people with a needed service and to help boost the economy at the same time, and we had a lot of fun doing it.

By the late 1990s, with the Trans-Labrador Highway finally built, people were less reliant on marine freight, and, at the same time, tourism was growing in the area, so shifting to tour boat operations seemed like a good idea. We swapped out the freighter and settled on an old Coast Guard boat, the *Garia Bay*, which we refitted at far too great an expense. It was worth it in the end, though, because it was transformd into a beautiful tour boat that we operated for several years. Even after our marriage ended, Jim continued to offer tours for a number of years, and he still lives in the old restored Anglican rectory, which is beautiful and stands tall in Battle Harbour overlooking the Atlantic.

Although I was in business with Jim and then on my own for more than a decade, it was never much of a money-making experience for me, which doesn't bother me in the least. My goal has always been to improve the lives of the people of Labrador, to support the communities they live in, and to build an economy to sustain them. Truth be told, when all was said and done, our losses were well over $500,000—most of it through our business in Battle Harbour—which was in my name, though we both helped pay off the debt. It may seem like a lot to lose doing something that was driven by passion rather than hard, cold economics, but when I go back to Battle Harbour and see what has been accomplished with Gordon Slade, local families, my ex-husband, and many others who contributed over the years, I'm satisfied. We preserved a great part of Labrador history. I am good with that and wouldn't change a thing. After all, if you amortize it over ten years, it only took me $50,000 a year to see a beautiful dream become reality. I never regretted a cent of it.

I was always one for coming up with big ideas and then plunging ahead to put them into action. I had a good job with decent pay, but these businesses were a side calling, something I wanted to do because I could, and because it would make a difference. Later, when the hotel in Mary's Harbour was about to close, I bought it, not because it was my lifelong dream to own or run a hotel, but because a hotel was essential to the community. The hotel was the only place to stay in town and had the only real restaurant. You couldn't expect people to come to Mary's Harbour in summer, to take excursions to Battle Harbour and the area, if they had no place to stay and nowhere to get a decent meal.

In 2001, I paid about $420,000 for the hotel and called it The River Lodge, because it was on the bank of the beautiful St. Mary's River, overlooking the slow running water and framed by tall spruce and birch trees. It was successful for a number of years. The hotel paid for itself and kept a number of people employed, but whatever profits it generated were plowed right back into the business, because it takes work and money to keep an old place like that up to snuff. Jim was not onside with the purchase and made it known up front I was on my own. He was getting a little tired by now of me being away from home; politics was demanding, and he felt that purchasing the hotel would just bog me down with more work. In the end, it proved more work than I could handle, given my increasing political responsibilities after the 2003 election, so I sold it to my brother for what was still owing on the mortgage, about $125,000. I knew if Keith didn't take it on, nobody else was likely to do so. I knew he would maintain it and keep it going for the good of the community.

I was following my passion, and what could be better in life than that? I may not have gained financially, but the experiences I had taught me a lot about life and a lot about myself, about the kind of person I was and where I wanted to be. *Making a contribution was what drove me and continues to motivate me to this very day.*

The time that Jim and I worked together, building up our businesses and restoring Battle Harbour, was a good time. In the early years, I was working as an outreach worker and employment counsellor in a number of communities. I was also on the municipal council in Mary's Harbour and eventually became mayor. I was one of few women on council during most of those years. The council saw leadership in me, and hope; they wanted me to run for mayor and so I did.

I was not surprised by the joy I got from being mayor, since my mother had inspired those ambitions in me at a young age. It is important to give back to community, in any capacity. I felt I had good leadership skills, I was willing to put the time in, and I knew there were good people around me ready to offer support. I was never shy about speaking publicly, and I was willing to advocate for better services and infrastructure for our community. I felt it to be my duty; after all, as a resident, I would benefit from any success, just as all other residents of the town would. And, as I would discover, it wasn't much of a leap from municipal politics to provincial politics.

Going into business with Jim certainly put a lot on my plate, but we were happy doing that work and had a few good years together. I remember how we supported and encouraged each other, but, as with many marriages, things eventually did start to fall apart. My entry into provincial politics in 1996 wasn't met with great fanfare from my husband. He supported me in my decision but wasn't always active in the campaign or in my subsequent political life. It meant a lot of changes in our lives, as I would now be away from home a lot more, in St. John's or visiting the many communities that made up the district.

Jim mostly stayed behind in Mary's Harbour or Battle Harbour, continuing to tend to our tour boat business, which took him to a number of communities along the Labrador coast, so we spent less and less time together. Politics often causes stress in relationships. You have to be very diligent to serve the demands of political life while also meeting the expectations and needs of relationships.

The biggest change that occurred in 1996 was that I got pregnant. We were so excited.

*I believe we must never lose hope when
facing life challenges. We must continue to
believe and be persistent in that belief!*

— Judy Pardy,
advocate for seniors

CHAPTER 4

PROUD TO REPRESENT THE PEOPLE

My provincial election campaign had been exhilarating, exhausting, enlightening, and rewarding. My district of Cartwright-L'Anse au Clair had nineteen communities, some only accessible in winter by small plane or snowmobile, stretched over more than 26,000 square kilometres. While I thought I knew the area well, I'd had an intense introduction to its many people and an in-depth education on the issues that concerned them over the weeks of the campaign.

Now, in early 1996, it was my job to bring those issues to the attention of the government and do something about them. Sitting for the first time in the green seal-leather-covered seats on the Assembly floor, I felt a brief surge of excitement. I was the first Independent MHA elected in twenty-one years and the first woman ever to represent Labrador. I hoped—no, I *knew*—that I would find a way to make the government and the other MHAs sit up and take notice of our great land.

The Newfoundland House of Assembly—Labrador had not yet been included in the name of the province—is contained in the upper floors of the East Block of Confederation Building, an eleven-storey structure constructed in 1959 to replace the Colonial Building. A seven-storey building, referred to as the West Block, was added in 1985. In addition to the Assembly, the two buildings housed the headquarters of most government departments. A small Service Annex Complex rounds out the legislative campus.

This was to be my second home for the next seventeen years, this building perched high on Confederation Hill overlooking the beautiful city of St. John's. I wonder if I had known then the struggles I would endure, would I have been quite so excited? Perhaps not, but I would have been even more resolute. I was doing a job I loved for a land and people I loved. I would put my head down and try even harder.

Before I even took my seat in the House of Assembly, I knew I would have to face the press. Everybody wanted to know who Yvonne Jones was, this young woman who was the first Independent MHA elected in more than twenty years. I wanted to make a good impression on that first day, and I didn't think the Ski-Doo coat and snow boots I wore at home or on the campaign trail were going to do it. I had gone out the day before to shop for a suit, and I had found a couple that I liked. It was early March and the media interviews would take place outside on the steps of the Confederation Building, so I needed a coat. I wanted a nice raglan, but at that time of year the only one I could find was in faded jade green, a colour I was not fond of.

So, there I was on the steps, wearing a coat I despised and facing reporters, and I thought, *This is not about you, Yvonne.* I was there to represent the people of my district, from Cartwright to L'Anse au Clair. These communities were built on resilience, by people who worked hard for themselves and their kids. It was a big area with a lot of towns, but not many of the problems they faced were like those in the rest of the province. It had been a hard-fought election, and my constituents had put their trust in me, as well as a lot of expectations. I felt a great weight on my shoulders, but I knew that if I focused on what was important, both my load and the ones that so many of them carried would be lightened.

In those first interviews, I spent only a few moments telling them who I was, and then I cut straight to the issues. I was one person in a big province where people and issues were vying for attention, so I had to be focused and creative in order to make the voices of my constituents clear and strong. I talked immediately about the need for a highway, the sub-standard housing, the high cost of living, and the scarcity of jobs. I pointed out the lack of proper municipal services in many communities and noted that existing infrastructure was aging and inadequate. Community members didn't have gathering places because the centres they had built themselves out of scrap lumber, hand-sawed logs, and free labour were forty or fifty years old, needing repairs and replacement. There were so many issues: big ones, sure, but also little ones caused by distance, and isolation, and a lack of government services. I was there to address them all, and I wanted to make sure that people in St. John's—and, more importantly, back home—knew that.

I remember taking my seat in the House of Assembly. It was exactly where everyone said it would be, in the very back corner where I'd never be seen or heard from again. Well, they were right about the corner, but I was determined they would be wrong about the rest. I just didn't know yet how I would make myself heard.

What I did know was that I had just turned twenty-eight, I was a freshman MHA, and that the people of my district had put me here with a strong mandate to make their issues known and to find solutions to the many real and pressing problems they faced. Looking across the green and white carpeting at the solid row of wooden desks occupied by government Members, then past them at the portraits of the many who had come before, and then up to the public galleries on the next level, I felt my excitement turn into calm determination. There were a few friendly faces smiling down at me, and although my first remarks were directed to the Speaker as per parliamentary custom, it was to those faces and to the people of my district that I was truly speaking. The first words I spoke on that March day in 1996 might not have been earth-shattering, but they came from the heart.

"Thank you very much, all of you.

"Mr. Speaker and Honourable Members, it is with great pleasure that I address the House today, on behalf of my district and the people of Cartwright-L'Anse au Clair.

"First of all, I would like to say I am very honoured to be part of a team of Labrador people who have just been elected to this House, and I wish my partners luck in their endeavours. I would also like to say that I am very proud to represent the people of Cartwright-L'Anse au Clair. Obviously, we have not chosen a candidate that follows within the party lines, but rather, we have chosen an Independent to be our representative within government and within the structure of this Province, and their decision has been well justified within the riding."

I was proud to represent the people of my district and, with others, the interests of all of Labrador. I was equally happy to assert my independence from the government, consistent with the wishes of those who put me there. I would congratulate the government when they did well and criticize and question them when they failed to serve the people I represented. Although I had initially run for the Liberal nomination, I now saw it as fortunate to have won as an Independent. Free of the constraints of party discipline, I could speak my mind and truly represent the people.

It was not going to be easy. As an Independent MHA, I could not access additional funds for research that were provided to party caucuses but had to rely on my limited Member's allowance. Nor could I rely on a party organization to provide backup support from outside the House of Assembly. My opportunities to speak in the Chamber were also rationed, based on the rules of the House.

A lot of the Members on the government side were very experienced, and the ministers, in particular, were very able and strong. I remember looking at people like Beaton Tulk, John Efford, Roger Grimes, Paul Dicks, Chuck Furey, Kevin Aylward, and Tom Lush; these guys had been elected and re-elected for several terms. I had been watching them in the news for years, and now I was sitting across from them. I knew they were strong ministers, and they had strong Members on their backbenches, too. They were good on their feet and great debaters. One of them in particular, Justice Minister Chris Decker, who was a Member from The Straits-White Bay North on the Northern Peninsula, was a tremendous orator—perhaps not surprising, given his background as a clergyman and mayor.

Up and down the line, the government caucus was strong. They had also just set a new record for electing the most women ever to the House of Assembly and the Liberal bench. Premier Brian Tobin had eagerly appointed a record number of them to the Cabinet: Julie Bettney, Sandra Kelly, Joan Marie Aylward, Anna Thistle, and Judy Foote. Mary Hodder and myself rounded out the female representation—a record seven women on the floor of the House, with the largest percentage ever at the Cabinet table. It was a breakthrough for women in politics in Newfoundland and Labrador, after many years of Lynn Verge and Pat Cowan doing the heavy lifting for women in the Legislature.

The Opposition consisted of nine Progressive Conservatives led by Loyola Sullivan. Then there was Jack Harris, the leader and only member of the NDP, and finally, sitting right behind him in the very back corner, me.

I would have to work harder than any other MHA if I was to be effective in my job. I had been brought up to work hard, and my experience as mayor of Mary's Harbour had already taught me that a woman in politics had to persevere and talk loudly to be heard. Moreover, I would have to be determined, repetitive, and patient in trying to educate others. I wasn't limited to bringing up issues in the House; I could work in Committee, talk with other MHAs and ministers, meet with departmental officials and outside organizations, cultivate contacts in the media and, of course, draw on the collective wisdom of leaders and volunteers back in Cartwright-L'Anse au Clair.

I also had a couple of secret weapons. The first was that Jack Harris and I had adjoining offices, essentially a shared space, which proved to be a great experience and a tremendous asset. Jack was already a seasoned politician and knew the ins and outs of the House and its procedures. He had plenty of wisdom and insights, which he generously shared with me; it was a tremendous help that first year. I had and still have tremendous respect for Jack for the many years of service he gave to the people of his district and to Newfoundland. His tips on bills and how the legislative process worked gave me a real head start. I also appreciated several Members of the Opposition who were very kind and supportive of me, such as Tom Osborne, Bob French, and Loyola Sullivan, as they took on the government on important issues. I had great political teachers on both sides of the House of Assembly.

The other advantage I had was that I found I really loved the process, loved the idea of debate. I knew with a little experience

I could get on my feet and give as good as I got. They could try to ignore me, and they did; they could mock and heckle, and they did; they could try to shut me up, and they tried, but they never succeeded. I like to think their efforts at ghosting me eventually came back to haunt them.

That first speech laid out many of the issues that I would pursue over the next few years. Like much of Labrador and rural Newfoundland, my district had been hard hit by the cod moratorium. Hundreds of fishers and plant workers had been thrown out of work and onto social programs managed by the federal government. Fisherfolk are nothing if not resilient, and those people were determined to carry on the traditional economy of their parents and grandparents, one way or another.

Plenty of other fishing opportunities had been identified—shrimp, crab, lumpfish, scallop, and even sea urchins—and I demanded the government provide the support and the quotas for the fishermen of Southern Labrador to explore them. It was a constant battle with both the provincial government, which could provide the support, and the federal one, which controlled the quotas. I didn't win every fight during the next three years, but I won enough that the fishery was more viable when I finished my term than when I started it.

I knew from my own experience in business that we could also develop a significant tourism industry, and not only in the summer but in the winter as well. All we needed was a hand up from St. John's and Ottawa, and the people of Labrador would do the rest.

Like today, back then economic development didn't take place in a vacuum. People always need access to education and to good health care. The cost of living is high in Labrador, some of it as a direct result of government policies, which makes it difficult for individuals to escape the traps of poverty and underemployment.

While work was proceeding successfully and I had ended my first session in the House of Assembly, my first term in office began with a personal tragedy, one of many I would suffer and overcome, and all of which would shape my broader understanding of life.

It was about a month after I was elected that I found out I was pregnant with our first child. It was a shock, if not quite a surprise; Jim and I had always intended to have a family. The timing wasn't ideal, but we were excited. I had just been elected as the first woman from Labrador and I knew the news would be met with a great deal of negativity. *We elected a woman, an Independent MHA at that, with no party behind her to back her up,* they would say, *and now she's pregnant, so what is she going to do for us?* These thoughts kept running through my mind, so we decided to keep the news to ourselves. I had to build a reputation as an MHA first, to prove myself before I shared the joyful news.

It was July 23 and I had been in St. John's that week while Jim was up in Carbonear, putting the freighter into dry dock for some needed maintenance. I was with a good friend, Ina Jeffries, who was one of the only people who knew about the pregnancy. She had three children of her own and, now that I was further along and starting to show, she had come to help me get things sorted.

We decided that I should go visit my grandparents for the weekend—my mother's parents, Malcolm Stone and Jean Pye, who moved out of Labrador in the 1970s to be closer to the hospital when grandmother was ill. They lived in Seal Cove, Conception Bay South, just forty minutes away from the city. Before I left, I dropped by the Sears store to order baby furniture and other things we would need to welcome our child, as well as some larger dresses and sweaters so that I could continue to disguise my pregnancy for a few more weeks. Some of the larger items would be delivered and the rest would be packed up so I could pick them up on my way back into the city.

I was headed into month six of my pregnancy, the point when you begin to think everything is okay. While the doctor had explained what would happen when I was due to deliver, what happened next was entirely unexpected. While I was at my grandparents' house I began to feel ill, and then fluid began to pour out of me, a heavy gush that soiled my clothes. It never occurred to me that my water was breaking. I spent Saturday night with a fever, and on Sunday I was so sick I knew I had to get back to St. John's.

I considered calling my mother; it was time to tell her and I knew she could provide me with so much support. I decided as soon as I was feeling better I would let my family in on the joyful news. Not wanting my grandparents to be worried that I was unwell, I called Ina and asked her to meet me at Sears, which was on the far side of St. John's from my home, to pick up my purchases and then to take me to my place. I had my own car but I didn't think I could make the whole trip on my own. So that's what we did.

By the time we got to the bungalow I was renting on Newfoundland Drive, I was once again burning up with fever and didn't know what to do with myself. Ina took care of me, putting me to bed with cold packs and Tylenol. When I woke up in the middle of the night in so much pain that I had to get her up to help me, she asked, "Did your water break while you were away? Is that what happened? Did the sac break?" For the first time it dawned on me that I was in labour, and had been for a day and a half.

By this time, I was in so much pain I was hallucinating, but the contractions were real. Ina was wonderful, so calm and caring, so knowledgeable. I doubt I would have survived the ordeal without her. She called ahead to the hospital to warn them I was on my way and in labour, and then drove me straight to Emergency. It was five o'clock in the morning, but they were ready for me. The doctors told me that I had an infection, either a urinary tract infection or one in the amniotic sac, which had caused a premature rupture of the membranes. My water breaking had triggered the early labour, but delivery now would be difficult.

Because of the infection, there was a risk that a natural birth could cause the baby to become infected, too, which would seriously compromise the baby's health. On the other hand, a Caesarean section could be life-threatening for both me and the baby. There were no guarantees of a successful birth in either case. Ina had reached Jim in Carbonear, about an hour or so away, but he had not yet arrived. Everything was happening so fast; time was running out, and natural childbirth became the best option.

A team of doctors was standing by, but the technology was not nearly so advanced then as it is today. The baby's lungs had not fully developed and she couldn't breathe on her own. She was baptized Eliza after my paternal grandmother and died that morning.

I looked up with red eyes as Jim entered the room. I was holding our little angel close to my bosom; Jim was also crying and heartbroken. What was to be the sacred bond of parenting had now been snatched away from us, and with it the dreams we had shared for our child.

It was a terribly sad and difficult time. First, I had to tell my family about my pregnancy and the death of my child on the same day. My mother was so angry that I had not confided in her, not trusted her to keep my secret. It took her a long time to forgive me and to understand why I made the choice I did. I don't regret keeping my pregnancy hidden; it was the only way I could have survived politically and done the things that I knew needed to be done for the people I served, and to establish myself as a politician in the district. However, I now wish I had told her. She understood politics as well as I did; she knew how hard it was to be a woman in that field. It would have been okay for her to know and to be there to support me.

Dealing with the grief was my most immediate struggle; it nearly overwhelmed me. I had been entering the final stage of my pregnancy and had been making plans for our daughter's arrival only a few days before. Now it was over. The grief of losing my child took a terrible toll on me. It took a similar toll on Jim. The cracks in our relationship that may have started with my election now widened and deepened with the loss of our Eliza. The year 1996 marked a fundamental change in our relationship after only five years of marriage. Although we stayed married for many years after, the beginning of the end was rooted there.

Though we never talked about it, I sometimes worried that my extensive travel that year, the long hours of work, and the pressure I was under had affected my pregnancy and led to our loss. I don't know if that was true; certainly no one told me that it was the cause. In the end I didn't blame myself, and I hope Jim didn't either. But that loss changed our relationship, and it changed me.

It took me several months to recover and then return to the Legislature, but when I did, I was more determined than ever to succeed. I dived deeper and deeper into politics. My work became my life. I had to prove myself over and over again to win the acceptance I craved and to become the best politician I could become. It may have started as a way of coping, but it soon became more than that. I found I was good at the job; I could provide real solutions for the people who had elected me. I became a fixer, and by fixing other people's problems I could forget about my own and move on.

By the fall of 1996, I was back in the House, focused completely on serving my constituents. That focus carried me through the next few years and helped me stay the course when sadness or other difficulties threatened my journey. I did become a better politician and, I think, a stronger person. Most importantly, my hard work paid off for my constituents. But my biggest success had to wait nearly to the end of my first term.

Oil had been discovered off Newfoundland's shores in 1979; the first barrel from Hibernia was produced in 1997. Disputes over Newfoundland's portion of the revenue would continue for years before Newfoundland and Labrador got their fair share.

More important to me, however, was the discovery of the vast reserve of nickel and other metals at Voisey's Bay in Northern Labrador in 1993. Newfoundland prospectors Christopher Verbiski and Albert Chislett had been looking for diamonds, but what they found would eventually prove equally as valuable. Inco purchased the deposits in 1996 for $4.6 billion and began the long negotiations with the federal and provincial governments and the two Indigenous groups on whose lands the deposits lay.

I knew it would take years to reach an agreement and then to build a mine and a smelter to process the ore. For too long, Labrador's resources had been harvested for the benefit of others, leaving the people of Labrador with few benefits. It was high time that changed, and I intended to use those years and whatever arguments I could make to ensure that change. I began to promote the idea of adjacency: that the people who lived closest to a development be the first—though not the only ones—to benefit from it.

When the agreement was finally signed in 2002, the Nunatsiavut land claim was well advanced. Premier Roger Grimes had agreed that while Inuit and Innu would get first priority at jobs and procurement contracts, all other Labradorians would be considered second in the hiring process. We were able to get a commitment on training for Indigenous people and settlers in Labrador to ensure they had the skills required for these new jobs, and we worked hard to ensure the remote mine would restrict fly-in/fly-out workers to Newfoundlanders and Labradorians, giving people at home the opportunities they deserved. Premier Grimes did not have an easy job, but he managed it well and was able to get commitments that would benefit the province for decades to come.

In Labrador we were equally successful on most fronts. What we differed on was where the smelter and refinery would be placed. I tried very hard, along with other leaders—especially Philip Earle, who was executive director of the Combined Councils of Labrador at the time—to land the new, high-tech operation for Labrador, but after three studies looking at ports in Forteau, Cartwright, and Goose Bay, the feasibility did not pan out, nor was there solidarity in Labrador around housing the infrastructure, which many felt would be environmentally damaging to Labrador lands, wildlife, and the cultural climate.

In the end, we were disappointed with the outcome but satisfied we had done our very best, and we accepted the benefit agreement we had secured with the Premier and the company to move Labrador forward. It has proved to be an incredible project for all Newfoundlanders and Labradorians, and the returns to the province are something Premier Grimes, the Indigenous governments, and Labradorians can be proud of.

Despite the promise of future wealth, the present looked dark for many people, and nowhere more so than in Labrador. The government had entered a period of austerity, trying to get a burgeoning deficit under control, but people were being affected unequally. Places that were underserviced already could ill afford further reductions in those services. As I told the House in the summer of 1996:

> "We have had enough exploitation of our resources and that
> is what has caused people in my district to protest to the
> degree that they have. This is what has brought about the
> talk of separation and the other upheavals of protest that we
> have seen throughout the districts."

I understood the frustration that people were feeling at losing or seeing reductions in such services as air ambulance, effective policing, education, and municipal infrastructure. I also felt it was incumbent on me to quell the calls for separation, and the only way to do that was to persuade the provincial and, sometimes, federal governments to change their approaches and the way they looked at Labrador: not as a place to be exploited, but as a place to be developed in partnership with those who lived there.

It wasn't easy. I was only one voice; the only way I could succeed was to lend my voice to others and help get their message across in as forceful a way as I could.

When the people of Black Tickle were facing a crisis over safe drinking water, I was quoted in the *Evening Telegram*: "If they have to live with Third World conditions, maybe they'll apply for Third World aid." Some thought these words were over the top, but they did focus the mind of the minister in charge to eventually look at options to solve the problem by investing $1.5 million into a water treatment facility for the community.

When the provincial sales tax was merged with the Goods and Services Tax (GST) to create the Harmonized Sales Tax (HST) in 1997, I pointed out that goods and services that were exempt from provincial sales taxes, such as home heating oil, would hit people in Labrador especially hard, as prices were already much higher there than in the rest of Newfoundland. Those on social assistance were often in dire need as they tried to heat their homes in the harsh Labrador winters.

Changes in tax rates were also hurting local businesses, who saw their customers from both the Labrador Straits and Labrador West drive across the border to Quebec for cheaper gas and cigarettes. It only affected a few—perhaps too few for the politicians and bureaucrats in St. John's to notice, so I added my voice to theirs and made use of contacts in the media to publicize their plight.

The government responded by adjusting tax rates on the border to create a more level playing field. I had less luck on the matter of fuel subsidies.

Ultimately, that is how democracy works. You fight for your constituents and do everything in your power to persuade or cajole the government to do the right thing. Some fights you win, others you lose, but you never throw up your hands and say, *I give up, I quit.* Sometimes you have to put your head down and fight the next one. Step by step, anyone can make their community, their province, their country a better place. It's not easy, but nothing worth fighting for ever has been.

I'd rather dwell on the arguments I won. When fishers in Southern Labrador complained that the area allocated to them for the crab fishery was unproductive, I worked with them and their representatives to get the federal Department of Fisheries to agree that if they could prove it, they would let them fish farther north. When they did prove it, the department was forced to live up to its promise. As a result, fishers and plant workers were able to keep earning a decent living, feeding their families for years after.

On another occasion, when the government proposed privatizing the air ambulance service, I worked with the Grenfell Regional Health Services board and local communities to show that such a change would *not* save money and would drastically reduce the accessibility and affordability of medical transport for the people of my district. The government listened to reason and cancelled the tenders.

One of the finest moments during my time as an Independent MHA was when we all came together to demand that the federal government develop a post-TAGS program for Newfoundland and Labrador fishers. TAGS, short for The Atlantic Groundfish Strategy, was an income support program put in place for the tens of thousands of people whose lives and livelihoods had been disrupted by the cod moratorium of 1992. It was meant to help people until the cod returned or until they could transition to other fisheries or industries through training or relocation. While tremendous efforts and sacrifices had been made, many families still relied on the program just to get by. Now it was coming to an end and there was no clear path to a replacement.

In April of 1998, following a unanimous motion of support in the House of Assembly, I joined a delegation to Ottawa. It was a great display of solidarity seldom seen in politics. Our success was limited, but not insignificant. Although the federal government did not replace TAGS with a similar program, they did relax some of the rules around EI benefits and provided additional training resources for those who wanted them.

A more subtle victory, one hard to quantify, was that of waking up federal politicians and bureaucrats a little to the importance of listening to those most impacted by their decisions—in this case, the fishers themselves. It was a temporary triumph and a fight we had to return to many times in the years since, but as I wrote in my journal in 1998, "I will try, until I can no longer, to ensure a better life for people in my district."

It was a lesson that obviously took time to sink in, because a few months later, the Department of Fisheries and Oceans unilaterally and without warning placed a year-long moratorium on the commercial salmon fishery and limited the salmon food fishery—a subsistence fishery for local people that was regulated by Ottawa and that so many Labrador families relied on. In the meantime, the sport fishery was allowed to continue, to the benefit of individuals and businesses from away. The compensation offered to salmon fishers was pitiful and did not even cover the expenses they had already incurred to gear up for the season. The response of DFO to criticism was "Take it or leave it." Like all things in life, it was a case of two steps forward and one step back.

The fight over salmon, and especially the food fishery, would take some time to resolve.

One element that set Labrador apart from the rest of Newfoundland was the need to take into account the constitutionally protected rights of the Indigenous people who lived there. At the time, only the First Nation reserve at Conne River had really established themselves as a distinct community in Newfoundland and Labrador. Indigenous people who lived off reserve had less notice. This was a factor in fishing, but also in all matters of resource development and land-use management. By the late 1990s, both the Inuit, who lived in the northern part of Labrador, and the Innu, whose territory straddled the Quebec–Labrador border, were well on their way to having their land claims settled and their right to self-government negotiated. As such they had to be consulted and accommodated on such projects as the Voisey's Bay development, and they had to derive significant benefits from the use of their territory.

However, a third Indigenous group, originally known as the Labrador Métis Nation and today known as the NunatuKavut Community Council, and whose ancestry and traditions included both Inuit and European people, was still struggling for recognition—a struggle that is only partially resolved.

*In the midst of struggles and surrounded by
negativity, always remember: your strength lies
in staying true to yourself. Integrity will always
protect your spirit and guide your way.*

— Sheila Downer,
VP Northern Community Engagement, Harris Centre

CHAPTER 5

SHIFTING INDUSTRY

Long before the moratorium, fishing was an uncertain business. Just like in farming, good years were often followed by bad, and even in a good year some individuals had poor catches. Out West, some people refer to the Prairies as "next-year country," and I suppose the same term could be applied to the fishery. Still, it was what we had, and few people had the vision to think there could be something else.

The biggest barrier to economic development was abundantly clear. The lack of a highway to connect communities to the outside world meant that we were dependent on infrequent and sometimes unreliable ships and expensive air transport. Not only did that drive up the cost of living and of doing business in our communities, it limited visits by tourists and made the export of our resources expensive and often impracticable.

The lack of a highway was not the only barrier to development. Most communities were reliant on diesel generation for electricity, which was both expensive and dirty. Rates for power were higher in our communities and it was a constant battle before the Public Utilities Board to keep Newfoundland and Labrador Hydro, a Crown corporation, from increasing the differential even more. Canada Post also got into the act, setting postal rates to isolated communities at almost unbearable levels. In 1984, the Bank of Montreal closed its branch in the area, leaving the entire south coast of Labrador without access to regular banking services. In a region already struggling with income uncertainty, where people were reliant on mostly seasonal work, the barriers to building an alternative economy were and are huge.

Yet local ingenuity and hard work often found a way.

In 1978, under the guidance of lawyer and union leader Richard Cashin, fishermen along the south coast of Labrador began to organize as a workers' collective, and in 1979, the Labrador Fishermen's Union Shrimp Company was established, bringing together fishers from L'Anse au Clair to Cartwright. The goals of the company were simple: to create greater stability in the local fishery, to create an integrated approach to the catching and processing of fish, and to provide local people a say in the management of the industry.

In 1982, the members decided to transform the co-operative into a limited company, but with the same principles and mandate. When other plants were closing in the difficult decades after 1992, the LFUSC kept operating and kept innovating. While the private operators in the Labrador area closed their doors one by one—the last were Quinlan Brothers in Black Tickle and P. Janes & Sons in St. Lewis—the Shrimp Company kept going. More than 40 years later, the company operates five fish plants in the region, employs over 500 people on a seasonal basis, and services more than 600 fishers and crew in Labrador. It has established numerous international partnerships, and it markets its products around the world.

However, the LFUSC is more than just a fisheries business. When the Bank of Montreal pulled out of the Labrador Straits in 1984, local people wanted to establish a credit union. They needed money to get started, so the Shrimp Company loaned them the funds. Today, the Eagle River Credit Union has assets of more than $185 million and six branches, three in Labrador and three along the West Coast of Newfoundland, and it continues to look for new acquisitions. The credit union provides a full range of banking services throughout the region and, like all co-operatives, pays regular dividends to its members.

The LFUSC invested in the communities it serves in other ways, too. When a $1,000 grant was needed to get a community project started, the Shrimp Company would look for that money in its budget. It was never big money, but there was always some. Often, communities had little in the way of fire protection services, and again, the company would find a way to augment those services by purchasing equipment or providing training. A few years ago, it was able to make a significant contribution to Air Daffodil, which provides transport for locals needing medical care and cancer treatments in St. John's.

When fishermen needed money for a new boat motor because it had broken down in the middle of the fishing season and they had no credit, the company was there to support them. It would let them borrow money to pay back when they could, which really helped give fishers and their families a hand up and brought some stability to their lives. While the primary focus of the company was on catching and processing fish, it always had the bigger picture in mind, recognizing that without supporting people and communities, there could be no fishery.

The company had tremendous leadership in two key individuals, Gilbert Linstead and Ken Fowler, backed by a strong board with members drawn from communities across the area. They did their job, managing money and building an industry to create jobs and sustain communities. They were constantly adapting and innovating and now have two of the newest and most modern plants in Newfoundland and Labrador, both in Mary's Harbour. They have built good marketing networks with the United States, Japan, and even the UK, which is a particularly tough market to break into.

Those people don't get involved in politics or in big lobbying campaigns. Instead, they continue to work as they have since the company was established, building relationships and supporting each other. It's a fantastic business model, and when I look at regions around Canada that have resource developments, I think it would be very successful for northern and rural communities.

A shifting perspective on industry also brought forestry to the forefront. Many of the communities along the south coast of Labrador, especially Port Hope Simpson and Cartwright, had been exploiting the abundant forestry resources for many years. Initially it was for lumber, but as time went on, pulpwood for manufacturing paper products became very important. It attracted big companies like Abitibi-Price and Kruger who came to buy logs and pulp in large quantities. After 1992, we hoped that logging would become an alternative to the fishery as a basic and sustainable industry.

For about eight years, we saw steady growth in the area, though some complained about the big companies taking our wood instead of processing it locally. Demands for a local pulp mill were made frequently, but nothing ever came of it. Still, a number of local entrepreneurs, like Melvin Penney, Glen Penney, and Simon Strugnell did a great job at building up their forestry businesses. The provincial government got involved by building forest access roads and starting reforestation programs, both of which provided secondary jobs.

By 2004, local businesses had grown, and after much lobbying, the provincial government established a forestry division in Port

Hope Simpson and Cartwright, with full-time government jobs in conservation, enforcement, planning, and seasonal fire services. The number of logging permits was doubled, and more forest access roads were built every year.

Early in the twenty-first century, however, the market for paper—and therefore wood pulp—changed. The increasing use of digital records and the explosive growth of e-books lowered the demand for paper. The total consumption of paper in North America dropped by twenty-four per cent between 2006 and 2009, leading to overcapacity in production and falling profits in the industry. Plants were closed in Canada, the United States, and Western Europe, while production grew rapidly in China. By 2010, China had risen from a distant third place to become the largest paper producer in the world.

In Newfoundland and Labrador, the two mills owned by Abitibi Consolidated closed their doors. The Stephenville mill closed first, in 2005, and production ceased at the Grand Falls-Windsor pulp and paper mill in February 2009. Abitibi-Bowater went into bankruptcy protection; when it emerged in 2010 as Resolute Forest Products, it had cut its newsprint production by one-third. It never returned to the province.

The bottom fell out of the market for pulpwood from Labrador, and one by one, forestry businesses across the region disappeared. We had gone from demanding that our forestry products be processed in Labrador to begging companies to buy our pulp. Without a market, there was little to sustain the industry. It had never developed a market for secondary products, so there was nothing to fall back on.

Today, we still have a small forestry-based business in Port Hope Simpson, mostly producing firewood and lumber for local consumption, and another lumber business in Goose Bay. However, there is no large-scale forest industry in Labrador. Very few people are even cutting wood because it is uneconomical, and in remote Labrador it was never feasible to develop by-products such as wood chips for particle board manufacture or pellets for high-efficiency energy production; even with best efforts and government support, the right timing and investment never materialized.

Labrador is blessed with dense forests, especially in the central and southern regions, but the trees are old and vulnerable to destruction in storms and pose a high risk for forest fires, which threaten our communities and add to climate change. We are at risk of losing this resource if we can't find a way to use it. Indigenous governments and their development corporations have a real opportunity to create a local market for lumber and wood pellets, and then to expand to serve international specialty markets for wood. Clearing older forests would also create jobs in reforestation and help build a sustainable environment in Labrador. Local control and local decision-making are key to unlocking the potential of this resource.

On a happier note, in the last decade, the paper industry has bounced back, with the demand for paper and paperboard growing dramatically in China and India, and more slowly in North America. I suppose all those Amazon boxes must come from somewhere. Labradorians built a forest industry from scratch once; I'm confident that with ingenuity and hard work, we can do it again in a more environmentally sustainable way.

Mining in Labrador is another piece of the economic puzzle that faced challenges and had to shift and evolve as an industry. Mining has a long history and a bright future in Labrador. Although iron ore deposits were discovered in western Labrador as early as 1892, isolation and expense delayed the exploitation of this resource for many years. With the development of railways and electricity in the area, the Iron Ore Company of Canada began exploration in Schefferville, Quebec, in the 1940s and opened its first mine there in 1954. Eight years later, it began operations at Carol Lake near Labrador City. With the opening of the Scully mine at Wabush in 1965, Labrador became the leading iron ore producer in North America.

In 2013, the Wabush mine closure was announced suddenly, throwing more than 400 workers out of their jobs. This was largely due to falling prices in Asian markets, but also to rising mining costs at that particular mine. Further partial closures and slowdowns at other mines in 2015 cost another 600 good jobs in the region and highlighted the boom-and-bust nature of resource extraction operations.

As a newly elected MP in the Opposition, I fought hard for Labrador and its people, calling on the Conservative government "to assist these highly skilled mining workers to integrate into new jobs and help transition and grow the local economy to create new opportunities in western Labrador." I got nowhere. In 2015, however, both the provincial and federal governments changed, and with the Liberal Party now at both levels, assistance and support made its way to the workers.

Overall, the mining industry has been a reliable part of Labrador's economy, with new opportunities developing all the time. I'm particularly excited by the opportunity for new mines in critical minerals in Labrador. The news that Search Minerals Inc. is in the advanced stages of developing a mine proposal for rare earth elements near St. Lewis in NunatuKavut territory has been met with much hope. The mine property is located right on the highway—yet another benefit of the Trans-Labrador Highway—and at tidewater, making it highly economical to develop. The mine is expected to operate for at least fifteen to twenty years by conservative estimates, first as a seasonal open-pit operation and then as a year-round underground mine. Other sites in Labrador are also being considered; in total, nearly a dozen mining companies are exploring or developing projects in the region. In 2022, the provincial gross domestic product for mining was over $6 billion ,with $5.6 billion coming from Labrador mines.

The tourism industry has always played a small but important part in the Labrador economy. The abundant rivers are an attraction to those seeking adventure in our pristine wilderness. Sport fishing for salmon has been going on for decades, though most of the outfitters came from the island of Newfoundland or even further afield, and there were few benefits to local people. Wresting those opportunities away from well-established businesses so that local—and especially Indigenous—people would benefit was a significant part of my political agenda in my first few terms in the Legislature. However, today the outfitters in Labrador have a good relationship with the communities and the people. More and more we are seeing locals either owning lodges or working in the industry.

Spectacular scenery is found in every corner of Labrador, and much of it is now contained in national parks. Labrador's diverse culture and rich history is gaining recognition provincially, nationally, and internationally. Red Bay was designated as a National Historic Site of Canada in 1979 and a UNESCO World Heritage Site in 2013. Basque whalers had used the area as a base for some fifty years, beginning in the 1540s, and had left behind a treasure of artifacts to be uncovered by modern archaeologists. Many of these have been restored in place, on ground and in the water, while others have been gathered in a fascinating interpretation centre. While the historic site has provided some jobs and business opportunities to local residents, the village of Red Bay has continued to shrink over time. The population has decreased by half over the last thirty years, and its school closed in 2021 for lack of students, demonstrating that tourism alone can only do so much to keep remote communities viable. Still, without the draw of the Basque Whalers' Station, and later the Trans-

Labrador Highway, Red Bay's viability as a community would have been challenged even more significantly.

As I've mentioned, many of the Labrador communities I grew up in were physically isolated from the rest of the province and country. When I ran as an Independent in 1996 in the dead of winter, my entire campaign was dependent on snow machines and winter trails. The one thing I heard over and over during that campaign was "We need a road!" The building of the Trans-Labrador Highway naturally became my number one priority as a politician, and I promised that one way or another I would get it done.

In 1997, the governments of Canada and Newfoundland came to an agreement to transfer the existing marine service—both freight and passenger—from the federal to the provincial government. Newfoundland took on the responsibility for maintaining and improving transportation in Labrador in exchange for two existing marine vessels and $340 million, plus interest. A significant portion of that money was dedicated to improving roads and airports in Labrador.

It was time to negotiate. Through discussions with Premier Brian Tobin, I committed to run for the Liberals in Cartwright-L'Anse au Clair in the next election if they would commit to building the Trans-Labrador Highway to Southern Labrador and start the work before the next vote.

Once the deal was inked with the federal Liberal government under Prime Minister Jean Chrétien, funds were set aside to construct a highway across Southern Labrador, all the way from the Quebec border west of Labrador City to south of Red Bay, a distance of over 1,100 kilometres. The Trans-Labrador Highway (TLH) would upgrade existing roads and include hundreds of kilometres of new road connecting many of the communities along the south coast of Labrador. Premier Tobin knew Labrador and shared the vision, and without his full support, none of this would have been possible.

The highway was finally completed in 2022, though the work to connect further communities to the TLH continues. Of course, we knew we were not getting a highway of a calibre that was remotely close to those in the rest of Canada or even close to what we had spent decades watching being built on the island of Newfoundland. But for us, for the generations of people who had struggled to survive and thrive in our isolated communities, it was a lifeline, one that would change our lives in ways we couldn't imagine.

With the gradual completion of the TLH, tourism has grown substantially over the last twenty years to become a significant, sustainable industry that not only provides good jobs and business opportunities but also contributes to preserving our history and promoting our diverse cultures. I have already described the work my ex-husband and I did—along with many others—to develop the Battle Harbour Historic Site. It continues to grow and develop to this day, thanks in part to generous federal funding. There is no doubt that Battle Harbour and its varied attractions have significantly contributed to the continuing viability of Mary's Harbour and nearby communities.

On the list of Labrador attractions, Red Bay and Battle Harbour have been joined by Pinware River Provincial Park, as well as by a number of lodges and campsites accessible by road. Further north, two national parks have been established: the Torngat Mountains National Park in Labrador and Kuururjuaq National Park in Quebec, as part of the Inuit land claims settlement. In 2015, the Akami-Uapishk^U-KakKasuak-Mealy Mountains National Park Reserve was established in the area north of Cartwright to Rigolet and Sheshatshiu. While all of these remain inaccessible by road, they continue to be a draw for wilderness adventurers and a real opportunity for local—and especially Indigenous—businesses to develop.

Another major turning point for Labrador tourism came in 2002, when the provincial government created Access North-Labrador 2002, a co-ordinated series of community festivals and events across Labrador that started with dog-team races in Hopedale in mid-March and culminated with a First Night Celebration on December 31 in Labrador City. Across Labrador, more than seventy-five events—some existing, some new—were held, highlighting local food and culture, northern games, and regional history. Some of these events were developed strictly for the Access North promotion, but others built on well-established local traditions and gatherings. That year also marked the 250th anniversary of the Moravian missionaries' arrival on the coast of Labrador; a three-day symposium for Moravian scholars from around the world was held in August in Makkovik and Hopedale in celebration.

Also in 2002, Port Hope Simpson and St. Lewis hosted "Come Home Year" festivals to invite everyone who had called those communities home—and anyone who wanted to visit—to join them in remembering the past and planning for the future. The Labrador Straits Bakeapple Folk Festival was the longest-running festival in the region and that event was promoted. Others built celebrations around the fishery, with a crab festival in Mary's Harbour, a salute to shrimp in Charlottetown, cod celebrations in William's Harbour, and a sampling of locally cooked whelk dishes to highlight the industry in Pinsent's Arm. Of course, food was only the beginning. There were also games, dances, and music, including performances by local and regional talents, for these two-to-four-day parties.

The year was a great success, proving to people from around the world, and most importantly to the people of our communities, that Labrador has a lot to offer visitors, whether former residents and their families or complete strangers. I was so inspired that

I helped form the organizing committee for a Come Home Year in Mary's Harbour in 2006 and put together a book to commemorate the community's history and the many people who had lived there.

Government services and support systems are also a critical part of the economy. Whether it is the provision of clean water, effective health care, recreation, or support for seniors, these services provide good jobs in local communities and give people freedom and stability to explore their own creativity or entrepreneurial dreams.

It may seem that I've spent most of my career talking about, promoting, and encouraging economic development, and indeed I have. Poverty is a cruel master, and a lack of opportunity can be devastating to people, families, and communities. Everybody wants and deserves a decent life, and Labradorians, in particular, are willing to work hard and think creatively to create something out of very little. But they aren't magicians; even the most industrious and intelligent person cannot make something out of nothing at all.

Ultimately for me, though, it's not about money or things; it is about preserving communities and sustaining a way of life. Growing up, I witnessed so many people being forced to leave their homes through the resettlement programs of the 1960s. They all made something of their new situation—and, in fact, many were highly successful—but almost everyone carried a burden of grief wherever they went.

Resettlement was always seen as an end, not a new beginning. My parents and grandparents had been resettled, so I grew up hearing stories of "back home," even though we lived in Mary's Harbour and all of us kids had grown up there. But it was never home for them. My mother's family was from Henley Harbour; my father's, Indian Cove. There was a sense of grief around missing something or losing something. My dad's father was resettled to

Mary's Harbour from Indian Cove, twelve kilometres away. Not that far perhaps, but it was over water and sea ice, so a difficult journey. He lived to go back every spring and never wanted to leave it in the fall. Today he is at eternal rest in his homeland. The joy of their lives was felt in the stories of the places they came from and belonged to, and not from the place where they now had to live. A sense of home and belonging runs deep in our families and cultures.

My job may take me away for weeks on end, to St. John's then and Ottawa now, but my heart and my home is still in Labrador, and always will be.

*Life is a journey! My dad always
told me, take it one day at a time, one
foot in front of the other.*

—— Cathy Smallwood,
personal friend

CHAPTER 6

NEGOTIATIONS MATTER

While I had been encouraged in 1996 to run for the Liberal nomination by those close to Premier Brian Tobin, the support stopped abruptly when I decided to run as an Independent. When I won and arrived to take my seat in the Legislature, the atmosphere remained chilly.

However, as I found my feet and began to push the agenda of the people who elected me, the climate changed again, and pretty soon I was building relationships with people from all political parties. I mentioned the help NDP Leader Jack Harris gave me, but I also made a few friends in the Progressive Conservative Party and, of course, I had my own informal caucus of advisers in St. John's.

Coming from Southern Labrador—one of the most Liberal parts of the province—I was naturally drawn to that party. I began to get a positive reception from some of the other MHAs and people in the Premier's office, including some who had formerly run both hot and cold. It helped a lot that Brian Tobin, the Premier, had spent time in Labrador and knew the lay of the land. He understood where I was coming from. He also understood that I had been elected as an Independent, and as such, was bound and determined to speak my mind in the best interests of my district, even if it meant criticizing the government when it was due and voting against government measures that I thought harmed my constituents. I spent three years pursuing the agenda I was elected on, and I think that earned me the respect I needed to keep the pressure up and be taken seriously.

The feeling wasn't universal, though. Two Members of the government were particularly unhappy with me. Cabinet ministers John Efford, and to a lesser extent Beaton Tulk, both gave me a pretty hard time during my first term. I eventually won Beaton over, and we became great friends and colleagues. John Efford was a different matter—he had made his mind up and continued to oppose me on many issues.

John Efford was a close friend to Danny Dumaresque, the Liberal MHA I had defeated. He had been mad when I chose to run as an Independent, and was madder still when I won. Almost from the first time I rose in the Assembly to speak, I could count on being heckled by Minister Efford. To be fair, he never crossed the line with his jibes and insults—which is more than I can say for some "Honourable Members" over the years—but it was disruptive to my train of thought and frustrating, especially when I was making constructive remarks on this or that government policy. No matter what I had to say, Efford was going to comment on it negatively.

Tulk, another of Dumaresque's close friends, had initially treated me in much the same manner, though perhaps with less rancour. Yet by 1999 we had reconciled and become good friends. I was happy to serve under him when he became Premier in 2000 after Brian Tobin returned to federal politics and before Roger Grimes became Liberal leader and Premier. As Prime Minister Justin Trudeau put it at the time of Beaton Tulk's death in 2019, he was known for "putting people first," and his passing was "the loss of a great Canadian and a great Liberal."

I had first met John Efford when he was Minister of Transportation and I was mayor of Mary's Harbour. He was making a few stops in the district with then-MHA Dumaresque, but Mary's Harbour was only a refuelling stop, and no meetings were scheduled. I got on the phone to St. John's and called the Minister's office, the MHA, and the Premier. Finally, after a few days, they agreed to make a short stop to look at the deplorable gravel roads filled with potholes and a bridge that was crumbling. Infrastructure investments were rarely forthcoming for rural and northern outports. The bridge that joined the two sides of the community was a wooden structure with a few concrete pillars that had been built in the late 1950s.

The bridge was long past its best-before date; planks had been replaced year after year with rough, locally sawed lumber, nails were protruding, the railing was going to rot, and the structure had not been tested in years. I was determined to give the Minister a good ride on our community road, so I asked Hughlett Acreman, a local businessman, if I could borrow his old Jeep; that thing knocked hard over the potholes. I picked up the politicians when they landed and gave them a bumpy tour of the beautiful community, stopping at the bridge. I parked the Jeep and invited them on a walk. It was a short trek across the dilapidated bridge to the airstrip nearby. They were pressed for time and the plane was waiting, so needless to say the Minister was not happy with my tactic, but I felt it was necessary for him to see the damage that had to be addressed. I was quite proud of myself when finally the approval came; we would get a new bridge and funding for upgrades.

While sitting as an Independent, I was always hoping for signs that John Efford would come around, too. At one point during that first term, I was speaking in the Assembly about how people from Labrador were not being treated fairly, about the inadequacy of services and other issues. I had been speaking for a while and was being pretty loud, so maybe I had gotten a little hoarse. Efford walked across the floor and plunked a bottle of seal oil capsules onto my desk, saying: "Here, why don't you take a couple of those and calm down a little bit?" While most people might not see that as an act of kindness, I chose at the time to see it as a little crack in the wall that he had built between us.

John Efford was now Minister of Fisheries. He was a very popular minister and nowhere more so than in Labrador. In 1997, the people in Black Tickle were lobbying for a crab licence, and Efford was going to give it to Quinlan Brothers to open a processing plant there, as he was very friendly with the company. They were a good reputable firm—but there were already four crab plants on the coast of Labrador, plus the Labrador Fishermen's Union Shrimp Company in Mary's Harbour and Cartwright, Torngat Fisheries in Makkovik, and P. Janes & Sons in St. Lewis. People were worried that a fifth plant would dilute production and reduce hours of work for existing plants and their employees. I had been lobbying for a turbot plant in Black Tickle, but the people there were sure that crab was the way to go. Efford knew they needed something to keep them going and a crab plant was just the ticket.

The Minister was going to Black Tickle to make the announcement and, since it was in my district, I wanted to go, too. However, flights in and out of Black Tickle only operated three days a week. Getting to the community and back to St. John's would take five or six days. The only realistic way I could attend the event was to fly on the Minister's charter, which would go and return on the same day.

I approached Premier Tobin's assistant, Seamus O'Regan—who, after a distinguished career as a journalist, went on to become a Liberal MP representing St. John's in 2015—and told him: "Seamus, the Minister is going to Black Tickle to make an important announcement in my district and I have to be there. The only way that can happen is for me to be on the Minister's charter."

There was some protest, but in the end, I made it onto that charter flight. It was a big day for Black Tickle, and I was happy to celebrate it with them—but it was a short-lived victory. As predicted, five plants were too many for the Labrador crab fishery; today, there are only three left. Black Tickle isn't one of them.

Being an Independent MHA was a great experience. You answer to no one but your constituents and you can speak your mind without concern about the "party line." I know a number of people who have served as Independents and they all say the same thing: "It's great to have the freedom to speak your open mind and follow your own path; it is also very difficult, because you don't have an official support mechanism."

As I was very new to provincial politics, I had no idea what I was missing as an Independent Member. I built my own circle of advisers, mostly friends I trusted plus others who had something to offer—although they always seemed to expect a little in return, usually me raising an issue in the Legislature, or bringing it to the attention of a minister or two. Still, my team of advisers was cobbled together with volunteers who weren't always available when I needed them. All I had in the way of staff was a single assistant—at that time, a young woman named Shirley Pye from Lodge Bay, whom I had grown up with. Shirley was very hard-working and a great help, but she was only one person. Into my second year in St. John's, Shirley was offered the opportunity to work for NunatuKavut Community Council as the assistant to President Todd Russell and moved back to Labrador.

I was left to look for a new constituency assistant. By now I had learned how important this position was to the work I was doing. As an elected politician, the people you hire around you are every bit as critical to the job as you are. They are on the front line of every call, and their ability to deal with people, follow up on their issues, and help resolve them could sometimes be the difference between winning and losing elections. A few months earlier, when Shirley was off on vacation, I had asked another friend to fill in. Bonnie Hicks was originally from Port Hope Simpson. Like me, she had grown up on the coast and understood the challenges people faced. She did a great job keeping everything together. Just days after she came to fill in for me, I ended up in a vehicle accident and was hospitalized, so she was left on her own to figure it all out.

Dad and I had flown into Blanc-Sablon, Quebec—near the Labrador border—after a family wedding and his medical appointments in St. Anthony, and I'd rented a pickup truck. There was no highway to drive to Mary's Harbour—the road ended at Red Bay. But we had planned to drive to St. Paul's River in Quebec to visit my brother Bradley, who was working as a manager at the Daley fish plant. We set out on the drive but on the rough gravel road I lost control, flipping the truck, and we landed upside down in a ditch. I was so scared for my father; he had a heart condition and was panicking. I got my seat belt off and crawled out the window, but I was not able to get Dad out of the vehicle. I was in shock myself and pretty shaken up. Thankfully, the car that pulled up and stopped was being driven by a nurse who helped us out and got us both to Long Point hospital in Blanc-Sablon, where we got great medical care. We were released after a few days with no broken bones or major injuries. It was a horrible experience though, and I was so thankful we were both able to walk away from it afterwards.

Through all of this Bonnie Hicks held the fort. Later I called her up to see if she would like to come back as my constituency assistant. At the time, she was nearing the end of a paralegal program, and I wasn't sure if she would be interested. But she decided to take the job on a temporary basis and, as they say, the rest is history. We have been working together now for over twenty-six years. Bonnie is a natural leader, smart and committed. She truly understands the needs of the people we serve, and we make a great team.

I was full of energy and, I suppose, youthful exuberance. That appealed to Bonnie, and so we got down to work. I learned that when you want something done, sometimes you just have to forge ahead and do it. That was pretty much what those first years were like. As an Independent Member, I was forced to set the agenda, identify what was important and move it forward. There was no time to be nervous and scared, no time to shy away from a challenging task. I was forced into the spotlight, the expectations were high, and the criticisms sharp—especially because I am a woman. I knew I had to do whatever was needed to get the job done, and that's what I did.

When I was first elected to the Newfoundland House of Assembly, Labrador was still fragmented, geographically and socially. Communities were dependent, for the most part, on ferry service in the summer and expensive air travel in the winter. A few towns had road connections to the outside world, but they were roughly built and poorly maintained. The economy, other than traditional hunting and trapping, consisted of a precarious fishery, a fledgling tourism industry, a few small forestry operations, and a couple of mines. Although lip service was being paid to providing jobs to Labradorians first, the reality was high unemployment and low incomes for us, and all the good jobs going to workers from Newfoundland or farther afield.

As an MHA, when I spoke I was honest and genuine. I saw no need to sugar-coat the issues. I was passionate, and boy, could I argue. I never stopped pushing for the things that mattered most to my district. To do that, I built productive relationships with those around me—and more and more, with the governing Tobin Liberals.

CHAPTER 7

BREAKING THE GLASS CEILING

My entire focus prior to the 1999 election had been on securing commitments to build the Trans-Labrador Highway as quickly as possible and to the highest standards possible. Those commitments led me to seek and win the Liberal nomination and the subsequent election. Never during those negotiations did I ask for, nor was I offered, a seat at the Cabinet table.

Nonetheless, I had my hopes. In the same article where he had touted me as the cause of the election, my biggest-fan-of-the-moment, columnist Michael Johansen, declared I "would be an asset at any Cabinet table." He wasn't alone in that assessment, and I admit I felt a pang of disappointment when the new Cabinet was announced and my name wasn't there. I was to begin the next stage of my career as a backbench Liberal MHA.

But my discontent was momentary. I understood the difficulties Premier Tobin faced in making his selections. Labrador only had four districts, while the island had forty-four. It was extremely unlikely that more than one minister would be named from among the three Liberals elected in Labrador, and Ernie McLean was a known quantity, having served in Cabinet since 1996. It was only logical, I thought at the time, and besides, I was still young. My turn would come.

Being a member of government was an entirely different experience from sitting as an Independent. The first thing I noticed was the tremendous support available to me as a member of the governing caucus. I didn't miss it in my first term because I had never had it in the first place. I knew I needed some help, and I had put together a team to provide it, but it was mostly volunteer and somewhat transitory. Now all of a sudden I had access to research staff who worked for the caucus as a whole and political staffers who could help when I had questions or needed direction.

On top of that, I could now build stronger relationships with my fellow Liberal MHAs. That process had begun toward the end of my first term as an Independent, but now, seeing them in caucus meetings on a regular basis, I could really get to know them and they could see what I could contribute. For the most part it was a pretty easy transition from being an Independent to becoming a government member, and with a few exceptions I succeeded in building strong relationships, many of which continue to this day.

In some ways, I had the best of both worlds. I now had these new professional supports but still had access to many of the people in St. John's and in my own district who had supported and advised me as an Independent. They provided me with personal support when times were tough and an external perspective on policy and politics that many other MHAs—having always been in a party caucus— didn't have. I continued to draw on their expertise for some time after becoming a government MHA. Gradually, those in St. John's drifted away to other interests, or I drifted away from them as they pursued political approaches I didn't agree with. However, the people in my constituency, like Agnes Pike and others I've mentioned earlier, stayed with me and remain important sounding boards after twenty-eight years in political life.

Being part of the government wasn't all sunshine and roses, of course. I still had to experience what almost every woman in politics has to endure: questions about our competence or commitment or, worse, personal attacks and insults. The House could be a bit raucous at times, and I had grown used to being heckled, shouted down, or talked over. Coming from a Labrador fishing town, there wasn't much I hadn't heard already, and I had survived a certain amount of bullying by developing a thick skin and a good sense of humour. Some would say I gave as good as I got, and maybe I did, but I never commented on how people looked or how they spoke or where they came from, or any of those demeaning putdowns that seem to be the focus of attacks on women, and especially on me at the time.

It didn't take me long to figure out what was acceptable and what wasn't. I made ample use of the rules to call out Members who crossed the line, whether with me or with other women MHAs. For the most part, successive Speakers did a good job at reining in the worst offenders and wringing apologies out of them when such was required. Not that I didn't occasionally run afoul of the Speaker myself, especially after I returned to Opposition and sometimes called out those opposite for skirting the truth—or, since I'm not bound here by parliamentary language—telling outright lies. Still, my attacks, I trust, were always directed at what people said, the policies they proposed or defended, and not at their personal qualities. I criticized what they did, not who they were.

Not all the insults came from within the House, either. I had one regular "correspondent" who, for years, starting after I was first elected, would send me long, handwritten letters questioning my ability to serve, attacking my appearance, the way I spoke and even my choice of expressions, many of which were rooted in my

Labrador heritage. They finally stopped after I was diagnosed with cancer in 2010.

The resignation of Premier Brian Tobin in 2000 and his immediate move to federal politics and a seat at the Cabinet table of Jean Chrétien came as a shock to us all and launched the Liberal Party into a fractious leadership race. Beaton Tulk took over as Premier and oversaw the contest, which pitted three Cabinet ministers—Roger Grimes, John Efford, and Paul Dicks—against each other. Efford was enormously popular, especially for his often-outrageous public statements in defence of the fishery and the seal hunt. Grimes was more understated, a solid and effective Cabinet minister who had dealt with many controversial issues over his eleven years without ever becoming controversial himself. Paul Dicks had his share of supporters as well, but it was always going to be either Efford or Grimes.

John Efford and I had often found common cause when it came to certain issues, especially support for the seal hunt, and I was often amused, even excited, at his populist approach, a way of doing politics that has a long history in Newfoundland and Labrador. I knew he could be a fine premier, but I also knew his confrontational style rubbed a lot of people the wrong way, including me at times.

Roger Grimes, on the other hand, had become a good colleague and friend, and I knew he would bring a steady hand to guide the province forward. He was far more likely to succeed in completing the negotiations on the Voisey's Bay mine and could work well with the federal government. Fighting with Ottawa also has a long history in this province, but it wasn't what we needed at the time. The combination of personal regard and professional respect is what brought me into the Grimes camp.

In the end, Roger Grimes defeated Efford by fourteen votes at the convention in February 2001. Paul Dicks refused to serve under

Grimes and retired from politics; Efford turned down a senior Cabinet post. He resigned his seat in May of that year, only to re-emerge a year later when he won a federal by-election to replace Brian Tobin, who himself had retired from politics to pursue business interests. That's how it is in politics: one door closes and another opens, and you never know who will come through it.

Backing a winner never hurts, and when the new government was formed under Premier Grimes, I received my first appointment as Parliamentary Secretary to the Minister of Health and Community Services. The role of a Parliamentary Secretary is to provide support to the minister in fulfilling his or her duties as the minister directs. It might include answering questions in the House when the minister is absent, working in the Legislature and its committees to help move forward legislation under the minister's responsibility, and generally, to participate in debates either in support of or in place of the minister. Although not a member of Cabinet, a Parliamentary Secretary may be given access to certain Cabinet papers related to their duties and are therefore sworn to uphold Cabinet confidentiality.

There is a public function to the role as well. As Parliamentary Secretary, I often engaged with the public by giving speeches or making announcements and presentations on behalf of the minister, or explaining government policy related to the portfolio. From time to time, I was asked to represent the minister and government at national or even international events.

This was all fairly new to me, but I embraced it willingly and poured all my energy into the tasks I was given. My workload increased dramatically, and I was soon glad of the additional support provided me as a member of government. That work was a tremendous learning experience, helping me to understand the inner workings of Cabinet, the role of ministers, and the relationship between political leaders and the public service. However, all of this meant less time at home and more time on the road. This was not sitting well with Jim, and his dismay was not hidden. It seemed to be the bane of our relationship that I would be away more and not around whenever he needed me. We tried to schedule important family events in advance and make more of an effort to spend time together.

As Parliamentary Secretary to the Minister of Health, I quickly learned that in Newfoundland and Labrador, health care is one of the most important provincial responsibilities. Along with education, it makes up the bulk of provincial expenditures. Given the large number of small communities scattered across the province, it was often very challenging to deliver good, affordable care, especially in Labrador. I felt I was able to bring a fresh perspective to regional concerns, and I worked hard with Minister Julie Bettney to improve the health care system. We were able to provide better transportation services for patients in Labrador to access the main hospital at St. Anthony, with regular medical flights and a dedicated bus system from St. Anthony airport to the hospital. This allowed patients to more easily access the system. It was at this time that large parts of the accommodations at the hospital were renovated to become a patient hostel—an affordable place for families to stay near loved ones who were admitted for care.

Along the coast we increased staffing at the local clinics instead of just a nurse or two; we started to add special care nurses focusing on diabetes, public health, and mental health. These were now full-time positions being recruited, not just visiting nurses. The experience also proved extremely valuable in later years when health care came to dominate provincial politics for several years under the Danny Williams government.

When Minister Bettney was moved to a new portfolio in April 2002, I was given a new job, too, this time as Parliamentary Secretary to the Minister of Works, Services and Transportation-Labrador

Transportation Initiatives. While not a promotion per se, it felt like one to me as it put me at the forefront of the issue that had brought me into politics in the first place, the Trans-Labrador Highway. It was while working with Minister Percy Barrett that I was able to lobby successfully for the extension of the Trans-Labrador Highway to Pinsent's Arm and Cartwright; both initiatives were given the green light and built under the Grimes government. I also obtained a commitment on William's Harbour in 2003, which unfortunately was subsequently cancelled by the Danny Williams government.

In February of 2003, Premier Grimes shuffled his Cabinet to put a fresh face on government and present a new team to lead us into the next election. He asked me to be part of that team. I was appointed Minister of Fisheries and Aquaculture, the first woman to ever hold that position in Newfoundland and Labrador—in fact, the first woman across Eastern Canada—as well as being Minister Responsible for the Status of Women.

Despite the cod moratorium of 1992, fishing remained a significant part of the provincial economy and an enormous part of our heritage and culture. The outgoing minister had been popular and respected, so as a woman I had plenty to prove to those in the industry. Of course, I brought assets to the job. I came from a fishing family, and my brother was still active and successful in the industry. Many around me worked in the fishery, too, either as crew in the offshore fishery or in fish processing plants. I was used to people doubting my ability and equally used to proving them wrong. I was a skilled communicator, both one-on-one and in the public sphere—where all too often, tough negotiations ended up. Most of all, I wasn't afraid of hard work, and there was nothing to keep me from throwing myself completely into the job.

The issues were huge. Only three days after my appointment in 2003, I attended a meeting of Atlantic Canada Fisheries ministers to discuss the devastating impact a rumoured closure of the Gulf cod fishery would have on the region. The Newfoundland and Labrador government had been proactively fighting such a move, harnessing our own scientific research and on-the-water knowledge from fishers to make the case for the sustainability of the fishery.

An All-Party Committee of provincial and federal politicians had made recommendations to the Fisheries Resource Management Council (FRMC) and directly to federal Fisheries Minister Robert Thibault, to try to get them to listen to what local researchers and fishers were saying, but to no avail. At the end of April, the federal government announced a fifty per cent reduction in the already small (by historic standards) cod quota in the Gulf fishery, slashing it from 7,000 to 3,500 tons. The northern cod fishery was closed altogether, other than a small sentinel fishery designed to monitor the state of the cod stocks. I was informed of the decision the night before but received no details until an hour before the announcement. There were concerns that shrimp and crab quotas were at risk as well, as a twenty per cent reduction in the snow crab fishery in the Grand Banks area had already been announced for 2003.

Despite protests across Newfoundland and Labrador and calls for Thibault to change his mind on the decision, it was clear he had no intention of moving. Both he and Gerry Byrne, a Newfoundland MP who was Minister for the Atlantic Canada Opportunities Agency, seemed reluctant to answer questions—both about the decision and about what support the federal government would provide to fishers thrown out of work because of it.

In fact, initially Byrne claimed that neither he nor Minister Thibault wanted to close the Gulf fishery, which begged the question why was the decision made. (Spoiler: It was them. They made the decision.)

The silence continued through the month of May. During a brief meeting with Minister Thibault on May 12, I asked him to review fishermen's logbooks that revealed a discrepancy between what the department scientists were saying and what was happening at sea. He essentially ignored the request. By the end of May, frustration was growing, and a proposal to change the terms of union between Canada and Newfoundland was put forward to allow for a shared management of the fishery that would give the province a meaningful role in policy and program development for the industry. By this time the federal minister was ducking and dodging, avoiding meetings and refusing to say much at all. There was no certainty over EI payments to displaced workers, nor about a rumoured $25-million make-work program to take up the slack.

Eventually, it became clear there would be no change on the cod closures and quota reductions. Still, I needed to get the minister onside about other aspects of the fishery, notably shrimp and crab quotas, and a related matter of getting licences for Indigenous fishermen in Labrador and allocating some of the quota to them. Given the turmoil in the fishery, the minister didn't want to do anything at all controversial and was simply rolling over quotas to existing licence holders (an unfortunate tendency that I still get into arguments with the current Minister about). The Minister didn't want to meet, and when we finally sat down briefly, he and the department would make no commitment.

I knew I couldn't leave it at that. I needed to talk to the Minister directly, without the filter of the formality of federal–provincial relations. I knew I could make a good case to him, and we could come to an agreement to move forward. Lawrence O'Brien was the MP for Labrador, so he was pushing for movement in Ottawa, and my staff were calling his staff relentlessly to set up this conversation. Finally, early one Sunday morning, my BlackBerry rang; when I answered it was Minister Thibault. Here I was in my pyjamas, with my hair in rollers and a big scarf on my head, sitting in my little apartment in St. John's. Thank goodness we didn't have Zoom meetings in 2003 because I would have been quite the sight.

We wound up having a good conversation—a negotiation, really, that covered a number of areas, including the shrimp quota, the allocation of licences, and some measures to stabilize the crab fishery and to provide supplementary income to those displaced by federal policy. On May 26, the minister announced a twenty-six per cent increase in the northern shrimp fishery, with a special allocation of 7,000 tons for small-boat fishers in Southern Labrador and surrounding areas. The result was a huge success for Labrador and for the province generally, and many of the benefits from those agreements are still being received.

Not all of my challenges came from the federal government. In May, the province was faced with a shutdown of the crab fishery when the processors essentially went on strike.

The system of negotiating prices for fish products, including crab, before the season began had broken down when the Fisheries Association of Newfoundland and Labrador (FANL) had withdrawn from the final offer selection process of collective bargaining for the 2003 fishery. The Fish, Food and Allied Workers' (FFAW) union, which represented fishers, had been left to try to bargain with individual fish processors, which often set one community against another and was likely to create chaos in the marketplace.

While FANL agreed to return for the 2003 fishery, the stage had been set for conflict. In May, the pot boiled over when FANL rejected the final price for crab as unsustainable. Fish plants began to close around the province, and when Fisheries Products International (FPI) joined the closures, the fishery practically shut down.

Caught in the middle were fish plant workers, most belonging to the same union as the fishers. While the boats could take their catches elsewhere, the plant workers were being laid off in droves. As seasonal workers, they had already expended their EI benefits, and the shutdown would create real hardships, both in the short and the long term.

As Minister, I felt it was incumbent on me to intervene to get the fishery running again. I held a series of meetings with the various parties and proposed several solutions to the logjam, including an increase in the amount of crabmeat processing (as opposed to whole crab). With parties unwilling to meet, I was talking to them separately, trying to find common ground. Inevitably, some of the negotiations began to take place in public, allowing Opposition politicians to attack our government's approach as mere "damage control." The media, on the one hand, encouraged our role in the discussions while also suggesting that the changing positions created "crab confusion."

When people's livelihoods are on the line, people can be loud and aggressive. Deadlines were set and missed, and accusations flew on all sides. At one point, the union accused FANL of manipulating the plant workers to try to gain advantage. It was another blow to a troubled industry and one of the biggest challenges I faced as a politician.

I recall the first meeting I held with the processors. We were gathered in a large board room at the provincial Department of Fisheries, seated around a long table. I was at the head of the table, flanked by my deputy and assistant deputy ministers, with the representatives of the companies arrayed around the table. Along the walls of the room were pictures of all the former Ministers of Fisheries for the province, with my own photo at the end of the row—the only woman framed on the ministerial wall and the only woman at the table.

Bill Barry, head of one of the larger processors, was speaking and outlining his position, when he suddenly stood up from the table and went over and took my picture off the wall and put it on the floor by his legs. He kept talking, asking questions in an aggressive way. Barry knew the industry well and I knew he would contribute to the discussion, but I remember thinking: He's trying to intimidate me. "Those are interesting points," I said, "but you'll have to wait for your answers." I turned to the next processor in line and asked for his perspective on the troubled industry. There was a brief silence, but I kept looking at him, so he made his presentation. Barry sat for a minute but then got up and hung my picture back on the wall. When I had finished with the processor I was talking to, I turned back to Barry and answered his question.

There was plenty of tension and odd behaviour in that meeting. Another processor named Terry Daley started to add to the conversation, but then turned to yelling and cursing to make his point. By this time in my life, I had heard pretty much every swear word under the sun. You don't grow up in an outport fishing family without hearing the words "fuck" or "damn" this and that. As I sat there listening to this torrent of abuse, I thought a couple of things: *I'm the minister, but I'm a woman, too, and I've been put in the position of trying to fix this mess where all these guys are losing money every single day it goes on, and they are pretty unhappy. Probably none of them have any confidence that I can fix it and they figure they're wasting their time talking to me. Which is why Terry Daley is cursing and shouting and not letting up, and not just at me but at the other processors.*

Finally, I stopped them—maybe I raised my voice a little, too—and I said: "Listen! I didn't come here to be sworn at and yelled at or to hear you curse at each other. If you want to do that, the door is right over there." I must have been convincing because after that, they did calm down and we were able to carry on. I thought: *They've settled down and they're talking again, so maybe we can actually do something here and find a solution.*

Over the next few days, I went from meeting to meeting with union representatives, fishers, fish plant workers, processors—back and forth—carrying messages, formulating proposals, finding solutions. In less than a week, all parties had come to an agreement and the crab fishing season was saved. I learned very quickly that no love was lost between the FANL, the processors, and the workers squeezed in the middle.

Those were challenging times, but by now I was an experienced politician with seven years under my belt. I had had some good mentors along the way, but I had also developed some inner strength and a thick skin. I didn't like being yelled at and insulted; who does? But I knew that if I kept my cool, remained focused and determined, listened to what people were saying, what they were concerned about, and offered practical suggestions, then solutions could be found where everyone could win a little.

Be patient and persistent.
Life is not so much what you accomplish
as what you overcome.

CHAPTER 8

THE STAR POWER OF DANNY

Even before Danny Williams became Premier, he had a larger-than-life quality about him. After finishing his degree in political science and economics, he studied at Keble College at Oxford on a Rhodes Scholarship where he pursued his lifelong love of playing hockey for the Oxford team. While still obtaining his law degree at Dalhousie University in Halifax, he negotiated his first big business deal when he led a group of businessmen to obtain the first cable television licences in Atlantic Canada.

As a lawyer, his firm became one of the biggest in Newfoundland and was frequently in the news, especially during the Mount Cashel Orphanage scandal when his practice represented many of the abused boys who were suing the Roman Catholic Church.

By the late 1990s, speculation about Danny's political ambitions began to heat up. His family had long ties to the Progressive Conservatives, and when the Liberals won another majority in 1999, the rumour mill began to run overtime.

Having built Cable Atlantic into one of the largest tele-communications companies in Atlantic Canada and become its principal owner, he sold the company in two pieces in 2000, for a total of $228 million, earning him the nickname "Danny Millions." That same year, he announced his intention to run for the leadership of the Progressive Conservative Party in the province.

It was a foregone conclusion he would win, and in April 2001 he was acclaimed as leader. Two months later he won a by-election in the district of Humber West. It was a fortuitous time for Danny to assume the leadership. The popular Liberal leader, Brian Tobin, had departed for Ottawa to serve in Jean Chrétien's Cabinet, and Roger Grimes had won a hard-fought leadership race that left the provincial Liberal Party divided.

The results were immediate, as the PCs dramatically rose in the polls. Over the next couple of years, they won all four by-elections under Danny's leadership. As well, in September 2001, Ross Wiseman crossed the floor from the Liberals to join the Progressive Conservative caucus. Danny was on a roll. He further burnished his reputation by donating his salary as Opposition Leader to charity—not exactly a hardship for him, but an impressive gesture nonetheless.

I had limited interaction with Danny Williams when he was Leader of the Opposition. I was focusing on my constituency, and after February 2001, my work as Parliamentary Secretary, first to the Minister of Health, and later to the Minister of Works, Services and Transportation. Still, when he was interviewed about why there were so few women in the PC caucus (one, to be precise), I had no choice but to respond. According to Danny, women "just don't have the artillery to win the nomination . . . they did not have the support, they did not understand the process, and they just got beaten at the nomination level."

Having fought hard to win the nomination in 1996 and been denied it by last-minute rule changes, and being surrounded by several strong, capable women who had won their nominations, won elections, and were now occupying some of the most senior positions in Cabinet, I replied: "While there may be hurdles for women to overcome in pursuing a political career, lack of intelligence about the nomination process is not one of them." While Danny's views toward women in politics did evolve, when he first started out he was still stuck in the old boys' mentality of traditional politics. However, throughout the rest of his political career he demonstrated support for women in politics and made tremendous efforts to give them important positions in his government.

No one was really surprised by the October 2003 election results. Danny Williams was like a soldier who had just come back from winning the war, waving the flag and leading the parade. People had real confidence in him as the guy who could solve all their problems. Going door to door was really tough for our candidates; most of us could tell the writing was on the wall. So, we were not surprised, but it was painful. Twenty of our Members, including six Cabinet ministers, lost their seats. The PCs won thirty-four of forty-eight seats, with almost fifty-nine per cent of the popular vote.

Danny Williams had the longest and probably the sweetest honeymoon of any politician in Canadian history—only Frank McKenna in New Brunswick could give him a run for that record. Other than a brief dip in 2004, in the wake of significant cuts to government spending and a month-long public service strike, he remained sky-high in the polls for nearly his whole time in office.

While an opinion poll in June 2004 showed support for the PCs falling to forty-one per cent—only two points ahead of the Liberals—there was little we could do to exploit the short-term drop. The next election was nearly three years away, and there was not even the prospect of a by-election to chasten the government. Besides, we were still recovering from the defeat a mere eight months earlier, trying to sort out who would be more effective as critics and how we might restore the party's fortunes, both politically and financially.

Even the resignation of Elizabeth Marshall, the Minister of Health in the Williams government, did not tarnish Danny's reputation much, even though it was obvious that her leaving was connected to the Premier's blatant but behind-the-back interference in her portfolio. This demonstrated, as I said at the time, how much of a one-man show his government really was; power was concentrated at the top. His efforts to reduce the number of seats in the Legislative Assembly was another example of this; it would have impacted rural—and especially, Labrador—representation, and it was an area that I and others pushed back hard on, so that in the end the cuts weren't made.

There's nothing like picking a fight with Ottawa to bolster support for a premier and his government. This tried-and-true tactic became part of Danny's repertoire while he was renegotiating the Atlantic Accord with the Paul Martin government late in 2004. Martin had offered an eight-year deal that allowed the province to keep 100 per cent of its revenue from offshore oil. For context, constitutionally the offshore was within federal jurisdiction, but previous versions of the Accord had allowed the province to keep a portion of the royalties. However, there was an expenditure cap to prevent provinces from exceeding the per capita tax revenue of Ontario. Danny claimed that would cost the province billions over the life of the existing oil fields, and he, along with the other Atlantic Premiers, walked away from the negotiations.

Always one for grand gestures, on December 23, 2004, Danny ordered all the Canadian flags flying on provincial buildings to be removed. It made national headlines and caused quite a stir in Newfoundland. It was less impressive to those of us in Labrador. There they did not take down Canadian flags, simply because at that time Labradorians felt more of an allegiance to Canada than they did to Newfoundland and to Danny Williams and his government. Still, the tactic was an effective wake-up call for Ottawa. Negotiations resumed, and by January 10, the flags were flying again. A few weeks later an improved deal was signed with Newfoundland and Labrador, and Nova Scotia. An opinion poll in March 2005 showed that support for the Newfoundland Conservative government had reached eighty-six per cent, a level that would be common for the rest of Danny's time in office.

I learned that defying Danny Williams never came without a price. Despite promises in the Throne Speech and the 2005 budget to open a Premier's office in Labrador to provide greater access to the government, the office never materialized and eventually disappeared from the books. I speculated in the House of Assembly that there might be a reason for that. "I looked at it and I said, 'I hope it is not vengeance …' Then I had to ask myself: was the whole flag flap the issue why Labrador, in itself, did not get addressed in this budget?" I never got an answer to that, though I took a lot of abuse for raising the subject.

I'm sure that Danny considered himself to be the sole reason for the ongoing strength of his government and the support given to it by the people of Newfoundland and Labrador. People did see him as the saviour of the party (and, by extension, the province), so wasn't he due the absolute loyalty of his MHAs? It certainly seemed that was his way of thinking. It certainly seemed it when PC politician Fabian Manning fell out of favour, even though he had been a loyal soldier. As I said in the House at the time: "He supported his party, he believed in his government, and when he made his speeches, they all tapped on the desk over there, Mr. Chair, praising him up until he dared to do his job. When he dared to do his job and stand up for the poor fisheries workers in this Province, Mr. Chair, he was given the boot." More than that, his actions were labelled treasonous—as if he had sold secrets to the enemy.

If Danny Williams had one weakness as a politician, that was it. He could not abide criticism. His reaction was often overreaction, and the more deserved the critical remarks were, the more outraged he became. In 2006, he threatened to discipline hospital pharmacists if they spoke out about working conditions or the lack of staff.

That same year, he was criticized for his bullying approach in negotiations over the Hebron oil field. Again, speaking in the House, I said, "These are the kinds of comments that they are making, the people who are working in the oil industry: as far as everyone is concerned globally, we are not open for business. We are not open for business, and no one wants to deal with him—referring to the Premier of the Province. All he does is fight, and the business community here is sick of it." Although a deal was eventually reached that saw the province take a small ownership share in the oil field, for a number of months it really did seem that Danny Williams' approach would scupper the whole thing.

One of the worst examples of his leadership style was evident a couple of years later, when the Cameron Inquiry investigating the provincial breast cancer screening scandal began asking tough questions of the government. Danny immediately went off on the Commission, making outrageous statements to the media. Then, he expressed surprise at learning that a number of people had taken offence to his remarks.

I addressed this during the budget debate in May 2008, as recorded in *Hansard:*

"The problem here is that all the soldiers are not marching to
the drum. He cannot line them up like he can his caucus and
his Cabinet. He cannot have them all play to the one beat

and, because of that, Mr. Speaker, he is scorching, so he goes out and he questions the Cameron Inquiry and the integrity of the people who are there. He calls it a witch hunt. A witch hunt, Mr. Speaker, is the phrase that he uses. He talks about it being a prosecution, not an inquiry."

Despite all this, the Premier and his government remained inordinately popular with the people of the province. When the election was held in 2007, he increased his majority, going from thirty-four seats to forty-four seats and gaining an astonishing 69.6 per cent of the vote. No other party in Newfoundland and Labrador, before or since, has reached such heights. As far as I know, no other party in Canadian history has garnered that much support. When Frank McKenna's Liberal Party won every seat in the New Brunswick legislature in 1987, they did it with just over sixty per cent of the vote. Not surprisingly, those results only added fuel to the fire.

With our caucus reduced to three Members—Kelvin Parsons, Roland Butler, and myself—it became increasingly difficult to hold the government to account. Cuts to our caucus financing after the election in 2007 further hobbled our efforts. It seemed to me and to some members of the media, as well, that this was a deliberate effort to muzzle the Opposition. I got into a bit of trouble in the House for suggesting bias on the part of the Speaker when he was acting as Chair of the Operations Commission. In that role, he sided with government Members in every instance, breaking tie votes on the allocation of funds.

Cuts were made to all three parties, but it seemed the cuts to the Liberal caucus were more extreme than those suffered by the NDP and the Progressive Conservatives. As the sitting government, the PCs could leverage plenty of research and advice from department officials. To make matters worse, the Chair subsequently allowed an appeal of the allocation to the NDP, providing that party with additional resources. No such appeal was allowed in our case.

We were forced to lay off some very good people as a result, and at one point, threatened legal action to rectify what we considered an unfair outcome. At the end of the day, I decided that we had made our point and that the best way forward was to show them exactly what three hard-working and determined MHAs could accomplish. How many resources you have is less important than how well you use them. So, we knuckled down, worked long but effective hours, and focused on areas where we could make a difference. As Interim Leader at that time, I felt our performance in the House was the best way to restore the party's credibility, while the party executive and constituencies rebuilt the organization and finances from the ground up.

It wasn't easy. Newfoundland had entered a period where, thanks to revenues from Voisey's Bay and offshore oil and the new Atlantic Accord, the government was running significant surpluses. One year it reached $2.4 billion, which, to put it into perspective, was almost twenty per cent of the provincial debt at that time. After the austerity of 2004 and 2005, the government under Danny Williams was suddenly awash in cash. While they prudently used a significant portion of the surpluses to pay down the debt, there was plenty left over to spend on infrastructure, improved services, and tax cuts.

It was very hard to question Danny or his government. The Progressive Conservative caucus and staff were all very loyal to him; there were no secret phone calls or brown envelopes being passed around hinting at dissent. Sure, some of the PC Members were upset at some of Danny's policies, but none of them would have the face to confront him. So no, they were not going to stick their neck out and feed information to the Opposition, nor were the public servants. Everything went quiet. There were some issues on the edge of government we could and did go after, but you could never really go after the Tories on policy because they never really talked about their policy. You could question what they did, but it was hard to find out or question why they did it.

Of course, despite his aggressive and frequently bullying ways, Danny Williams could be charming—even chivalrous. When, during the 2007 election, my Progressive Conservative opponent, Dennis Normore, suggested the riding would be punished if it continued to send a Liberal MHA to St. John's, the Premier promptly intervened. "This is not the way we operate. There is not a question of any district paying at all for not having a government seat." He went on to say that he was "very annoyed" at these "improper comments." Not surprisingly, Normore apologized. The people of Cartwright-L'Anse au Clair also spoke out loud and clear; while Liberals were losing their seats all across the province, I got my second-highest vote of my entire time in provincial politics—seventy-two per cent.

Danny might attack you one day on one issue, and then be complimentary or helpful on another issue the next. On occasion he would even speak privately with me to apologize for a particularly harsh remark. He was very good at building relationships and at getting people on his side—even if your job was to oppose him. That was why he could appoint so many of his buddies and partners to good government positions and almost no one would question him. If you could show him it was wrong, he might back down or shift a little, but it was a hard job to ever convince him he was wrong.

Still, we Liberals did have our victories, such as getting Danny to admit the government might have overreached in limiting the role of the Auditor General in reviewing the operations of the House, or finally demanding that Andy Wells resign as mayor of St. John's before being appointed as head of the Public Utilities Board. As much as he bristled at being criticized or questioned, I believe he secretly appreciated a good fight and a strong argument and, in the end, respected his opponents. At one point during my time as Interim Leader of the party, he declared that our hard work, careful research, and focus made our caucus of three a more effective Opposition than the one he had faced in his first term, when we were a caucus of twelve.

I can't end my Danny Williams saga without discussing the famous ABC—Anything But Conservative—election of 2008. When Stephen Harper was campaigning to become Prime Minister in the 2006 election, he promised not to include revenue from non-renewable energy sources in the equalization formula, but when he became Prime Minister, he reneged on that promise in the 2007 federal budget. Danny was furious, saying they'd had a firm commitment from Harper and the change would cost Newfoundland dearly. When an election was called for October 2008, Williams launched his "Anything But Conservative" campaign, going so far as to register the movement as a "third party" with Elections Canada.

Although the ABC campaign was nationwide, its impact was strictly local. The Harper-led Conservatives lost all their seats in Newfoundland and Labrador, and saw their share of the vote drop by twenty-six per cent. Six Liberals and one New Democrat were sent to Ottawa. The impact elsewhere was less profound; the federal Conservatives gained seats in an increased minority government and went on to win a majority (but with only one Newfoundland and Labrador MP) in 2011. Of course, by then, fences had been mended and Danny Williams went back to his strictly partisan ways.

Over the years, I had other deep disagreements with Premier Williams, especially when it came to the development of Muskrat Falls—a subject that deserves its own chapter—and the development of the province's oil fields. I and my team fought the good fight despite the overwhelming popularity Danny enjoyed.

Even the media treated him like the guy who had all the answers, so they would generally simply go to him for advice on what was happening. When he was under pressure, he didn't sit back and wait or let someone else deal with it; he would charge right in and lay it all out. He had such an aggressive style that no one really wanted to take him on; when they did, they soon regretted it, retracting stories or issuing apologies in the face of his real or pretended outrage.

Then in November of 2010, Danny Williams announced his departure, surprising even his closest colleagues. I was as shocked as anyone. He left just after I became the official Leader of the Opposition. If I were conceited, I might claim that was the reason, but in reality he quit while he was on top. And he was very much on top of his game and could easily have won another term. No one forced him out, there was no looming scandal—he was still massively popular. He had had a health scare, which might have been a factor, though he never said so in public. His fans might have said he put in his years and did a good job, signed the deal on Muskrat Falls, and deserved to get on with his life— attaboy, Danny.

I sometimes wish things had turned out differently and that I'd had the opportunity to go head-to-head with Danny Williams in the 2011 election. I am confident I would have given him a good fight; truth be told, my four years facing him across the floor as Interim Leader of the Opposition had honed my own political skills. One thing he taught me was that no leader, however popular, is infallible. The more they think they are, the more vulnerable they become.

CHAPTER 9

LEADER OF THE LOYAL OPPOSITION

When I was first elected as an Independent in 1996, I had one thing on my mind: to improve the lives and economic fortunes of the people of my district. My primary goal was to get the Trans-Labrador Highway built to connect the communities of Cartwright-L'Anse au Clair to the rest of Canada. Even after I switched to the Liberal Party for the 1999 election, my ambitions were modest. No Cabinet seat was promised, and none was forthcoming, and while I admit to being a little bit disappointed, I understood that I was new to the caucus and had to pay my dues.

But by the time of the next election in 2003, I had been appointed to Cabinet as the first woman Minister of Fisheries in Eastern Canada. While I was confident going into that election—I was re-elected with sixty per cent of the vote—it soon became clear that we were in for a rough ride in the rest of the province. When the votes were counted, the Liberal Party received its lowest percentage of the popular vote since the province had joined Canada; only twelve Liberals were elected to the House of Assembly. Nearly half the

Cabinet was gone and not a single Liberal was elected in St. John's or its suburbs. The party was dispirited and, what's more, deeply in debt.

The caucus felt a little lost after the 2003 election. Aside from myself, none of them had ever sat in Opposition before. A few, including the party leader, Roger Grimes, had been in government since 1989. Now, they had to operate without access to the bureaucracy, with reduced personal staff and caucus resources; they had to learn how to ask questions instead of answering them, how to attack government policies and actions instead of defending them. In defeat, the divisions in the party may have grown deeper, making it harder to work as a cohesive and effective Opposition.

Meanwhile, Danny Williams continued to grow in popularity and strength, and he would later say that the Opposition during his first term was "largely ineffective."

I, on the other hand, had always enjoyed the freedom and excitement of being in Opposition. I'd had three years as an Independent MHA and had learned when to excoriate the government and when to acknowledge they did something good—if only to encourage them to do even more. I thought Opposition was the best place you could ever land in politics. I still believe that—not for the people I represent but for me as a politician. I didn't have to deliver for a political party; I could just be the voice of the people. It was easy to say what people wanted to hear, and have them suddenly think you were a great Member. This was the shallowness I could never understand; you were not measured by what you delivered but by what you said. Still, I absolutely loved being in Opposition.

It was a bit of a comedown, of course, to go from being a minister to an Opposition Member, but then again, given the controversies and criticisms that went with the Department of Fisheries, it was a bit of a relief, too. I could go back to what I had entered politics to do: stand up for the interests of my constituents. By now, I brought a broader perspective to the job. I could see how the difficulties faced by the residents of Southern Labrador were shared not only by other parts of Labrador, but also by much of rural Newfoundland. Increasingly, I was able to develop that perspective into an overall approach to pushing the new government to do more for rural areas, to spread around the new-found wealth that was coming from oil and other resources in order to help people in their daily lives.

Having been in government and in Cabinet, I had a clear view of what government could and should do to help people. I had learned a lot from the more experienced Members of the caucus and Cabinet, and now I was focused on expanding my knowledge and understanding, both in those areas I had been assigned to act as critic for, but also across the whole range of government responsibilities.

It came as no surprise when Roger Grimes announced his resignation as leader and MHA in May 2005. He had been in the House for sixteen years, twelve of them as Minister or Premier. Danny Williams was still ascendant and the prospects of Grimes returning to the Premier's office were slim to none. It was, as he said, the right time to retire from provincial politics.

Gerry Reid was appointed Interim Leader of the party, but he expressed little desire for the permanent role. We had two years before the next election—time enough for a good candidate to emerge and for the party to get its finances in order. But gradually, it became clear that no one in caucus wanted the job. When a leadership vote was held in February of 2006, the lone candidate was a lawyer, Jim Bennett. He won the leadership by acclamation.

Jim Bennett had grown up on the Northern Peninsula of Newfoundland in Daniel's Harbour. He was familiar with the people and culture of the province, and he was smart and well-educated. He was a lawyer who practised in the province but had also practised in Ontario where he had lived for a number of years. That alone made him attractive—he had history here but no real history in the provincial party. He was a fresh face.

But for whatever reason, people didn't gravitate to him. A lot of his ideas about government direction or remedies for certain problems were controversial, which caused people to pay attention to him—but not in a positive way. Things came to a head when Bennett proposed a two-tier minimum wage system for the province, which the caucus vehemently opposed. Jim Bennett was forced to resign at the end of May 2006, and Gerry Reid once again became Interim Leader.

There was discussion again in 2007 about holding a leadership race, and the media again questioned whether I would be a candidate. By this time, however, no one—including me—had any appetite for such a contest. Danny Williams, after his brief slump in 2004, was once again sky-high in the polls and the attitude was that we needed to consolidate and hold on to as many seats as we could until Danny's popularity began to wane.

The election of 2007 was a disaster for the provincial Liberal Party. We didn't even have a full slate of candidates. Our popular vote dropped by eleven per cent to a new record low, and we were reduced to a mere three seats. Gerry Reid suffered a particularly heartbreaking loss, losing his seat by only six votes after a judicial recount. Our caucus consisted of myself, Kelvin Parsons, and Roland Butler. A single New Democrat, new leader Lorraine Michael, made up the rest of the Opposition. Across from us sat forty PC Members, led by the seemingly unstoppable Danny Williams.

In November, the party turned to me and I accepted the role of Interim Leader, with a leadership convention scheduled for October 2008 to pick a permanent one. I was comfortable leading the party in the House. "In an interim basis, I'm going to lead a party I'm very proud of. I believe in the principles and policies of this party and

I'm energized with the opportunity that lies ahead and I'm up to the task at hand," I said. After ten years, more than half of it spent in Opposition, I knew the ins and outs of the House of Assembly. I was used to hard work and knew I could do well by choosing my fights carefully.

Our initial focus would be on Labrador and rural Newfoundland, especially the West Coast, which had been hard hit by closures of pulp and paper plants and a gypsum mill. "Low unemployment in St. John's is fabulous, but surpluses need to be spread around to other regions," I pointed out. I was happy to praise the government for addressing pay equity and reducing the debt in the teachers' pension plan. These were good policies, but our job was to make those policies even stronger. Investment in tourism and forestry, as well as support for the fishery, were essential to creating a balanced economy and should have been a priority—yet they weren't part of any government plan. By focusing on those omissions and any errors the government made, even a caucus of three could be an effective Opposition.

Kelvin Parsons and Roland Butler were perfect complements to my own strengths. I had developed a reputation as a "scrapper," according to the *Newfoundland Herald*, and had an in-depth knowledge of the fishery, health, and women's issues, as well as business experience and personal first-hand knowledge of the difficulties of living in rural and remote areas. My work as a journalist had honed my communication skills and helped me formulate tough questions.

Kelvin Parsons was a lawyer who had first been elected in 1999. He had served as Minister of Justice and Attorney General for three years in the Grimes government and brought those legal insights to his work in Opposition. Kelvin and I became more than simply colleagues; he became a very close friend who supported me through my toughest times. With his wife, Jeanette Fleming, he became an important part of my life and remains so to this day. When I had to step away from the leadership during my battle with cancer in 2010, he took over as Interim Leader, doubling his workload without a hint of complaint.

Roland Butler was first elected in 2001 in a by-election in the district of Port de Grave, formerly held by John Efford; Roland had previously served as Efford's executive assistant. He had completed a program in business administration, but what he was really known for was his deep involvement in his community. A long-time resident of Shearstown, where he lived with his wife, Maude, and family, Roland was an active member of the Lions Club and volunteered with numerous sports and recreation organizations, as well as being an active member of his church. He had been named Shearstown's Citizen of the Year in 1993. Roland was so rooted and well-liked in his community that he actually increased his share of the vote in his district in 2007, defying the blue wave elsewhere in the province.

This deep knowledge of community often proved invaluable during our time in Opposition. Roland was very much an "elder statesman" and a calming influence in the caucus and in the House. He took a lot of pride in representing his constituents on the issues that affected everyday people. He wasn't as interested at that time in the bigger picture of politics, what the policies of the party would be or how we created our vision to handle the issues to meet the needs of people. Rather, he was very much a strong constituency MHA who worked hard every day to deliver for the people who had sent him to the House of Assembly. On issues like reducing medical wait times or adding a new drug to combat Alzheimer's to the provincial formula, or addressing unemployment and the needs of small communities, he would speak very eloquently and had a lot of impact, because these matters affected all Newfoundlanders and Labradorians, not just people in his riding. He had a very grounded approach in terms of delivering his message, keeping it relevant to his own constituents and therefore relevant to others across the province.

Roland was very much a family man and his wife, Maude, was a big part of his political career. She supported him consistently. Whatever events went on, she was always there. They brought a family perspective to our small caucus. They would have us for dinner at their apartment in St. John's, where Maude would cook while we got together to have our caucus meeting over a meal at their kitchen table. Roland had a huge heart and never wanted to hurt anyone, so he was always careful in what he said and how he said it, even in the most heated debates. I think he helped keep us balanced in our approach of acknowledging when the government was doing good, while holding their feet to the fire to make them do better.

Those first few months were busy for all of us as we settled into our new roles. Even as 2008 had barely begun, the media had begun speculating who would come forward to run for the leadership at the convention planned for October. My name was bandied about in various outlets, some encouraging, others dismissing me as part of the "old guard." Kelvin Parsons was also a subject of speculation, as was my old opponent, Danny Dumaresque, who was now president of the party. Roland Butler had announced he definitely wasn't running and was the first to suggest what we were all thinking—that we weren't ready for a leadership race. The party was at its lowest level of support ever, it was deeply in debt, and in many ridings, we had little or no organization on the ground.

The executive agreed, and much to my relief at the time, the leadership question was put aside until 2010. Make no mistake, I fully intended to become the permanent leader, but for now, it was more important to show we could be an effective Opposition in the House while we rebuilt the party apparatus from the ground up. I was fully committed to those tasks, and we had a lot of work to do on both fronts. With no one clamouring for the job, the permanent leadership could wait until we had something formidable for the eventual winner to lead.

As 2008 unfolded, the task ahead become ever clearer. Although the provincial budget forecast a surplus of over $500 million—which later grew to well over a billion dollars—dark clouds were on the horizon. A worldwide financial crisis triggered by sub-prime mortgages had begun with the United States falling into recession in December 2007 and staying there until June 2009. Canada fared considerably better because of the strength of our banking sector and the fact that commodity prices—a key part of the Canadian and Newfoundland economies—continued to rise until the middle of 2008. The recession, when it finally arrived in Canada in December—brought on by falling exports, especially to the US—was relatively mild and ended when the economy began to pick up south of the border.

Still, the April 2008 budget forecast a significant downturn in 2009 and projected a deficit of nearly $750 million for 2009–10. As it turned out, the province was once again saved by high oil prices, which shaved that deficit by nearly sixty per cent. Still, the years of large surpluses were over and, with the exception of 2010–11, budget deficits were the norm for the remainder of the PC government's life.

Tighter finances—even just the expectation of them—meant tougher choices for the government and, to some extent, that made an easier job for the Opposition. Money spent in certain areas of the economy generally meant less for others, which was certainly the case when it came to the fishery and the forest industry. If one region received more than its share of expenditures, other parts of the province might go wanting. It was certainly my view and that of my colleagues that rural Newfoundland and much of Labrador, where the needs were the greatest and the cost of living the highest, were being short-changed.

However, before we could focus our criticism on the government's failures, we had our own hurdles to overcome. While spending was up overall in the 2008 budget, one significant cut that directly impacted our ability to do our job was a large reduction in the allocation to our caucus. Technically, this decision was made by the Management Commission that governed the internal affairs of the House, but there was little doubt in my mind that it was an edict that came directly out of the Premier's office. Danny Williams and his team didn't like being questioned, didn't like having their mistakes discovered and revealed, didn't like criticism of any kind. What better way to limit that than to reduce the resources of the political parties who were doing the questioning? The government side argued that we now had a smaller caucus, conveniently forgetting that, as the Official Opposition, we were duty bound to hold the government accountable for all of its programs and services. If anything, our workload and our reliance on trained researchers had increased.

We, of course, appealed the decision, as did the NDP, who had also had its resources cut. When the votes were held in the Management Commission meeting, the Chair, who also happened to be the Speaker of the House, broke the tie to grant the NDP some relief, but voted against increasing our budget. Case closed. Although even some members of the media called on the Speaker to "take the high road" and suggested we could resort to the courts to seek a remedy, I knew that would be a waste of time and resources.

I wasn't going to take this lying down, though. Outside the House, I made sure that anyone within the sound of my voice knew that Speaker Roger Fitzgerald was acting out of partisan bias when he cast that vote as Chair of the Committee. I was immediately accused, as I knew I would be, of attacking the integrity of the

Speaker. A point of privilege was raised in the House by Government House Leader Joan Burke, suggesting that I should be forced to apologize or be otherwise disciplined.

It was during the debate on this matter than Kelvin Parsons really shone. In a well-researched, well-argued, and lengthy submission, Kelvin delved into the long-standing traditions of Parliament, as well as the specific Act that established the Management Commission in the wake of the 2007 spending scandal that had impacted several sitting and former MHAs, and ultimately sent one to jail. He even quoted Fitzgerald himself, to underline how there could be no point of privilege regarding the Speaker, since Fitzgerald was not in his role as Speaker when he had cast his vote:

> "Even though it is not in there and reflected in *Hansard*, the Leader of the Official Opposition, I do believe, in our meeting of November 18—and this is very important—asked the question of the person occupying the seat at the end of this table here, who is the Member for Bonavista North, the Speaker of our House of Assembly, specifically asked him: In what capacity do you sit here in this Management meeting? The response of the Speaker was: I am not here as Speaker; I am here as Chair of the Management Commission."

Kelvin must have been very persuasive, as he won over NDP Leader Lorraine Michael and, moreover, led the Speaker himself to rule there was no point of privilege involved (though he did suggest we should all be more respectful of the Management Commission Chair).

The question of bias was left to another day. In 2010, I accused Fitzgerald, this time in his role as Speaker, of being biased in his rulings in the House when it came to controlling heckling, silencing me more often than government Members who were disruptive in the House. I refused to be silenced by hecklers—yahoos, as I frequently called them—or by the Speaker's rulings or non-rulings. The Speaker demanded that I apologize, which I only did because, as I told the press, I "did not want to cause more chaos in the House."

In the end, our caucus did not receive additional resources, forcing us to lay off several of our loyal staff, a necessity that pains me to this very day. They all went on to careers in other fields, but at the time it was traumatic for all involved. As for the caucus, we resolved to work even harder to hold the government to account, which we did with vigour and determination for the next two years.

There were countless issues that arose in those days. Some were of major importance—the breast screening scandal, the Muskrat Falls development—and merit their own chapters. Others occupied the agenda for a few weeks or months, and, although they eventually faded into obscurity, with each one we were able to raise questions about the government's intent or actions and gradually chip away at the shield of invincibility that seemed to protect the legend of Danny Williams. Every time we were able to show government failures, it reduced the aura of competence that they tried to project.

Several matters come to mind that are worth mentioning. A report of the provincial Fire Marshal highlighted the lack of adequate fire alarms and other protective equipment in the province's schools and institutions. The government initially tried to downplay the scope of the problem but, in the end, allocated sufficient resources to solve it. Cutbacks in health and education, lack of community infrastructure, the high cost of living—especially in remote areas—were the kinds of everyday issues we were raising whenever we could.

Of course, not all the mistakes the government made were small-scale. Legislation in 2009 to claw back the water and timber rights from the Abitibi paper mill after the company announced its closure "accidentally"—in the words of the Premier—included the mill and the polluted grounds on which it stood. This saddled the province with tens of millions of dollars in environmental expenditures and eventually cost the federal government $130 million in compensation because of the provisions of the North American Free Trade Agreement. The damage to the province's reputation with the international business community was incalculable. The government tried to claim that the recovered rights more than compensated for the costs and tried to get the courts to allocate the damages to the company, but in 2012 the Supreme Court turned them down. In the end, they had to apologize and accept the liability—or rather, taxpayers did.

By working hard and staying focused on issues, criticizing the government when they failed, by praising them when they did well while pushing them to do better, we were able to have a real impact. The 2009 provincial budget addressed many of the issues we had been raising, and we even began to inch up slightly in the polls. Our caucus was praised for our hard work and effectiveness by the provincial media, and even by the Premier and some of his ministers.

By the end of 2009, I had reached a level of professional confidence that allowed me to think it was time to change my title from "interim" to "permanent" leader of the Liberal Party. The convention was still a year away, but I decided that I needed to act like the party leader, not just in the House, but on the hustings. The perfect opportunity arose when a by-election was called in The Straits-White Bay North for October 2009. The seat became vacant when Minister Trevor Taylor abruptly resigned. He claimed it was for personal reasons, but his decision did come after the government announced it was moving some key medical services out of his area. That issue became the focus of our campaign.

Marshall Dean ran for us in the district. He was very well respected in the community, very smart, very well-spoken. Marshall was a former Salvation Army officer and a local businessman. His wife worked at the hospital and they had a beautiful family; he was probably the ideal candidate. I knew a strong candidate wasn't going to be enough though, so I went to St. Anthony with my Chief of Staff at the time, Joan Marie Aylward—herself a former minister in the Tobin government. We rented a hotel room, unpacked our bags, and stayed there for the entire election. I knocked on doors every day with the candidate. We were out doing rallies, meeting groups and individuals. We were doing everything that we possibly could to win that seat. We did not relent for one minute; when it was all over, we were able to win it despite the love felt for Danny Williams across Newfoundland. People on the Northern Peninsula knew they could do better, that they *deserved* better. Health care was the main industry in the area, and the Williams government's tampering with those services and threatening their future was the card we needed to win.

This gave us a great deal of momentum. It was my first real foray into the field as leader. Danny Williams was still strong and had a strong bench, but we were able to beat him in that seat because people there needed a voice. Winning in St. Anthony was huge for me, because it allowed me to establish a higher level of credibility as a leader. People began to take notice of what we were doing in a different way, recognizing that we were working hard and raising good issues, and they wanted to support us.

During the weeks I was in St. Anthony supporting the campaign, Jim came to visit. I had not had much contact with him in recent months and our marriage had become very strained, with me away and dedicated to my work rather than the relationship. We parted ways that fall knowing the end was near and that it was time to get our legal affairs in order. Our post-nuptial agreement was activated, and for a legal fee of $500 each it was settled in the spring. Life takes many twists and turns; this time I was driving off the marriage road. It had been over for a number of years, and my new leadership role had sealed our fate.

At this point I was no longer in fear of the public aspersions that would be cast upon me as a divorced woman in politics. Gossip and chatter were already happening around me; it was harmless, but I knew it was time to make our breakup legal and move on. Our post-nuptial agreement was valid and agreeable to us both, which took away the bitterness and fighting that can come with divorce. My family and friends were supportive, and Jim and I were both ready to move forward separately. The most difficult part for me was moving away from his mom, Marjorie, who had lived with us for the nearly 20 years we were together. She was a beautiful, kind, soft-spoken woman who held a special place in my heart and my life. She was so kind and accepting of me and provided a sense of simple tranquility that I had longed for in my life. We remained in contact until she passed away in the summer of 2023.

A month after The Straits-White Bay North by-election, another had been called in the district of Terra Nova. Unlike the seat Marshall Dean won for us, which was historically Liberal, Terra Nova had swung back and forth between Liberal and PC for nearly thirty years. The vacancy arose with the resignation of Health Minister Paul Oram, who claimed health concerns as his reason for leaving. This time, no single issue in the district could be laid at the government's door. The candidate running for the PCs, Sandy Collins, was well known in the area, having served as Oram's constituency assistant. Oram had won the seat with seventy-four per cent of the vote in 2007, so it was going to be a tough election for us. Oram was well-liked and respected, and although his name wasn't on the ballot, he still influenced a lot of voters.

I couldn't spend as much time in Terra Nova as I had campaigning for Marshall Dean, but I was there for about half the campaign, and the other two caucus Members went in to support John Baird as well. Without a strong local issue to focus on and with people wanting to remain part of the government side, it was a tough sell, but we did everything we could. While John didn't win, he did increase our vote by over twenty per cent from the 2007 election; I took a certain amount of comfort and confidence from that.

John Baird was a strong candidate for us, but people didn't gravitate to him in the same way that they had with others. He had worked his entire life as a forestry conservation officer. He understood the connections between people and the environment. He had a lot of good ideas around conservation and building a greener economy, but people were in a different mindset in the province at that time. Things have changed a lot since 2009, and an environmentalist like John might have a better chance at being elected today, even in a place like Terra Nova—which remains a PC stronghold.

Three more by-elections took place in 2010 and early 2011, including the district vacated by Premier Williams. They were all districts that had voted overwhelmingly Conservative in 2007, and, in each case, there was no whiff of conflict or scandal around the vacancies. All three districts returned government Members, but in two of the three the Liberals increased their share of the vote by fifteen to twenty per cent, another indication that our fortunes were on the rise.

That summer I was spending even more time on the road campaigning, getting better acquainted with the various districts, and recruiting support for the party. However, it was at the Labrador Expo in June 2010 that things in my personal life took an unexpected turn.

The year before, in 2009, I was giving a speech at the Expo's opening conference in Happy Valley-Goose Bay. It was a forum to focus on future resource development across Labrador and to network with people from diverse industry backgrounds. I was one of the speakers welcoming people to Labrador and calling out the mining companies by name to thank them for their partnership and investments in Labrador communities.

As I was walking off the stage in the arena, I could see a man waiting at the end of the steps, hand outstretched. He introduced himself as Joseph Lanzon and went on to ask me why I hadn't mentioned the name of his company in my remarks. I had no idea what company he represented, so I asked him. He said, "I'm with Labrador Iron Mines and I have my chairman and the president of the board here. I would love for you to come and meet them all." I could tell right away Joseph was a guy of high energy and certainly knowledgeable about the mining industry. I agreed to meet with him and his company team for lunch and got to know them all a little bit better. I worked with them on their operation in Labrador, helping them connect with the right people to move the project along.

A year later I was back at Expo Labrador, this time after having spoken to a friend, Premier Bob MacLeod of the Northwest Territories. I had known Bob for quite some time and was a great admirer of his leadership and the work he was doing in the western Arctic. Bob had said, "I'd love to introduce you to a friend of mine. I think the two of you would be very compatible," then he told me the friend's name: Joseph Lanzon. I started to laugh. I told him we had already met but that I had been under the assumption that Joseph was married with family. I learned very quickly that was not the case.

I guess Bob operated as a mediator between us, because when we met in 2010 we exchanged phone numbers and emails and decided that we would keep in touch—and so we did. I was planning to attend a legislative conference in Saskatoon, and Joseph suggested I stop over in Ottawa on the way back. We could get together for the weekend and get to know each other a little better, away from work. It was an interesting proposition. However, I was non-committal, and for good reason: I had just undergone a biopsy for breast cancer, and I didn't know when the result was coming back or what it would be.

July came and off to Saskatoon I went. By now I had gone for a second biopsy and was still waiting on the result. The day after I arrived in Saskatoon, I got a call from my doctor telling me that my results were negative and that everything was good. I was excited and happy at this positive news, and I went out and celebrated with some of my political colleagues from across the country that I had known for a number of years. I called Joseph to tell him that I would meet him on Friday in Ottawa and that I was looking forward to our weekend together. The conference was great, and I was full of anticipation about getting to know Joseph better, about what the prospects would be for us, and even thinking, *Who knows, maybe this would just work out.*

When I got off the red-eye in Ottawa from Saskatoon, I wasn't necessarily looking my best, but I was excited and ready for a nice, relaxing weekend with great company. We left the airport and were driving to Mont Tremblant, where Joseph had booked a cottage for the weekend. On the way, we stopped at Montebello in Northern Quebec, a resort on the St. Lawrence Seaway. As I was getting out of the vehicle, my phone rang. I took the call; it was my doctor again. First she asked if I was alone or if someone was with me; I said I was with a friend. She said: *Unfortunately, I have bad news for you; your first biopsy results came back negative, but the second biopsy showed positive cancer detection.*

I was stunned with the news, and I could feel tears stinging my eyes. I thanked her for the call and told her I would be fine and would connect with her on Monday. I now had to tell Joseph what was going on: that I had just been diagnosed with breast cancer in my left breast. I went on to tell him that it was most likely I would have to have surgery, chemotherapy, and radiation based on the discussion with my doctor. That day we walked along the St. Lawrence River for about two hours, talking and thinking, as I composed myself and tried to come to grips with the next stages of what I would have to face. He suggested he bring me back to the airport so I could get the earliest flight back home to Newfoundland and Labrador, but I said absolutely not. *I am here now. This is our weekend together and we are going to enjoy it.* In that moment, I put the breast cancer to one side as much as I could for the next two days, as we set out to get to know each other.

Sunday afternoon, as I was leaving Ottawa, I said to Joseph, "Give me a year. Let me get through this, and I'll give you a call if you want to pick up where we left off. I'm happy to do so, and if not, I fully understand."

He looked at me and said, "I will be part of this journey with you, or I won't be a part of your life; this is where it starts. It is your decision, and you can tell me when you decide." The conversation ended there. I began a journey through uncharted woods, not knowing what each step would bring, but knowing there were people who cared about me who would be there to support me.

The leadership convention was scheduled for November 2010, with nominations closing on July 31. On July 9, I was the first to file my papers. Despite rumours that there were other candidates, I was also the last. The campaign turned into a coronation. Some political pundits speculated that no one else wanted the job because Danny Williams was still unbeatable, but I had a different view.

As Interim Leader, I had spent the last three years in the House on my feet every day defending the interests of Newfoundlanders and Labradorians. I had gone on the campaign trail, winning one by-election and improving our results in three others. The polls showed that the party and my own approval ratings were creeping up, and with fourteen months until the next election, I knew I could push them even higher. In response to the critics, I said: "I keep my head down, I work hard, and I take my job very seriously." I was more ready than I had ever been to take the fight to Danny Williams. *Now that the leadership is settled,* I thought, *the work will really begin.*

But my body had other ideas. Halfway through July, there were early indications that I was not well, despite feeling strong and full of energy. More tests followed, and by early August the diagnosis was clear: at age forty-two, I had breast cancer and was facing a serious course of treatment. On August 13, I had surgery and shortly thereafter announced I would take a leave of absence from the leadership until I had recovered. The convention was postponed until May 2011.

CHAPTER 10

WHEN THE SYSTEM FAILS
THE BREAST CANCER SCREENING SCANDAL

The first hint that there was a problem with the interpretation of breast cancer hormone receptor screening tests came in June 2003 when a pathologist, Dr. Gershon Ejeckam, identified problems with the quality of lab work conducted by the Eastern Regional Health Authority. However, those reports were either ignored or never reached the desks of senior management. Nearly two years passed before the test result of a single breast cancer patient was re-examined in April 2005 and found to be inaccurate. A comprehensive review of tests, 2,000 of them going back to 1997, was undertaken.

Three months later, on July 19, 2005, George Tilley, the CEO of Eastern Health, met with Health Minister John Ottenheimer. That same day, the minister sent an email to Premier Danny Williams' office, informing him that a communications strategy was being developed. In the end, Ottenheimer decided alerting the public would cause unnecessary stress.

That's when it all began to spin out of control.

Although the Chair of Eastern Health, Joan Dawe, was informed by email the next day of potentially major clinical issues involving breast cancer screening, it was clear that Tilley still thought the matter could be resolved internally. Tests could be reviewed, patients could be retested, and treatments changed if required. Even as the number of affected women began to rise, Eastern Health must have been convinced it could control the damage.

The problem was so vast, however, that it was bound to attract attention, and even though officials at Eastern Health knew it was inevitable, they had no plan in place as to how to deal with it when it did. In September 2005, a reporter at *The Independent*, a weekly paper in St. John's, caught wind of a number of retests being undertaken—though they initially thought the problem had to do with mammograms. Fearing the panic that information would cause, the director of communications for Eastern Health, Susan Bonnell, told the reporter it was hormone receptor tests that were being redone and asked that the newspaper hold off on the story until the retests were complete. As a former journalist and current politician, I could have told her exactly how that would turn out. The paper printed the news on October 2, but it generated limited response.

The next move by Eastern Health officials, on the advice of their lawyer, was to stop sending patients letters advising them that their tests were being redone and to start phoning them instead. Coming only a few weeks after the newspaper story, this lack of a searchable paper trail seemed an effective strategy—deliberate or not—to prevent reporters from seeking documents through freedom of information requests. Eastern Health may still have thought they could contain and resolve the matter internally, but when it came out, it's not surprising that accusations of a cover-up were made, including by me.

My concern was less with what the bureaucrats were up to and more with what those politically responsible for them—the Minister and, ultimately, the Premier—were doing. Did they know? What did they know? What did they do with that knowledge?

But it was early days yet. Breast cancer screening failures were not on the public radar, and they weren't on mine either. In 2005, we were questioning the adequacy of mammography clinics in the province and the need to send some patients out of province for those tests. We also were concerned about the lack of support for breast cancer and other cancer patients and their families when they were sent from rural Newfoundland and Labrador for treatment in St. John's. From various media reports, I was now aware there were inadequacies in the system, but I had no idea of the scope of the problem and what would emerge over the next two years. To be fair, I don't think Premier Williams or his Cabinet colleagues knew either—at least not in 2005.

Having said that, one minister should have known. Health Minister John Ottenheimer met with the CEO of Eastern Health the day before Tilley warned his Chair of a "potentially . . . major clinical issue." The Minister was certainly sufficiently concerned about it to propose that a communications strategy be developed— an idea, he later told the Cameron Inquiry, that was dropped on the advice of Eastern Health officials. Perhaps the Minister of Health was too focused on his own health to pay sufficient attention to the issue. A few months earlier, heart troubles had required him to have a pacemaker implanted, and he had stepped away from his Cabinet role for two months to recover. In March 2006, he requested a less stressful portfolio, citing health concerns, and was shifted to Intergovernmental Affairs, with Tom Osborne taking over at Health. Osborne was subsequently replaced by Ross Wiseman in January 2007—just as knowledge of the testing scandal was coming to the forefront.

Wiseman later admitted he had failed to read the briefing note provided him on the subject, while Minister Osborne claimed he was never even informed of its existence.

Eventually, however, the Premier did know. In August 2006, he was sent a briefing note—an update of a short report sent in October the previous year—on the expanding number of faulty tests. Eastern Health still believed the matter could be contained, and there seemed to be no urgency for the Premier or his new Health Minister to act or inform the public. By then, it was clear this was not an isolated event, but the actual number of faulty tests was unknown. It was only in December 2006 that Eastern Health admitted that 117 breast cancer patients had received inaccurate test results, which then required a change in their treatment plan.

Every province faces its own difficulties when it comes to delivering health care to its citizens, and Newfoundland and Labrador is no different. We are particularly challenged by the fact that we have a small population spread over a large land mass. There are approximately 560 communities, 500 of which have fewer than 1,000 people living in them. Some have fewer than 200. Yet even residents of these small communities expect and deserve a level of health care comparable to that provided in larger centres.

In every province, the medical system consumes an inordinate amount of the provincial budget. In 2003, my final year in Cabinet, it totalled $1.6 billion and represented nearly forty-five per cent of provincial expenditures. In 2022—in the midst of the COVID pandemic—the provincial health budget had grown to $3.6 billion and made up roughly forty per cent of a much larger provincial budget. Other provinces can tell a similar tale.

With that scale of expenditure, you might think that elected officials would spend an equal amount of time scrutinizing the system, making sure it was delivering the level of care needed by citizens. At one level, you would be right: we are very attentive when problems arise, questioning the adequacy of the ambulance service, and reacting to reports of crowded ERs or unreasonable wait times. We engage in vigorous debates over what role, if any, the private sector should play and what treatments or drugs should be included or excluded from provincial drug coverage. As individual MHAs, whether in government or Opposition, we are constantly alert to issues around fairness and levels of service.

At the same time, the range of services is so broad and complex that much of it is left in the hands of the professionals. While we often question medical experts or the Minister of Health, who is expected to have a more in-depth knowledge of the system on issues such as the adequacy of medical transport, or the staffing levels at local facilities, or even whether we have enough specialists to do the job, questioning the system itself is a much rarer thing. There is an assumption that the system, writ large, functions well— even if it sometimes needs a little push such as extra resources or a different focus.

When the system itself fails, as it did during the breast cancer screening scandal in our province, it is much harder to discover the problem and correct it. The doctors, administrators, and politicians responsible may at first underestimate the seriousness of the issue and think they can correct the problem internally. When that fails, when the self-monitoring and self-correcting mechanisms built into every government system can't resolve the problem, perspective is lost and panic sets in. If that only resulted in money lost or careers unfairly ended, it would be bad enough. But this failure resulted in cancers misdiagnosed, treatments being botched, and women dying who might have lived.

For most of 2006, the public—as well as my colleagues and I on the Opposition benches—remained uninformed as to the full scope of this problem. Ironically, the government was in the midst of developing a new cancer strategy to better deal with all aspects of the prevention, detection, and treatment of this pernicious disease, which affects people in Newfoundland and Labrador at higher rates than anywhere else in Canada. It was during discussions of this strategy—long before my own diagnosis—that I first began to advocate for lowering the age at which women would be tested for breast cancer using mammography, from age fifty to forty.

But while the bureaucrats, journalists, and politicians had failed to reveal the entire ugly truth about the botched breast screening results, the courts did not. On May 15, 2007, documents relating to a class-action suit filed in July 2006 by Verna Doucette of the Port au Port Peninsula—the representative plaintiff for the 2,000 impacted women—and Klein Lawyers revealed they were aware of over 300 patients who had received inaccurate test results. These women, in the midst of personal health crises, had stood in solidarity to challenge the health care system in the courts. They were not walking away, and neither would we. I was in my office in Confederation Building that night, working to be ready for the week at the House of Assembly. I could not shake the impact of what was happening and of how many women's lives might have been saved.

On May 17, I moved the following motion in the Legislature, as recorded in *Hansard*:

> WHEREAS it has been revealed that there were error rates of forty-two per cent in breast cancer screening tests conducted by Eastern Health and the circumstances surrounding the release of this information has shaken confidence in the health care system in this Province;

> BE IT RESOLVED that this House of Assembly calls upon the government to appoint a judicial enquiry into the circumstances around faulty breast cancer screening results and the release of this information.

The next day, Tilley apologized on behalf of Eastern Health for failing to fully review the results that showed patients had been failed by the system.

Within a week, the government announced that it would establish a judicial commission of inquiry to investigate hormone receptor testing. They eventually appointed the Honourable Margaret A. Cameron, a justice in the Supreme Court of New-foundland and Labrador as the Commissioner, with Bernard Coffey, Q.C. and Sandra R. Chaytor, Q.C. appointed co-counsels. However, the inquiry did not officially begin until ten months later, delayed by a failed legal action by Eastern Health to prevent the release of peer reviews of doctors and specialists.

We had reason to be concerned about this. As I reported in the House a few days after the inquiry was announced, "The Minister, in a scrum outside, made this comment to the media . . . 'I understand and appreciate the dilemma they found themselves in, trying to balance their responsibility to the patients who needed a change in treatment and their responsibility to protecting the interests of the organization in the event of litigation.'"

To my mind, this was not the way to start the process of looking into potential wrongdoing or incompetence—by defending the choices made in keeping this information from the public. Too many people's lives had been impacted and someone needed to be held to account. Their responsibility needed to be to the patients, not protecting the government from a lawsuit.

One of the victims who spoke publicly at the time was Donna Howell of Mount Pearl, fifty-three years old and a nurse of twenty-eight years. She was one of over 1,000 women who were retested as part of the review into faulty hormone testing. While she did not want to be critical of the doctors and nurses who provided her with good health care, she realized that it was important to speak up. "I want to make things safer for our daughters, granddaughters, whoever might get this disease, so they have the best possible chance of living for as long as they can," Howell told CBC News.

Howell, like many cancer patients, was given the hormone receptor test to see if she would need to be treated with tamoxifen. A drug for women who test positive for hormone receptors in their cancer, tamoxifen had been shown to increase survival rates in breast cancer patients. Howell's test reported as negative. It was two years before she learned the test result was wrong. Her cancer had returned, this time in the form of bone cancer throughout her body. Would tamoxifen have made the difference? We don't know for certain, but it has helped save the lives of many women who've battled breast cancer. It might have helped save her. "You know, maybe (tamoxifen) would have made a difference in whether I get to live to see grandchildren, or I simply get to see my children educated," she said in an interview.

Donna Howell passed away in 2009.

Women like Donna Howell, Verna Doucette (who died in March 2015), and hundreds more, put human faces to this issue, making it difficult for anyone to continue to hide information. In the end, it was all revealed. Donna Howell and Verna Doucette helped ensure the safety of many women and men in our health-care system.

Every day new information was surfacing, and I vowed the questions that arose would dominate debates in the House and in the public for the next two years. How much involvement did the Cabinet have in this issue? Had the Cabinet been engaged in this matter since 2005? How long had they had knowledge of it, and why had they decided to keep this information in the privacy of the government domain and not allow it to be shared with the public? These questions are always at the heart of any failure on the part of governments and their agencies. Who knew, when did they know, and what did they do with that knowledge?

At that moment, I was able to state what I had always believed deep in my heart about the role of government and of elected officials:

> "When you deal with issues like this, political parties are irrelevant, the places that we hold in this Legislature are irrelevant. The real relevance here is the women and families who have been impacted by something that has erred in our system.

> "I do not care if it was in 1997 or in 2007. I do not care who was in government and who was not in government. When these events occur in our history that affect the lives of women, of families, no government should ever be pulled kicking and screaming to deal with an issue like this. It should be the top priority. It should be the number one concern, because governments are elected to protect the interests of the public and the people, not to hide information from them, not to renege on their responsibility. You must hold to account the proper authorities to deal with these particular issues."

I believed that then and I still believe it.

On March 18, 2007, one day before the inquiry began, the government announced that 108 of nearly 400 patients with faulty tests had died. It was impossible to know how many would have benefited from the treatment proper testing would have granted them. The number of dying patients was growing, and so was the number of those impacted. The full picture was yet to be known.

The stories and testimony of the women who were affected, and that of their families, were heartbreaking, as they spoke in the media, to the courts, and at the inquiry.

When the Commission began its hearings, it quickly learned of the 2005 meeting between Tilley and Ottenheimer, about the exchange of emails with the Premier's office—initially calling for a news release and then insisting it was unnecessary (what the Premier later called a "stand-down order" from the Department of Health). It also heard about the briefings provided to the Premier in October 2005 and in August 2006, which apparently downplayed the scope of the problem.

Day by day, however, the pressure increased, forcing the Premier to declare to me in the House on April 7: "I can tell you and the people of this province that neither I or anyone in my government under any circumstances would attempt to conceal or prevent the disclosure of information that would affect the health of people in this province."

Yet, more and more damning testimony came out. After the minister claimed, in late May, that all impacted patients had been contacted, it was revealed by patients and the Canadian Cancer Society that, in fact, many had not yet been reached. The Premier suggested it was the fault of officials in the Health Department and especially those at Eastern Health. "Policy was not followed, Mr. Speaker; and, secondly, there was no protocol between the health authorities to say who was responsible for doing what. As a result, there was a passing of the responsibility back and forth between each other."

Eventually, the appearance of cover-up began to dominate the discussion, to the point it was eventually raised on CBC's *The National*. Premier Danny Williams called their reporting biased and threatened to sue the corporation if a retraction wasn't issued. The fact that the next day, CBC anchor Peter Mansbridge—the face of the national news in those days—issued a "clarification" was perhaps indicative of the power of a Premier in full flight. Commissioner Cameron, meanwhile, in the face of the Premier's demands for a speedier process and a less "prosecutorial" approach by Commission lawyers, refused to be budged into making changes to the process, indicating the limits of a Premier's power.

As the inquiry proceeded in its steady, thorough, and systematic way, Premier Williams grew more and more testy; his distaste for criticism and disagreement pushed him to lash out at those who contradicted the preferred narrative. By early May, he had referred to the process as a witch hunt. He—and sometimes his Minister of Health—had developed the habit of holding press scrums to dispute the testimony of the day and, often, to attack the people who gave it.

It certainly provided plenty of fodder for Question Period and debates in the House, and I admit I rather enjoyed taking the government—and, especially, the Premier—to task; he was an entertaining and worthy opponent. Here's a sample of what I had to say during the budget debate in May 2008. You can sense the stress and desperation in my words as I looked for answers in what was looking more and more like a cover-up, whether an intended one or not:

"We saw it last week with John Abbott, we saw it with Justice Cameron, we have seen it with legal counsel like Bernard Coffey and Sandra Chaytor, we are seeing it today with the president of the Medical Association and the list goes on and on and on. I bet you before midnight tonight he will be out there taking a swipe at Justice John Gomery who did the Gomery Inquiry, who was on the radio this morning saying that the Premier was out of line and that he was inappropriately making comments in the middle of this Inquiry. I bet you, before the clock strikes midnight tonight, the Premier will be looking for a way to cut the legs out from under Gomery as well, Mr. Speaker. Because: how dare you question me? How dare you take an opinion different from me? If you do, I will stop at nothing, I will stop at nothing to disparage your reputation, to ruin your professional credibility. Mr. Speaker, when it comes to this government, they always have to be right and no one else is entitled to have an opinion different from what they have.

"Well, this is one issue where there are a lot of opinions, Mr. Speaker, because there are a lot of people impacted. For the life of me, I cannot understand, and may never understand in my lifetime, why a Premier who wanted to be sincere and was portrayed to be sincere in launching a public inquiry into the largest health disaster in our history in this Province, would now go out and tear it to pieces like he has, undermine it in the way that he has and attack every individual involved in it. Even those who are not involved but have opinions that support this Commission, he has attacked them and attacked them on a very personal level; like today, Mr. Speaker, out demanding letters of apology from physicians in this Province. How dare they have the opportunity to speak out on an issue, Mr. Speaker! It is absolutely ludicrous, ludicrous in leadership, like you have never seen before."

By the end of May things had calmed down a bit and the government had agreed to Commissioner Cameron's request for an extension of the inquiry to February 28, 2009. The government now adopted a change in tone as Health Minister Ross Wiseman said they would allow the inquiry to unfold.

And unfold it did. Testimony continued until the end of October, with more and more revelations about how badly Eastern Health had failed patients.

Eventually, the inquiry released its report, delivering a digital copy to the minister a few minutes after midnight on March 1, 2009.

(Commissioner Cameron even publicly apologized for being a few minutes late!) The final report was 470 pages long and contained sixty recommendations for improving the health system to ensure similar situations could never occur again that could cost the lives of the people of Newfoundland and Labrador.

The government's response was quick. They committed $21.4 million to begin implementing the most urgent recommendations, notably to add seventeen new staff to ensure quality control at the lab, to develop an integrated information system to eliminate gaps in patient files and care, and to hire ten dedicated staff to act as patient advocates within the system. The general response of the medical community and of both Opposition parties was that it was a good start—but only a start. Even Eastern Health said it would take at least $100 million to respond to all of the inquiry's recommendations.

As the CBC reported: "We're only able to do so much this year," said (Health Minister Ross) Wiseman, adding that this year's spending "will get us rolling" on a plan that will ultimately take years to achieve. It then became my job as Leader of the Official Opposition to make sure the government honoured its commitment.

The inquiry also found that Minister Wiseman was lacking in judgment and in care, citing him for his "indiscriminate acceptance" of the information he received from Eastern Health on the testing scandal, saying "His duty of diligence demanded more." Wiseman refused calls for his resignation, but in July 2009, he was shuffled out of the Health portfolio and replaced by Paul Oram, who lasted only three months before quitting politics, citing health issues and unfair media scrutiny of his business dealings. It was left to Jerome Kennedy, an experienced minister, to complete the implementation of the inquiry's recommendations. From the time the breast cancer scandal was first realized in 2005 until 2009, the PC government appointed and removed five Cabinet ministers.

It was just five months later in 2009 that the Supreme Court under Justice Carl Thompson ruled on the class-action lawsuit against Eastern Health by breast cancer victims of faulty hormone receptor testing, granting them $17.5 million in a settlement. A breast cancer patient from Wabush, Labrador, Elizabeth Finlayson, spoke with the media, saying, "I am glad it is over with because the last year has been hard on me and my family but no money in the world will ever make me better. I've been battling infection for the last three weeks. I'm just exhausted from all of this." She expressed what many patients were feeling. "I'll never get rid of this cancer," she said. "I will eventually die with it."

Elizabeth Finlayson passed away in hospital on July 1, 2011 in Wabush.

Fifteen years have passed since the Cameron Inquiry released its report. The passage of time has shifted my perspective away from the vigorous pursuit of accountability that engaged me in 2008. I think once the government realized what had happened, things were too far advanced. They were trying to find a way to soften the blow and ensure they communicated information in a way that sidestepped their responsibility as government. Obviously, Eastern Health fell down on the job of reporting the error to the government as they tried to control the messaging. Worrying about saying the right thing caused delays in communicating to the public and to patients. That's why the semblance of a cover-up existed, because nobody came clean at the beginning. Telling the truth is critically important when public safety is in the balance.

If this were to happen today, the government would be more upfront; disclosure tends to be instantaneous now, within hours—not days, weeks, or months. In fact, in August 2022, it came to light that a large number of mammograms had to be re-examined because of issues around the technical quality of digital monitors. The four health authorities involved reported the need for review immediately and set up a clear method of communicating with patients. Not everyone was satisfied with that process, but the issue was dealt with openly, and within a couple of months the review was complete and the small number of patients requiring follow-up were contacted and dealt with by the system.

Back then, it was an old-school way of thinking, that we can fix this, we can deal with it. They thought they could control the narrative, but they couldn't. So many lives were impacted. Every time they tried to control it, or fix it, or review it, it looked like they were doing something underhanded. Perception was important.

I don't think there was any intention to deliberately hurt anyone. It was more about how do we not scare everyone? How do we control this? And how do we fix this in-house and make sure these women are retested? How do we do all this and not scare everyone and cause a complete catastrophe in the province? In their efforts to manage the fallout, that's exactly what they caused. It was a total catastrophe, where people died as a result of faulty information, where people were not told at the earliest point possible that errors had occurred and they had to be retested. More emphasis was put on reducing fear, controlling the message, protecting the government and the integrity of the health care system than on protecting patients.

As for Danny Williams' outrage, that was his style of leadership. For all that he accomplished in some areas and for all his popularity, this was a fatal flaw. He and his ministers couldn't handle the political weight that was coming down on them over this issue. I think what they were trying to do was deny that it was real, to say it was just politics, just a group of people opposing the government—a witch hunt, a conspiracy.

It was anything but that. If you listen to the testimony and the cross-examinations, the motive for the inquiry—from the beginning— was to strengthen the health care system going forward, and that meant strengthening the way government deals with these kinds of problems.

When the report came out, with its criticism of the Health Minister and its recommendations of how things could be done better, I think it was a difficult for the government to accept, but they took their medicine and did what they had to do. Part of their reaction was because we never let up on them in the House or in the media. We monitored the situation following the inquiry, looking to see if new technologies were being pursued and new protocols introduced, how screening was being conducted, and what labs were doing the work.

The changes that both government and Eastern Health implemented did strengthen the system in a way that was needed so that people could feel confident in it once more. When the time came that I announced my own cancer diagnosis and that I would be taking a leave, I emphasized that I was going to have my treatment done at Eastern Health in St. John's and that I had full confidence in the system to see me through to good health. They certainly did, and I still feel I had the very best care I could have possibly received anywhere in Canada at that time.

CHAPTER 11

CANCER STRIKES

In July 2010, it seemed that I had finally reached the mountain-top. No one opposed me for the leadership of the Liberal Party, affirming the value of all the hard work I had done. It was now only the formality of the convention in November before I would be named to lead the party into the 2011 election.

However, life had other plans.

I had barely had a minute to savour becoming leader when a routine mammography revealed a lump in my breast. Cancer had raised its angry head, and I was now forced to focus on a fight that was non-partisan—and that would require all of me. Though I was only forty-two, with no family history of the disease, I had championed the idea of early testing, and I was practising what I preached. I was further motivated by the news that several friends in their forties had recently received a diagnosis. A biopsy of the lump quickly showed that the cancer was aggressive, and surgery was scheduled for August 16.

Despite its geographic size, Newfoundland and Labrador is a pretty small place, and it wasn't long before speculation started and calls began coming into my office asking what was wrong. I decided that since I couldn't keep it quiet, I might as well be completely open about it. I had been deeply engaged in cancer care, first as the health critic after the 2003 election and then as the Leader of the Opposition throughout the breast cancer testing scandal. I would publicly share my journey with cancer in the hopes of promoting early screening for women and to show confidence and solidarity with others.

It was Friday, August 13, when I revealed what was happening. I called a press conference at Confederation Building in St. John's, where I said: "I wanted to take this opportunity to inform the people of the province that I have been diagnosed with breast cancer and I will be away from my work at interval periods over the next couple of months." During my absence, Kelvin Parsons would take on the interim role of Opposition Leader, as I fully intended to return to work as soon as my health allowed. "I certainly want to give assurances to the people of the province that the Opposition office will be open; we will be there to continue to advocate on behalf of the people of the province and everything will operate as normal," I said.

I went on to explain that, even though there was no history of breast cancer in my family, I had become very sensitive to the matter from talking to some of the young women who had been adversely impacted by the failures at Eastern Health. In January, during a routine checkup, I asked my doctor to arrange for a mammogram; although I was under 50, I was not feeling well and wanted to explore all possible options. It was fortunate that I did.

The next few months were not easy. Surgery was followed by chemotherapy and then radiation. One thing that I quickly learned is that most people are inherently kind. When someone is sick or struggling, the natural human instinct is to help.

Even those people you've spent years arguing with and criticizing show they understand that life is bigger than politics. NDP Leader Lorraine Michael said, "We all know that Yvonne is a fighter and we know that she will face this challenge with her usual determination. My concern for Yvonne goes beyond any political differences we might have. She has fought many battles in her life, but none as demanding as the fight she now faces."

Danny Williams added: "I was terribly saddened to hear that Ms. Jones had been diagnosed with this terrible disease . . . I know first-hand what a determined, strong, and courageous woman she is, and I am confident that she will face this challenge with the utmost strength and dignity. I wish her nothing but the best in the time ahead. And I offer my prayers for her speedy and full recovery."

These words did comfort me, but the gentle loving support of my family and closest friends was amazing. I had counted on Kelvin Parsons to hold the fort in the House, but he did far more than that; he carried the load as colleague and friend, encouraging me and supporting me on the journey of fighting cancer as well.

In the months before my cancer diagnosis, I had met Joseph Lanzon, the man who would become my second husband, and had started a long-distance relationship with him. I had such admiration and respect for Joseph that I knew he was the person I wanted to have in my life, and he quickly proved me right. Though we were in the early stages of our life together and many men might have had second thoughts after my diagnosis, Joseph strongly supported me, offering the love and encouragement I needed to get healthy. He stood by me then and he stands by me still; I consider myself incredibly lucky every day we are together to have found my true soulmate, friend, and partner in life.

It was a difficult fall. The treatments I had were invasive and I had a tremendous number of side-effects from them. I don't think I could have prepared myself for what I went through;

I don't think it is ever possible to prepare yourself fully to take on chemotherapy or to fight cancer. Despite that, and despite how completely drained I felt, I couldn't entirely step away from the things to which I had devoted my life. Politics was as much in my blood as those chemicals.

I was approving press releases even while sitting in the chemo lab, and I was thankful the House only sat eight days that fall, because it allowed me to keep my mind focused on treatment and wellness and not the House of Assembly. Joan Marie Aylward would go to every treatment with me in my three-week chemo cycle. I would relax on the bed in the cancer unit as they connected the medicine to my port, using the time to say hello and catch up with the other patients and staff. As always, I would have a funny story to tell about my wig or of having hot flashes in the middle of the night. Joan Marie would have office files for review and signing; with my BlackBerry in hand we would get through quite a bit of work for the first few hours until my eyes were heavy and then I would sleep. You get used to the noise of equipment in the chemo lab, of people moving around, and it becomes a soothing white noise, some form of calmness that lets you rest.

I was deeply immersed in the health care system and getting a first-hand education. Hundreds of women were going through treatment every year, and I met many of them along the way. I was inspired by their strength and determination, and moved by their stories. Many of them were afraid, wondering how it would all turn out, but they were also full of hope and resolve, wanting nothing more than to get well and return to their homes and their loved ones.

During this time I decided to do two things. First and foremost, as soon as I returned to the House I was going to introduce a private Member's bill to lower the breast cancer screening age from fifty to forty. I was only forty-two when my cancer was discovered, and

I met many women my age and younger who had the disease. I had pushed hard for my tests but not every woman was in a position to do that, especially if they were from rural or remote regions of the province. I did a lot of research into the effectiveness of early screening, which has not been universally adopted in Canada to this day, and while there are some risks, the data—in the words of Dr. Martin Yaffe of Sunnybrook Health Sciences Centre in Toronto—"has unanimously found an overall reduction in breast cancer deaths in women who are screened for breast cancer, including women aged forty to forty-nine." I did introduce that bill and persuaded the government to make the change so that the screening age would be dropped, but it never materialized until Premier Andrew Furey announced in May 2024 that they would implement the new benchmark for breast screening in Newfoundland and Labrador.

The other thing I decided to do was to go through my treatment in public. It was not an easy decision. Cancer, especially breast cancer, is a deeply personal issue. It not only impacts your body but also your self-image and your emotional life. Cancer in any form strips you of dignity and pride and it makes you vulnerable, and that is what I found most difficult. However, I felt that as a public figure, and one who had been so involved in the breast screening scandal of a few years before, I had a duty to show people that the system could work and that there was hope at the end of the treatment tunnel.

In January 2011, I shaved off what remained of my hair and called it a celebration of hope. Surrounded by family, friends, and survivors at my friend Mary Berghuis's home in Torbay, I confronted the inevitable, as every blonde strand fell to the ground. The presence of people I loved sharing this moment with me helped build my resilience for what was to come. *Labrador Life* published a lengthy article on my journey though cancer. In it, I described how I had come to understand I was slowly being transformed through the physical, emotional, mental, and spiritual experience that is cancer. These changes were not all negative—far from it, in fact. Without realizing it, overcoming odds and accomplishing things throughout my life had prepared me for this challenge. From the beginning, I made a choice: I would face cancer head on. Rather than becoming a victim, I decided I would be the navigator on this journey.

In many ways, the hardest step in this public fight was the first one. Holding that initial press conference on August 13 and sharing my news with the world was the most difficult moment in my entire public life. After that, sharing my progress and insights seemed easy, almost natural. I talked about how difficult the treatments had been and what was still to come, both chemo and radiation therapy. I used the opportunity to express how unhappy and frustrating it was not to be fully engaged in my work and not to be able to do more to help other cancer patients across the province. There were days of extreme sickness and tiredness, where I felt my body would just cave on me.

I was living in a condominium building at the time that had big windows; the sun would pour in and heat me like a blanket as I rested. One day I was agitated; there was no comfort, and I felt overtaken with agony and bad energy. I felt that way for days and wallowed in my self-pity, crying and sobbing as if it would bring relief. My mother sat with me in the living room in the afternoon sun as I whined and tossed and turned in discomfort, thinking life would never be normal again. She would encourage me to open my mail and read the beautiful messages people had sent to me.

One of those cards was from Linda Coles, a local artist I knew. The painting reproduced on the card was called *Around the Corner*. It was of an old saltbox house, the kind found in many outports across Newfoundland and Labrador. Off the back door of the house was a gravel path, which turned a corner, allowing the viewer to see the beauty of the ocean. It was in that moment I was sure there were better days just around the corner for me, as well. It is now my motto in life, that whatever you are dealing with today will pass, for there is always something positive to come around that next corner. You just have to be strong enough to keep going.

On November 3, while still receiving treatment, I held a news conference to announce I would join with other national leaders in the campaign to see breast cancer screening guidelines lowered to the age of forty. "As women, we have to take responsibility for our own breast self-examinations, but I am asking the government to partner with women across this province on our path to better manage our own health." I would do my part in promoting early screening in Newfoundland and Labrador, but cancer respects no boundaries, and spreading the word to other provinces was equally important.

It wasn't always easy to keep fighting. I went through a roller coaster of emotions during my cancer experience: fear, anger, humour, but most importantly, gratitude. Cancer can be tough, devastating, and dark. I've learned that it can also make us come alive at other levels. In certain ways it was a breakthrough that transformed my life. I learned right from the beginning that I needed to have an attitude of gratitude, not just for the early diagnosis, but for the incredible support I received from my family, friends, constituents, and all the caring people across the province. I came to look forward to every new day, even when I knew it would be a tough one. It was mine to embrace.

In February 2011, two weeks after my final chemo treatment, I was back in my office at the House of Assembly. I was limited in what I could do, but I held meetings and briefings for a few hours every day and even managed to get out to Corner Brook for a weekend of campaigning for Mark Watton in the Humber West by-election. It was Danny Williams' old district and, while we didn't win, we nearly tripled the Liberal vote.

I returned to the House when it opened in March, arranging my work around the weeks of radiation therapy I was still undergoing. The treatment leaves you quite fatigued, but I put in as many days and hours as I could manage, working myself up to the election scheduled for October. It never once entered my mind that I wouldn't be ready for the fall campaign, and as the spring rolled along, I worked hard to get the party ready. Cancer had been tough and had certainly changed my view on life, but more than anything it made me determined to live life to the fullest. Every day I got up and I was just so enthusiastic, so energized, and I didn't think that would ever change.

In June I was honoured to receive the Medal of Courage awarded by the Canadian Cancer Society at a special ceremony during the Society's St. John's Relay for Life. I was humbled when they described the award: "The Medal of Courage is an award granted to an outstanding individual, who in his or her personal battle with cancer has exhibited outstanding and unusual courage and has significantly helped to further the mission of the Canadian Cancer Society or that of the cancer control community." In accepting, I said: "I've never received a gold medal in my life, unless it was for a grade three sack race that I can't recall winning, but I guarantee you this is the one gold medal that really matters to me."

The summer was booked solid, with trips to various regions, speeches, and fundraising events. I was looking forward to the coming campaign with energy and optimism. However, just as I never gave up in my fight against cancer, cancer wasn't ready to give up in its fight against me. During the summer, my health took a sharp turn for the worse. My immune system collapsed, and with all the travelling and meetings, I would wind up in the emergency department or hospital every three or four weeks. My doctor finally told me that things were not going to improve in the short term, especially if I was in the midst of a campaign. I laid it out for the party executive: I was prepared to carry on, but it might mean that some of the campaign would have to be from my hospital bed in St. John's. My body would not allow me to campaign fully every day by bus or plane all over the province, but I did think I could be effective.

The executive decided they needed someone else. A week later, the party executive selected Kevin Aylward to lead the Liberals. Aylward had left politics in 2003, but I was not surprised he was ready for a resurgence. He had first been elected to the House of Assembly in 1985 at the age of twenty-four. He'd served as an MHA for many years and was in Cabinet in the late 1990s and early 2000s, before leaving politics. His lengthy experience was cited as part of the reasoning for his selection as leader.

He led them to third place in popular vote. The party gained three seats and remained the Official Opposition; Alyward, however, lost his own seat, finishing a distant second to the PC candidate. It was never going to be an easy race for the Liberals, regardless of who the leader was.

I won my own district with seventy-one per cent of the vote, and felt I could have done just fine campaigning from a hospital bed. Regardless, despite my four years at the helm, I knew my time as leader was over. It was time for a new person to take over— and for me to find some other way to continue to serve the people and province that I love.

At the time, I admit, I was disheartened and disappointed. But, ten years later, I look back at photos from that time, both public and private ones, and feel triumphant at having beaten cancer. Those of us who are survivors never stop worrying; you just live the best life you can. You love harder, you celebrate more, you understand differently and you never stop reaching out to others who are on the cancer journey because you know what they face each day. Cancer patients need more than medical care and treatment; they need family and friends, they need positive energy and hope. They need to know you are there. It keeps them strong, gives them courage, and gives them the drive to fight harder. I will never forget the support my family and friends gave me. Having them next to me and beating cancer was the greatest gift of my life.

My mother Barb and my brothers Keith and Brad would travel back and forth from Labrador to St. John's to support me during my treatments. The encouragement of my family was incredible during those days. My sisters Sherry and Nancy, and so many of my friends, became a source of strength along a difficult path; I truly valued their positive support. Joseph and I had grown in our relationship through my struggle with cancer. He came from Toronto to spend two or three days with me in St. John's after every chemotherapy session. He never once reneged on his commitment to share this difficult journey with me. In fact, the time we spent together allowed us to learn a lot about each other, especially me in my vulnerable state. Battling cancer is about hanging on to hope and seeing a future, and I could see a great future that was yet to be lived.

The universe has surely blessed me in my life, surrounding me with strong, caring, and loving individuals. I first met Joan Marie Aylward when we were both elected in 1996, me as an Independent, she as a Liberal. She was a newcomer to the political scene but certainly not a new face to Newfoundlanders and Labradorians. As the leader of the provincial nurses' union, she had raised many issues regarding health care, especially as it affected the equality of work for nurses. When she was elected, she was automatically appointed to Cabinet for her skills and expertise as a communicator. A hard worker and strong advocate on a number of issues, she was an asset to the Tobin government.

While I admired Joan Marie from the first, I didn't really get to know her until I joined the Liberal Party in 1999. We immediately became good friends and political colleagues. She raised the bar for women in politics and became the first female Minister of Finance in the province at a time when Newfoundland and Labrador's financial situation was challenging. Joan Marie was prepared to break the glass ceiling wherever and whenever she needed to. She not only came from a nursing background—which gave her a tremendous understanding of health care in the province—she also understood the value of teamwork and of embracing the people around her to get things done.

Joan Marie had left politics by the time I became leader of the Liberal Party of Newfoundland and Labrador, but I invited her back to be my Chief of Staff, and she accepted. She had the political experience to advise me, as well as a deep understanding of what it meant to serve people. What I didn't imagine at the time was that once I was diagnosed with cancer, she would also be the one I relied on more than any other. She gave me the reassurance I needed to maintain hope and optimism as I fought cancer. There was not a day we didn't chat or sit together or research my diagnosis and treatment. I realized how important it was to have such a remarkable friend and colleague to lean on.

I urge anyone who is going through a difficult medical experience not to go through it alone if you can help it. Having someone by your side when you walk into a doctor's office to review diagnostic tests or treatment options is invaluable.

Do the best with what you have.
Reward is in the doing, not the getting;
in the trying, not the triumph.

— Hon. Gudie Hutchings,
MP for Long Range Mountains

CHAPTER 12

VOTING IN THE NEW

Although cancer had stopped me from leading the Liberal Party into the October 2011 election, I was not sure I was done with politics yet. I had a tremendous amount of backing in my district, and I knew that if I chose to run, people would support me. I had worked hard for people, and despite the fact I was getting over cancer, I felt people would be there for me. It didn't take much thought for me to decide, and so, for the fifth time, I stood for election in Cartwright-L'Anse au Clair. The results spoke for themselves, and I was very humbled by the seventy per cent of the vote I received. People appreciated the hard work I had done, and I appreciated the opportunity to keep working for them.

When I went back into the House of Assembly, I knew I wasn't going back to be the leader. That boat had left the harbour. I also knew that we had to be smart about leadership. We had had the experience with Jim Bennett being party leader and of Gerry Reid as Leader of the Opposition in the House. There had been conflicts and miscommunications and ultimately the disaster of the 2007 election, when we were reduced to three seats. I began to have conversations with people in the party and in the caucus, and it was soon clear to me that the obvious choice to lead the party was Dwight Ball—but would he do it?

Only six Liberal MHAs had been elected, myself included. One was Jim Bennett, who had properly won a seat and was still interested in leading the party. However, given his failed leadership in 2006, the Liberals overlooked him. Another was Andrew Parsons, Kelvin Parsons' son, who had succeeded his father in his district when Kelvin decided not to run again. He came from a strong political family, but at thirty-two he was newly elected and not ready for a leadership role. Randy Edmunds was a rookie MHA from Northern Labrador, with little profile outside his district. That left Eddie Joyce, who was certainly no rookie. He had been involved in the Liberal Party since the late 1980s. He was first elected in 1989 but gave up his seat a day later for Clyde Wells, who had won the election but lost his own seat. Eddie worked as a political assistant to Wells, and subsequently to Brian Tobin, before returning to the House in 1999. He had been defeated in 2007 but made a comeback in 2011. He had plenty of political experience, but that wasn't necessarily a selling point at that time. Eddie was also not expressing any real interest in being the new leader.

Dwight Ball was a successful businessman, owning a couple of pharmacies and several long-term care homes. He was not exactly new to politics, having served in the House for a couple of months after winning a by-election in early 2007, only to lose his seat in the subsequent general election later that year. Both elections had been very close, and 2011 was no different; he won with a sixty-eight-vote majority. However, he was a fresh face as far as the general public was concerned and that counted for a lot.

I had several conversations with Dwight after the election, and he was clearly interested in the leadership, but he needed some time to deal with some of his businesses and other issues. I agreed that I would accept the interim leadership, not of the party but of the Opposition in the House of Assembly until he was ready. So, I became Leader of the Official Opposition once again, until Dwight assumed interim leadership of the party on January 3, 2012. He took over as Leader of the Official Opposition the same day. Dwight also announced his intention of running for the permanent leadership whenever the party was ready to move forward and would step down from the interim role three months before the vote to give others an equal chance to run.

Dwight appointed me as Opposition House Leader for the party, making me responsible for co-ordinating our approach and response to government legislation and budgets. It meant I would spend all my time in the House of Assembly, engaging in debate and keeping everything flowing smoothly for our team.

The last election had left us in an odd position. The NDP had surged in the polls throughout the year, perhaps building on the success of Jack Layton at the federal level. Layton led the party to its greatest electoral success, both in popular vote and seats in May 2011, including two seats in Newfoundland—both in St. John's. In the provincial election that followed, the NDP finished second in popular vote, pushing the Liberal Party into third place, our worst showing ever. However, the NDP vote was heavily concentrated in St. John's, in four seats, all won with significant majorities.

The Liberals won six seats in smaller rural districts, a couple by margins of fewer than 100 votes. Kevin Aylward, who had led the party in the election, lost his own seat. As a result, while we finished third in votes, we had won six seats, leaving us as the Official Opposition, with all the benefits of resources and speaking rights in the House that the title brings. However, we knew we had a lot of work to do to rebuild the party's base, finances, and credibility with the public. The Progressive Conservatives had a clear majority, so there would be no election until 2015.

Still, I was there when the initial cracks appeared in the Dunderdale government. Kathy Dunderdale had been Deputy Premier under Danny Williams, and he clearly considered her his successor. She won the PC leadership unopposed, after four Cabinet ministers assessed their chances and decided not to run. A party outsider submitted his nomination papers an hour before the deadline but was disqualified when it was determined he hadn't gained the signatures of fifty party members.

As good as she was, Dunderdale had neither the charisma nor the star quality of Danny Williams, and trouble soon brewed within the caucus. The initial source was unexpected. In April 2011, Danny—who was still very popular—refused to attend a tribute dinner in his honour to be held in conjunction with Dunderdale's formal election as leader, and later claimed the Premier and her staff were "distancing themselves from him." In May, the government rejected a proposal to provide an annual subsidy to the AHL hockey team, of which Danny Williams owned a major share. Danny declared himself "shocked." Significantly, he did not campaign for the party in the 2011 election.

I certainly understood why the new Premier would resent interference by the previous one. I myself had no intention of interfering with the work of the new leader of the Liberal Party, other than doing everything I could to support whomever the party chose. Still, it must have been a bit of a shock to Danny Williams loyalists to see him publicly bickering with the party.

It was soon clear that not everyone was entirely happy with the new Premier. In September 2012, long-time MHA and Cabinet minister Tom Osborne quit the Progressive Conservatives to sit as an Independent, citing Dunderdale's leadership as the main cause. In August 2013, he joined the Liberal caucus.

Through 2012 and into 2013, support for the PC government began to fall, and by March 2013 a public opinion poll showed that it had dropped to thirty-eight per cent. Most of their losses initially turned into support for the NDP, but as Tory support continued to collapse, all our hard work at rebuilding the Liberal Party began to bear fruit. In May, the PCs were down to twenty-two per cent, with the other two parties in a virtual tie for support.

By 2011, I had been an MHA for over fifteen years—well over half of my adult life. I still had a strong urge to serve the public, but was no longer certain that politics was the best way to do it. I had beaten cancer and was in a new relationship, feeling very happy and secure. Joseph was a consultant, based in Toronto, whose work took him all across the country. He was very supportive of me and any decision I made. So, as 2012 rolled into 2013, I began to consider an entirely new career.

I was in my forties, fully recovered from cancer, and full of energy to boot. The University of Saskatchewan was offering a law degree with a specialty in Indigenous law, and it seemed right up my alley. I started checking out the program, talking to people who had graduated from it. I thought it could work for me; at the time, my youngest brother Bradley was working with the RCMP and living in Saskatchewan with his family, so I would have some family connections. Joseph and I talked it through, and we decided that this would be a good next step for me. I was putting together my application and contemplating what life would be like so far from the ocean—Saskatoon is about as far from the ocean as you can get in Canada—but, as John Lennon put it, "Life is what happens while you're busy making other plans."

Peter Penashue was the federal Conservative MP for Labrador, elected in 2011. However, new information had come to light that the Penashue campaign had been caught accepting illegal funds during the 2011 election. Dozens of donations totalling tens of thousands of dollars had been flagged. The campaign had been ordered to pay more than $45,000 to the Receiver

General. Moreover, the campaign had taken a large interest-free loan—which is disallowed under Canadian election law—and the federal Conservative Party was forced to transfer funds to cover it. Eventually, seven companies admitted to making illegal donations, and Penashue's official agent was charged with three counts of accepting illegal corporate donations. In March 2013, the MP resigned his seat while declaring he would run in the by-election when it was called.

I was sitting in the House of Assembly when the new provincial Minister of Natural Resources, Jerome Kennedy, walked across the floor and leaned over my desk. He and I had been constantly sparring verbally those days, so I had no idea what was coming. As he got closer to the desk he showed me the story on his BlackBerry, that Penashue had resigned over the financing scandal and that he was running in the upcoming by-election, which had been quickly called for May 13.

My political instincts were immediately aroused. I thought back to the 2005 federal nomination race. Back then, I had hesitated before putting myself forward, allowing others to get the jump on me. I also thought of what I had said publicly at the time about why I wanted to run. "I have passion for Labrador, my heart is here, and my soul is here, and there's nothing else I would rather do than look at being the federal Member for Labrador." It was true then, and I realized it was still true in 2013.

I had first considered a run at federal politics years earlier. After the 2003 defeat of the Liberal Grimes government, I had gone from being a Cabinet minister to a front-bench critic facing an enormously popular Progressive Conservative Premier who seemed likely to be in power for a number of years. My own party was in disarray, with a large debt and uncertain leadership. On the federal scene, Paul Martin had replaced Jean Chrétien as Liberal leader and Prime Minister, and had led the party to a disappointing victory in 2004. Then, the unfolding sponsorship scandal had cost the party its majority.

The seat in Labrador had become vacant at the end of 2004 with the untimely and sad death of Lawrence O'Brien, who had succumbed after a long battle with cancer. A by-election was called for 2005, and I decided to throw my name into the nomination race. I knew I had a strong base of support in my own district and thought that my work as a Parliamentary Secretary and then Fisheries Minister had raised my profile in the rest of the riding. In the end, there were four candidates vying for the job: Todd Russell, Wally Andersen, Olivia Letemplier, and me.

As it turned out, my support at that time was insufficient to win the nomination; I finished third after Russell and Andersen. In retrospect, I could see where I went wrong. I had failed to develop as wide a network of grassroots support across Labrador as I had in my own provincial district. As well, I campaigned on a pro-development platform, while a number of environmental and Indigenous groups were not fully supportive of development, expressing concerns about consultation and the impacts development could have on the environment and traditional Indigenous economies. In choosing Todd Russell, who was then the President of the Labrador Métis Nation (which became the NunatuKavut Community Council), they chose the candidate who best reflected their views.

Todd Russell, a long-time friend and colleague of mine, ran a strong campaign and won handily against four other candidates with over fifty-one per cent of the vote. He won re-election in 2006 with a similar mandate and in 2008, garnered over seventy per cent of the vote during Danny Williams' ABC campaign against the Harper government. In 2011, he lost the seat by fewer than 100 votes to Peter Penashue, who had a long history of leadership in the Innu Nation.

That afternoon in 2013, I left the House and thought about things in my office for an hour or two before calling Dwight Ball and Kelvin Parsons, who was now Ball's Chief of Staff. I asked what they'd think if I quit the House to run for the federal nomination. They were very supportive, as were some of my other close confidants in St. John's. The consensus was: do whatever makes you happy, what makes you comfortable. I knew they would all have my back no matter how it turned out. I spent the rest of the night trying to reach Todd Russell to see if he was running again. If I had reached him and he said he *was* running, I would probably have supported him. He was a very competent man and extremely well respected. At the same time, I knew he was thinking of returning to Indigenous politics.

I called every number I had for Todd, sent emails to all his known addresses, left messages with his friends and family, but I couldn't reach him, and he didn't call me back or respond to any of my emails. After a sleepless night, I got up the next morning and called *Labrador Morning* on CBC Radio and asked for time on their morning broadcast. For what, they asked? I immediately told them: to announce that I will be seeking the nomination for the federal Liberals in the upcoming by-election in Labrador. The words were no sooner out of my mouth than they had me on the air.

As people across the Big Land were waking up to CBC *Labrador Morning*—which everyone listened to—I was announcing my candidacy on the air and preparing for a campaign. Not five minutes later, Todd Russell called me and asked me why I had done it without talking to him. I mentioned all the messages I had left for him, and he said, perhaps a little sheepishly, that he hadn't called me back because he hadn't decided, and he knew that that was what I was calling to ask.

One thing I have learned in politics is that if there's something you want to do, you'd better get out and do it. If you're thinking about running today and it's what you want to do, then get started. Don't stand in line and wait, because the longer you stand in line, the more likely someone more determined, more eager, and more interested is going to be out there before you. When you're the first out of the gate, the perception is that you're the one who's making the decision. You're not hemming and hawing. You know what you want to do and you know exactly what you need to do; you're out there running. And that's exactly what I did. In the end, Todd didn't run against me; in fact, nobody did, and I became the Liberal candidate.

It was entirely my decision. No one from the Liberal Party of Canada asked me to run. Bob Rae was on the way out and Justin Trudeau was on the way in, and they were going through a leadership race until the middle of the by-election. I suppose the fact the Liberals were absorbed in their own race might have had something to with the timing of Penashue's resignation and the date of the by-election. Of course, once I was the candidate, the national party got involved.

It wasn't the easiest campaign I ever ran, but compared to my first one in 1996, it certainly wasn't the hardest, either. I had plenty of advantages. My time as Liberal leader had ensured that I had solid contacts throughout the riding and among the general population, and it gave me strong name recognition. I was able to fundraise quite well (without taking illicit donations!), and the national party gave me plenty of support. Of course, Bob Rae—who was acting as interim Liberal leader—came and campaigned with me at the beginning of the election. He was really well received in Labrador.

A month before voting day, Justin Trudeau won the Liberal leadership in a resounding fashion, and this was the first test against the Harper government. The Conservatives had now been in power for seven years and their support was beginning to fray around the edges. By the date of the by-election, they had fallen behind the Liberals in national polling, with the NDP a close third. Trudeau, like his father before him, was popular in Labrador, and you had a sense that his leadership wasn't a flash in the pan, as some pundits predicted.

Still, I think the Conservatives expected to win the race in Labrador. They certainly acted like they planned to win it. Stephen Harper had a number of his people in there. Jenni Byrne was running the by-election in Labrador for the Conservative candidate. She had been the *de facto* campaign chair for the 2011 general election, taking over for Doug Finley while he battled cancer. She had held several positions in the Prime Minister's Office and was considered one of the top political organizers in Canada; she was even once called "the most powerful woman in Ottawa." However, her Ottawa power would gain her no traction in Labrador towns.

Byrne assembled a strong team of local people, augmented by top party people, to run the by-election. My candidacy threw a wrench into all their plans. They definitely weren't expecting me to run; they thought it would be a rematch between Todd Russell and Peter Penashue, and they had prepared for that situation. They didn't prepare for Yvonne Jones leaving provincial politics after seventeen years and suddenly popping up on this ballot as the Liberal candidate. I'd knocked them off their game immediately, and that really helped me off the starting line.

I had a tremendous profile in Labrador, and not only because I was the MHA from the south coast. I'd been standing up for Labradorians for my entire political career, in every region and on every issue. People knew me and felt comfortable with me; they knew they could trust me. All those things really helped me go into the election with momentum. It was still a very tough campaign, because I was running against a sitting government Member who was a former Cabinet minister. People knew that if they re-elected

Peter Penashue, he was going to go right back into the Cabinet of the Harper government.

That was the biggest stumbling block I faced during that election. People knew I would stand up for them, but it would be from the Opposition benches and as a member of the third party. The question I forced voters to answer was "How effective had Peter Penashue been as a Cabinet minister?" There's nothing you can really point to that he had delivered on during that time. Even though he was a Cabinet minister in a majority government in Ottawa and a high-profile Indigenous person, there was no real legacy of what that government did for Labradorians, or what he was able to accomplish.

That was his weakness and one of the reasons for his downfall. No one could point to what he had done; no one could say: we needed this and he made that happen. One of the biggest issues at the time was 5 Wing Goose Bay. Penashue had brought no stability to the military base; they didn't have a new operational requirement, and their contract was running out. This became a political volley-ball during the campaign. The Harper government had said in the previous election that they were going to do something at 5 Wing Goose Bay. And they essentially told Labradorians: if you don't vote for us, you're going to lose your air base.

They did the same thing in the by-election, but thankfully, people didn't buy it the second time around. The Conservatives under Harper and Penashue had had the opportunity to do something real, but they had not done it. Now they were back making the same commitment. It was helpful that their message was hollow.

Justin Trudeau won the Liberal leadership midway through the by-election campaign. He was immediately very popular with Canadians, including in my riding. When he showed up to help with my campaign, there was great fanfare. He came to Happy Valley-Goose Bay and Labrador City, where he was met with large crowds of Liberal supporters—both mine and his. That really gave me the confidence I needed. He was a breath of fresh air coming in as the new leader of the Liberal Party in Canada. All these things helped me boost the percentages that I needed to win. Going into voting day, I felt good that I had built a concrete platform of deliverables for Labrador. I won with forty-eight per cent of the vote, nearly 1,900 votes ahead of Penashue, who finished second with just over thirty-two per cent.

I was very excited to go to Ottawa to represent Labrador in the House of Commons. We had a small but mighty caucus of thirty-six members, including four other Newfoundland and Labrador MPs.

Meanwhile, the provincial Liberals were gaining ground and momentum as well. In June 2013, they won their first by-election when Lisa Dempster handily won in my old district. That was not particularly a surprise, but it did give us an idea that we were moving in the right direction. It was the first by-election victory against the Dunderdale government, but it wouldn't be the last.

It's impossible to know what might have happened if the provincial NDP had retained its support through the 2015 election, but such was not to be the case. In October 2013, a letter came to light from Lorraine Michael's four caucus mates calling her leadership into question and demanding that a leadership vote be held in 2014, before the next scheduled election. Michael agreed to a review, but not a full-fledged convention, and subsequently two of her Members—Dale Kirby representing St. John's North, and Christopher Mitchelmore representing The Straits-White Bay North—left the NDP caucus to sit as Independents. In November, a poll showed that support for the NDP had collapsed, and the Liberals, now led by Dwight Ball, were sitting at fifty-two per cent support. The Dunderdale government had entered the lame-duck category.

The first PC Member to leave was powerful Cabinet minister Jerome Kennedy, who resigned his seat on October 2. Liberal Sam Slade won the subsequent by-election at the end of November. On

January 20, 2014, PC Paul Lane crossed the floor to the Liberals. By February 2014, he was joined by the two now-Independent, former NDP MHAS.

Meanwhile, Kathy Dunderdale had read the writing on the wall and tendered her resignation as Premier and leader of her party on January 24, 2015. At the end of February, she quit politics altogether. The future became abundantly clear in April when her seat was won by Liberal Cathy Bennett. Three more by-election victories to replace resigning Progressive Conservative MHAS increased Dwight Ball's caucus to sixteen heading into the election.

In November 2015, Ball led the Liberal Party to an overwhelming victory, winning thirty-one of forty seats with over fifty-seven per cent of the vote.

On June 4, 2015, I rose for the first time in Parliament to ask a question of the Minister of National Defence on the issue of search and rescue—a particularly vital topic to Newfoundlanders and Labradorians, especially in light of the tragic death of Burton Winters, the sinking of the *Ryan's Commander*, and the Harper government's decision to close the Search and Rescue Centre in St. John's. For a province that earns its living from the ocean, whether in fisheries or oil and gas, a provincial search and rescue (SAR) co-ordination centre was critical. Lobby efforts were led by Merv Wiseman, a former employee at the SAR co-ordination centre in St. John's. He truly knew what the consequences of this decision would mean to Newfoundland and Labrador, and he was supported at rallies and protests by unions, politicians, and thousands of people. I said:

> "Mr. Speaker, the Conservative government, and it knows this, has really gutted front-line search and rescue services. The Minister of National Defence made a fly-through announcement in response to the Auditor General's report

and did little to address any of the deficiencies. Why does the Conservative government not fix search and rescue in Newfoundland and Labrador before more lives are lost?"

It was an issue I would return to a number of times during those two years in Opposition, as well as other issues of particular significance to the people of Labrador, such as the future of 5 Wing Goose Bay, support for the fishing and sealing industry, cutbacks in federal services, and recognizing the accomplishments of prominent Labradorians.

As an Indigenous woman from a northern region, I was appointed party critic on northern issues—including search and rescue—and frequently questioned the government on matters impacting the three northern territories, such as the unsuccessful Nutrition North program and the impacts of climate change. I also took the lead on legislation impacting the North, such as the changes to the powers devolved to the governments of the Northwest Territories and Yukon, and the formation of the Nahanni National Park. Inevitably, these responsibilities crossed over into discussions of Indigenous issues, and I often spoke with great personal conviction on the matter of Missing and Murdered Indigenous Women, having known several Indigenous women from Labrador who were senselessly murdered.

I will admit to taking a certain amount of satisfaction in pointing to the growing number of ethical lapses on the part of the Harper government. Having just defeated an MP who had been forced to resign due to election irregularities, I was well placed to comment on the Senator Mike Duffy scandal and the resignation of Dean del Mastro from the House of Commons over the "robocall" affair. Del Mastro was eventually convicted for his role in the scandal.

One of the great things about being in Opposition is that you have significant freedom to pursue matters that interest you.

Rather than defending a platform or a program, you can speak about values and principles. The goal for most days is to shine a light on areas where the government has failed, or better yet, where they could do better. It is in those latter cases that you might even succeed in shifting the government's approach. I was consistent with the overall direction of the party, but at the same time, I could raise issues that reflected my own experience and the priorities of my region. As an MP, I frequently spoke about issues from a particularly personal and Labradorian perspective. Speaking about the seal hunt, I said:

> "I want to ensure it is noted on the record: my father went to the ice. My brothers still go to the ice to hunt seal. My mother has sewn sealskin until her fingers have been sore. To this day she makes a living from making this product. I cannot determine what the views of individual Members of Parliament are in this House of Commons or in the Senate. I cannot determine how other Canadians will reflect upon this industry. However, I will tell Members that it is a part of who I am, and it is a part of Inuit culture I am proud to say I belong to. We continue to promote this industry, we continue to hunt, we continue to use the product and we do so in a very humane way. It is a part of who we are, and we make no apologies for that."

I was also able to voice my support for the NunatuKavut Community Council, which at that time was struggling to be recognized by the federal government:

Labrador is home to three distinct Aboriginal cultures. This adds to the colourful tapestry of our history and our lineage. As I alluded to earlier, for thousands of years, the Inuit travelled throughout Labrador, and the Innu between Labrador and Quebec, hunting and fishing and later trading with Europe. Today, the NunatuKavut Community Council, which is led by former Member of Parliament Todd Russell, represents some 6,000 Southern and Central Labrador Inuit and continues to press the provincial and federal governments for their own land claims, self-government, and recognition. I will push for them as well, under Canada's Indigenous self-governance model, because they have the right to be represented as Inuit of Labrador.

Throughout the next two years I was able to speak many times on issues of national and local interest, to promote the interests and profile of Labrador and its citizens in the House of Commons, and to be a public critic of the government's Indigenous and Northern policies.

While speaking in the House is important, it is actually a small part of the work of an MP. A great deal of time is spent helping individual constituents to get passports or pardons and to access government programs for such things as mental health support or employment training. Making sure that businesses are aware of regulations that might impact them or grant programs that could help them improve their operations or reach new markets is equally important and time-consuming. It is shaping the policy of government to reflect the values and priorities of those you represent that takes real time and work, as does securing large-scale investments for infrastructure. Whether it is ensuring legislation around reconciliation, replacement workers, environmental benchmarks, or income security, you have to do the research, pose the tough questions, and push hard to ensure that all Canadians are treated fairly. It was work I loved doing; helping people gave me the energy to carry on and work harder. There was no greater reward than seeing a job done well that benefits millions of people.

In the midst of all this, in the fall of 2014, Joseph and I were settling into our new routine. He was working more and more from

Ottawa, as was I, and we were getting to spend a little more time together. I had gotten to know his four grown children, all of whom were in college or university and living away. They were and are remarkable, independent young men and women, who had their focus set on careers and families.

Joseph and I decided that we would marry in 2015; the decision came on the heels of another medical diagnosis. This time it was endometriosis. While I'd had an ablation in earlier years, it had continued to be a problem that required a biopsy every three to six months; my paternal grandmother had died of ovarian cancer. I reflect back now on my years of infertility and believe that this may have played a large role in my unsuccessful efforts to conceive. In any case, after having suffered breast cancer and knowing that it was estrogen-driven, my doctor recommended a full hysterectomy. On January 2, 2015, I was admitted to the Health Sciences Centre for the procedure. This was less than fifty days before my wedding to Joseph. During the time of my surgery and recovery, we planned the wedding, sent out our invitations, and brought everyone together on February 28 at Montebello, where we'd had our first date and where I had first learned that I had breast cancer.

Like every woman who dreams of marrying the man she loves, I dreamed of what the wedding would look like, and while I got married in Northern Quebec, it was very much a Labrador wedding. The ceremony was outside, with the reception held indoors. Wearing a white wedding dress and cape, all trimmed in sealskin by my mother Barbara, I was driven by dog team across the frozen snow, ushered by my brother Brad in his RCMP uniform, then led down the aisle by my brother Keith, decked out in sealskin hat and mitts. It was as Canadian as you can get: a glorious, beautiful day, with the sun shining high in the sky and the temperature at 5° Celsius. Water was melting off the eaves of buildings all over the resort.

Keith and Brad walked me down the red carpet toward Joseph, with family and friends sitting on both sides. I lifted my eyes to see him at the end of the aisle, and in the background Canada, Quebec, and Labrador flags were flying proudly. The inuksuks that marked the end of the path stood strong and determined, and in front of it all stood Joseph, smiling and patient as always. I knew I was making the right decision, because I could not wait to marry this wonderful man.

We had come from very different backgrounds; his parents were first-generation immigrants, while my family had been here for thousands of years. Joseph's father was born in Malta, an island in the Mediterranean Sea. He had grown up in a fishing family during the Second World War. For a tiny country they had endured fierce battles, as they were strategically located on the main supply lines to North Africa and the Suez Canal. They were forced out by the war and fled to Latvia for safety. His grandfather drowned while making a living from fishing, leaving Joseph's father, his siblings, and their mother—Joseph's grandmother—with very little income or a way to move forward in life.

At the age of fifteen, Joseph's father stowed away on a ship and immigrated to Canada, where he knew he could find work and send money back home. He made it—the ship docked at Pier 21 in Halifax, where he was quarantined for three months before being released and given permission to stay and work in Canada. Montreal would be his home and where he would meet his wife, a young woman from an Italian immigrant family. They married and had one son: Joseph, now my husband. Growing up in the city, Joseph embraced an urban life of riding the subway and living in a multi-generational home with both his grandparents and parents.

When Joseph was just ten years old, his mother's parents went back to Italy; his mother would soon follow, taking Joseph with her and enrolling him in a private school in Rome, where he was taught by the Jesuits and subjected to a higher level of learning than he was accustomed to in Montreal. His father moved to Brazil, where he worked with General Electric, and Joseph would go to be with him in the summer. As a result of his early learning, he became fluent in a number of languages—including Portuguese, Italian, French, Latin, and English. By the time that I met Joseph, he had reconnected with his Canadian roots, had attended the University of New Brunswick, had taken jobs across Canada, and spent more than fifteen years working and living in the Arctic town of Yellowknife, Northwest Territories.

We come from different backgrounds, but we had both emerged with a love for the North and the Arctic, embracing all that Canada had to offer in every aspect of our lives.

Newly married and with the support of my husband, in 2015 I was confident that I had done the necessary hard work to win re-election. As the campaign progressed, it was increasingly obvious that both the governing Conservatives and the New Democratic Party—the Official Opposition at the time—had badly underestimated Justin Trudeau's ability to capture the public imagination.

CHAPTER 13

A NEW DAY FULL OF HOPE

In October 2015, Trudeau led the Liberals to a comfortable majority in the House of Commons, winning 184 of 328 seats—a stunning increase of 148 seats. In my own riding, I once again faced Peter Penashue running for the Conservatives, along with Edward Rudkowski for the NDP, but this time it was no contest. I garnered over seventy-one per cent of the vote and Penashue finished in third place.

I was going back to Ottawa—not as a member of the third-place party, but as a member of the new Liberal government.

After the election, I had hopes that my hard work the previous two years might earn me a call to the Cabinet table, but I was also realistic about it. We had run strong Liberal candidates in Newfoundland and Labrador, winning all seven seats, and I knew that by tradition only one would get a Cabinet post. As well, the first Trudeau Cabinet was relatively small, at thirty-one Members, including the Prime Minister. In addition to regional representation, the PM had committed to gender balance in his appointments. It was no surprise to me, then, that he selected Judy Foote, who had won her riding of Bonavista-Trinity-Burin with an astounding 81.8 per cent of the vote. She had first been elected federally in 2008, the same year Trudeau entered federal politics and won his seat in Papineau, Quebec, so he knew her very well. Indeed, after the 2015 election, she was seated right next to the Prime Minister in the House, indicating the closeness of their personal and political relationship.

Judy Foote and I shared a long political relationship, as well. She was first elected to the House of Assembly the same year as I, in 1996, and immediately entered Cabinet. After 1999, we were both in the Liberal caucus and, in 2003, sat together around the Cabinet table, so I was well aware of her considerable abilities and experience. She served in the Assembly until 2007, quitting just before the 2007 election to enter federal politics (as I had tried to do in 2005).

We also shared something more personal. Like me, Judy fought two bouts of breast cancer, the first in 2000 and then again in 2014. The disease was a factor in her leaving federal politics in 2017—thankfully, not because of an active case. In 2018, she was appointed Lieutenant Governor of Newfoundland and Labrador, the first woman to hold that position.

The work I had done as an Opposition critic was not ignored, of course. On December 2, 2015, I was appointed Parliamentary Secretary to the Minister of Indigenous and Northern Affairs, the Honourable Carolyn Bennett. When added to my role representing the interests of my constituency and the needs of individual Labradorians, this made for a significant workload—not only when Parliament was sitting, but between sessions as well. Although it meant I often had to work three weekends out of four, I have to admit I loved the challenge. Being able to deepen my understanding of and connection to all of northern Canada and the many Indigenous peoples of our country was deeply satisfying and energizing. I tackled the work put before me with all the skill and stamina I could.

When Judy Foote resigned from Cabinet, the Prime Minister was forced to shuffle the deck and bring another representative from Newfoundland and Labrador into the Cabinet fold. Although I was again somewhat hopeful, I was not shocked when he chose Seamus O'Regan from St. John's. Seamus was new to Parliament, having been elected in 2015, but he was a well-known journalist and had once been named as one of *Maclean's* magazine's "100 Young Canadians to Watch." Seamus had grown up in both Goose Bay and St. John's, so he had broad experience with both regions of Newfoundland and Labrador.

I had known Seamus since 1996. When I was first elected provincially, he was working for Justice Minister Ed Roberts, and then Premier Brian Tobin, as an executive assistant in their offices. He was also someone the Prime Minister had known for many years and trusted deeply. I had no doubt that Seamus would make a good minister, and I understood he might be there for a while. I just kept working hard for Labrador and the North, and figured, who knows—someday it might be my turn.

I continued to be appointed to act as a Parliamentary Secretary, generally in relation to Northern and Indigenous Affairs. At the same time, I worked hard to make sure my constituents were well served. As the 2019 election approached, I felt confident that I would be re-elected. However, it proved to be a much tougher fight than I expected.

Nationally, the party saw its share of the vote drop by over six per cent, with thirty-seven fewer seats than the previous election, as new Conservative Leader Andrew Scheer fell just short of replacing the government. In my own riding, I was in a tough three-way race and, although I won, it was with a substantially reduced majority.

Our administration was now a minority government, relying on support from the NDP and sometimes the Bloc Québécois to pass its budget and legislation. Parliament had become ever more fractious and polarized. In the midst of all that, the global COVID-19 pandemic hit, forcing MPs to operate in a hybrid Parliament; a small number of Members debated in person, while others joined in virtually. It was new to all of us, and there were plenty of glitches, but overall I think it worked quite well. Still, the lack of personal contact did reduce collegiality and further increased the rancour between parties. While internal party solidarity was strong in the Liberal Party, the Conservatives quickly replaced Andrew Scheer with Erin O'Toole.

The so-called Freedom Convoy of trucks that occupied downtown Ottawa for more than three weeks didn't bring anyone together either, especially when some Conservative MPs saw fit to meet with the organizers, some of whom had called for the overthrow of the government.

Again, I was overlooked for Cabinet, and I began to accept that I might never get a chance to sit around that table. It was disappointing, but I knew it was how things work. Seamus O'Regan was a solid performer with a positive reputation, and there was no reason to think he was going anywhere soon. Still, I thought that as an Indigenous woman from a region of northern Canada, I would bring a different and useful perspective to the Cabinet table, and that there was room for both of us.

After two years, COVID-19 was waning. As a government we had provided tremendous amounts of support to individuals and businesses, while achieving one of the highest vaccination rates and lowest death rates from the disease in the entire world.

The Prime Minister knew that a tremendous amount of work lay ahead to help Canada return to better days. We needed a plan that would restore the economy while transitioning the country to a more sustainable path. Trudeau called an election for September 2021 in the hopes of gaining enough seats to form a majority.

I was ready to go. The campaign team had been assembled and Christian von Donat, my campaign lead, and Bonnie Hicks were already setting the wheels in motion. The campaign venues were booked, volunteers lined up, and the campaign funds were in the bank. I was hot on the trail in Labrador, going community to community, meeting with groups and organizations and reminding them of the support they had received from the federal Liberal government.

Joseph, who had been working hard with me, took sick during the election campaign. We had left Goose Bay one morning to head to the south coast, about a 450-kilometre drive. We were getting near the end of the election, and I was going to attend a dinner at the community centre in Charlottetown that evening. Joseph was not feeling well enough to drive (I know he's unwell when he lets me in the driver's seat) or to attend the event, so he went to our home in Mary's Harbour while I met up with my mother, who accompanied me to the community supper in Charlottetown, about sixty kilometres away. Before supper had ended, I got a call saying that Joseph had been admitted to hospital in Mary's Harbour and they had ordered a medevac for him.

It was an attack of diverticulitis, which he had been diagnosed with in 2019, right before the election. At that time, he'd had an attack in Happy Valley-Goose Bay and was taken to the hospital and admitted. He had been there for three days when they finally found out he had a bowel disruption and that his body was going septic. There was no time for a medevac to get him from Goose Bay to St. John's. If not for the excellent skills and medical performance of Dr. G. Narsing Pradhan, who was able to do the operation right there and then get him to St. John's, he might not have survived. We are forever grateful for Dr. Pradhan and his skills; he had saved many lives in Labrador, and my husband was now one more.

Joseph did very well for the first couple of years after that, but during the election of 2021, being on the road with me every day and campaigning certainly took a toll, and the illness caught up with him. Fortunately, after being attended to at the hospital in St. Anthony, he was released and able to travel back to Goose Bay. With my husband back home, I moved on to Labrador West to finish knocking on doors. With only two days left to campaign, I was trying to reach as many constituents as I could.

On September 17, 2021, another distressing call came in. A vessel with two young men from my home area had been lost at sea and the search was on. Marc Russell and his crewmate, Joey Jenkins, were reported missing when their vessel, the *Island Lady*, did not return to port after a day of fishing. Local boats were searching and the Coast Guard had been called in. The next day there was still no sign; the families and communities were frantically searching with all the supports they had, but more was needed. As the Coast Guard boats and military aircraft started combing the area, people kept up hope that the men would be found alive. Marc and Joey, while young, were used to working on the water. Marc owned the vessel and had spent all of his working life as a mariner and fisher with his father. There was reason to hope.

I had given up on the campaign by now; with just a day or so left, I had to turn my attention to supporting the search for Marc and Joey. I had left Labrador West with one of my campaign workers to drive back to Happy Valley-Goose Bay. The next day was election day, but I felt so heavy from the worry I carried for those boys, I could focus on nothing else.

As we got to Churchill Falls, it was around 9 p.m.; I was back in cellphone range after being out of it for hours. I checked my messages to find out that the search was being called off and would be turned into a recovery operation. The families were devastated. I reached out to Marc's dad, Dwight, a seasoned mariner, and his uncle, Todd Russell, who was co-ordinating operations for the family. They told me that both the Coast Guard and the military were pulling out of the search. It was there on the side of the road that I reached National Defence Minister Harjit Sajjan, who finally was able to get planes back in the air the next morning and Coast Guard vessels back on the water. But it was to no avail; the boys were never found and brought home to their families.

That election came and went in a blur, as the grief I carried could never be displaced by any victory. The loss of Marc and Joey rekindled the grief and emptiness I already carried from my brother Keith's drowning the year before. The pain was so raw it was numbing.

The day after the election Joseph took the flight back to Gatineau, Quebec, where he was seeing a specialist for his medical issues. Less than a week later he became ill; I was not surprised when I received a call saying he had been taken to hospital by ambulance and would once again require surgery. After surgery and nearly six weeks in hospital, Joseph was seeing improvement every day; he made a full recovery and has been doing great since.

It was a new election but virtually the same result. The Liberals gained three seats but remained in minority territory; the other parties were virtually unchanged in the number of seats they won. The leaders of both the Green Party and Conservative Party lost their jobs, forced out in both cases by internal dissension. For me, the results in Labrador were much the same as in 2019: another victory in a three-way race, with my own share of the vote barely shifting. After the 2021 election, I expected nothing to change. I was wrong.

On the night of October 25, I went to bed reconciled in my own mind that I would not be going into Cabinet because there would not be two Cabinet ministers from Newfoundland and Labrador. I understood and accepted that Seamus O'Regan was not only very capable but was a loyal friend of Justin Trudeau. That night,

I had a dream that two Cabinet ministers were appointed from Newfoundland and Labrador, but the second one wasn't me: it was Gudie Hutchings, who had been elected in 2015. I'd known Gudie for years; she used to run several fly-fishing lodges in Labrador and, at the time of her election, was chair of the Battle Harbour Historic Trust, which had played such a huge role in my life.

I got up that morning, poured my coffee, and said to myself, *Don't be so foolish. You know it's just playing on your mind and that can bring you into the very slums of despair and disappointment if you go down this rabbit hole.* As I was having my coffee and checking my email, I got a text from Gudie. She said: "I love you dearly, sister, but you'll see me on the big screen today as I'm being sworn in as the Minister of Rural Economic Development."

Everything inside of me changed. While I was proud of Gudie and excited for her to have this opportunity, the disappointment was hard to hide. Immediately I could feel the bitterness of loss, and my mind turned to negative thoughts of not being good enough. I felt stamped on and pushed back down; I was suddenly back to being that abused little girl. I was at our house in Gatineau, Quebec, sitting in the living room, watching the leaves falling from the trees outside the windows. It was raining and windy and my husband was recovering from a major operation and not doing great, and I really didn't want to worry him, but controlling my emotions was very difficult, and I broke down in sobs.

Don't get me wrong—I was very happy for Gudie and for Seamus. I knew they were both very capable people and I have tremendous respect for them. I also knew it was not their decision; it was the decision of the Prime Minister, but it left me feeling empty inside, questioning everything about myself and how others saw me. That vulnerability is what I had fought against my entire life, and now it was in front of me again. The feeling of never measuring up to society's expectations is hard to escape. I worked hard all my life. For the last twenty-eight years I've worked for my riding, for Labradorians and all northerners, for people and regions of the country I care deeply about. I tried to tell myself it was going to be okay, and for a few brief seconds, I'd believe that. But in the next moment I would revert to the depths of despair. The knots in my stomach were so tight; as the day went on, it hurt even more, and I felt like I was ready to crumple to the floor.

When you fall like that, you need to grab hold of something to pull yourself back up. I knew I was not alone in my disappointment; I thought about friends who had lost elections, especially one who lost in a municipal election and for two years went through a period of depression. Another friend lost a provincial election. These were two of the most capable individuals I have ever met, yet they never got the opportunity to serve and contribute because the people had chosen differently. I realized that this situation was out of my control. Only one person gets to make decisions about Cabinet and it's the Prime Minister; he has his reasons, which I may never know.

But it still bothered and hurt me that this one person could have such an impact on my life, especially when I seemed to be everything that he said was important to have represented in Cabinet: I was an Indigenous woman from an isolated region; I was experienced, with over two decades in office; I was a former provincial Cabinet minister and the former leader of a provincial party; and I had won eight successful elections. I had taken the lead on difficult negotiations, and had done as much to represent Northern interests in Ottawa as anyone had. In my own mind, I was qualified and deserving.

Yet that little abused child inside me could never quite believe it. Because of that unhealed trauma, I couldn't watch the television coverage as my good friends and close colleagues were sworn into office. I had to stay off Twitter and avoid all news of government business for several days after.

As the trauma of childhood followed me, I began to think about the troubles other people were facing. In my home community, a friend had just buried her husband, who had died suddenly of cancer. A cousin was caring for her husband, who was suffering with terminal cancer and had just had a leg amputated. I suddenly wondered how damned selfish I was, that I was not satisfied with my lot in life.

To think that for years I had been advising so many people not to worry what others think, that it's what you think of yourself that matters. And yet I was questioning myself. Do my family, my constituents, the people I've sat across the table from for the last twenty-five years think that I'm a failure or that I am not worthy? I had literally to shake my head and snap myself out of those thoughts. But I *didn't* feel good about myself. I knew I had to haul myself out of the slump, and I knew I could, because I also believed I could do anything that was within my control, that I could be focused and strong. So I would carry on, for I had a job to do and others were counting on me.

I'm sure I'm not alone when I say that the one way to take your mind off your problems is to realize there are people around you who need you. I was definitely needed by my husband, to help him with his post-op treatment. I remembered that his son, Quinn, and Quinn's wife, Katherine, and their little baby, Oscar, were coming to visit. I met Oscar for the first time just a few days after the Cabinet announcement, and he was a breath of fresh air in our home.

I knew at that moment that we may work all our lives to achieve things and to advance our careers, yet there will always be people who make decisions that impact us but that are completely out of our control. In the end, it doesn't matter. What matters is the health of those we love, and our own health. The time with our families, that sense of togetherness, that sense of loving one another and sharing, is the most important thing.

Two days after my great disappointment, I took little three-and-a-half-month-old baby Oscar into my arms and cuddled him, and I told him that things would be okay. He could be whoever he wanted to be. As I reassured Oscar that working hard toward goals in life was a good thing, I reflected on the many times in my life that things did not go the way I wanted. Those are the times that defined me and made me stronger. It was the greatest disappointments and the biggest battles that built my strengths and my character.

This little guy with big blue eyes was looking back at me with drool coming down his chin, his little arms and legs dangling and moving as he was fighting his way toward independence. I thought what a wonderful, beautiful thing life really is. We should not limit our existence by one event or one disappointment but in terms of how we can do better, how we can make a bigger difference. Ultimately it's not about title or position; it's about being able to hold your head up high and be proud of what you've done and to focus on where you want to go next.

As I'm writing this, I've already had my first cup of coffee, and I've said good morning to my little grandson, Oscar. I've told him what a wonderful world he is about to experience, and in his little face I see so much hope and so much potential. In sharing our experiences and what we've learned from them, and in supporting each other, we save each other.

Will I ever sit at the federal Cabinet table? All I can do is my best, take the challenges handed to me—such as being Parliamentary Secretary now to *two* Cabinet ministers!—and do what I've always done: turn difficulties into successes.

*Forgiveness is one of the greatest gifts we give
ourselves; by compassionately forgiving ourselves and
others, we develop the courage to let go, make peace,
and most importantly, build personal resilience.*

— Hon. Joanne Thompson, MP for St. John's East

CHAPTER 14

POLITICAL DECISIONS

In the course of any person's life—let alone a politician's—there are places and events that cause dramatic change to the human, political, and geographical landscape. While I have mentioned some of these in passing, there are a few I want to mention specifically.

MUSKRAT FALLS

It would be impossible to write a book about my life and my relationship to Labrador without touching on the Churchill River and the massive hydroelectric developments that surround it. It would be equally impossible to cover the entire past and future of those developments in a single chapter. Books, I am sure, are already being written on the subject and its impact, both positive and negative, on the province. The report from the public inquiry into the decisions and actions surrounding the Muskrat Falls hydroelectric development is also freely available for those who want a deeper dive into the subject.

In 1965, Joey Smallwood renamed the Hamilton River (named after a nineteenth-century colonial governor) the Churchill, after former British Prime Minister Winston Churchill. The Indigenous people who lived along its banks had their own names for it, roughly translating as the Grand River. The Grand River is a good name for it; it's the longest river in Labrador by far, with a vast catchment area and a deep cultural and economic significance to all the people of Labrador.

Smallwood had great plans for the river and for the falls of the same name. Since the late 1950s, the Hamilton Falls (Labrador) Corporation Ltd., a subsidiary of the British Newfoundland Development Corporation (BRINCO), held a ninety-nine-year lease on hydroelectric development on the river. However, despite a decade of trying, BRINCO was unable to raise the capital to construct the massive project and, after resisting for several years, Smallwood signed an agreement with Hydro-Québec, a Crown corporation of that province. Quebec would provide the capital and expertise, and in exchange they were given an exclusive right to buy ninety per cent of the power for forty years from first power at a fixed rate, with favourable terms of renewal—and it did renew in 2016, for twenty-five more years. The deal is scheduled to expire in 2041.

At the time, the deal was hailed as major victory for Newfoundland. The project would be constructed without using public funds from the province and provincial coffers would be augmented by a regular stream of revenue from the sale of power. The remaining power could be retained for local use or sold through the Quebec transmission grid. The deal was seen as so positive that no one in the province seriously questioned its terms, and when it was put to the House of Assembly, even the Opposition voted for it.

However, the province soon soured on the agreement. As various unforeseen events came into play, the price of electricity soared. While Hydro-Québec made billions in profits, revenue to

Newfoundland remained fixed at 1969 levels. By 2019, the province estimated Hydro-Québec had made $28 billion in profits while Newfoundland and Labrador Hydro received a mere $2 billion.

The Upper Churchill tapped roughly sixty-five per cent of the hydroelectric potential of the river. By the end of the twentieth century, interest turned toward the remaining potential and the development of the Lower Churchill, consisting of two large projects, one at Muskrat Falls and one at Gull Island. The Tobin government arranged to sell surplus power from the Upper Churchill to Hydro-Québec in 1999—power that originally was meant to fuel industrial development in Labrador. The agreement was renewed in 2004 for five years by the new Progressive Conservative provincial government. Discussions about the development of the Lower Churchill, which would undoubtedly cost billions, took place at the same time as the initial sale agreement. However, the deal was never made (and I expect, based on later developments, that the offer out of Quebec was pretty meagre relative to its real value).

In any case, the government of the day was focused on another major development—the Voisey's Bay mine—which would result in major benefits to the province that continue to this day.

In 2004, Premier Danny Williams signed an agreement with a consortium of companies to explore the development of the Lower Churchill. My biggest concern then was what benefits, if any, Southern Labrador would reap from the development, especially in terms of access to cheaper, cleaner hydroelectric power. The adjacency principle—that those closest to an industry or development should be the first to benefit—that had guided my politics from the very start of my career, should apply as much to electric power as it did to the fishery or to mineral development. Labrador faced the highest power rates in the province and much of it came from noisy, polluting diesel generators.

Williams assured me that Labrador would certainly "be taken into consideration" in any development of the river, but Labradorians had heard that before from both Liberal and Tory governments. I vowed to keep an eye on the government and not let up on the adjacency principle. The 2004 agreement to sell recall power would generate $45 million a year for the province ($220 million over the life of the agreement) and with the Atlantic Accord signed in 2005, the province was in a strong fiscal position. Why not use the money generated in Labrador to expand Labrador infrastructure by paving the highway and building transmission lines to mining developments? After all, the power being sold was supposed to be used in Labrador, and could be if we had the necessary infrastructure. The response to those suggestions was lukewarm at best.

Other questions arose as the months turned into years. The route by which power would be transmitted to potential customers in southern Canada and the United States was still up in the air. The so-called "Anglo Saxon" route (now renamed the "Maritime" route)—first proposed in the 1960s when BRINCO was trying to develop the Upper Churchill—was back on the table. This route would see transmission lines run south through Labrador to eventually cross the Gulf of St. Lawrence to join the grid in New Brunswick. While admittedly this was far more expensive than transport through the Quebec system, it made sense to have an alternative available, if only to strengthen our negotiating position with Hydro-Québec. While acknowledging the extra expense, the Premier said it was a "compromise the province might be willing to accept."

Meanwhile, the matter of redress—that is, compensation for the unfairness of the Upper Churchill—which had been a key part of the PC platform and a condition for the development of the Lower Churchill in the run-up to the 2003 election, was no longer being discussed by 2006. Newfoundland and Labrador was not the only party seeking redress, of course. The Innu Nation had never been compensated for the flooding of their traditional territory and the loss of hunting and trapping lands and were seeking a fair settlement in their ongoing treaty negotiations.

As well, a loan guarantee from the federal government that had been promised by the Harper Conservatives during the 2006 federal election was slow to materialize. In 2007, during debate on the creation of a new energy corporation for the province called Nalcor, the Premier himself described the status of the loan guarantee quite succinctly: "There is a letter of commitment from the Prime Minister, which is probably not worth the paper it is written on." He went on to say that it was pointless to press the government in Ottawa on the guarantee until pre-engineering work was completed and a solid proposal on sanctioning the project could be put forward. That, he said, would happen in 2009.

The creation of Nalcor Energy as a provincial Crown corporation was meant to bring all the province's burgeoning energy interests under one roof. Newfoundland and Labrador Hydro, responsible for generating and delivering electricity in the province, would become a subsidiary of Nalcor and would have four subsidiary corporations governing the Upper and Lower Churchill—with Muskrat Falls and Gull Island in separate companies—and a company to manage the assets of the defunct Twin Falls power plant on the well-known but strangely named Unknown River, a minor tributary of the Churchill River. Nalcor also had divisions or subsidiaries to manage Newfoundland and Labrador's interests in oil and gas development, energy marketing, and the Bull Arm Fabrication Site, where offshore oil platforms are built. The proliferation of companies with varied reporting mechanisms was confusing and called into question the ability of regulatory agencies to oversee their operations.

The new company created as many questions as it answered. We now had an idea about who was going to manage the development of energy resources, and particularly the massive Lower Churchill development, which could generate as much as 3,000 megawatts of power between Gull Island and the smaller Muskrat Falls power plants, but we didn't know how they would do it—other than that we would be going it alone in the process, according to the Premier.

"Going it alone" was an interesting concept, particularly since the corporation had limited borrowing power ($600 million initially), far less than would be required to build either plant, let alone the transmission line. Obviously, another investor or another source of funds would be required, but as to who it might be, the government was unable or unwilling to say. As it turned out, "going it alone" was not so lonely after all; in January 2008, Nalcor signed a memorandum of understanding with Nova Scotia Power and a private Nova Scotian firm called Emera, to study the feasibility of the Maritime route while still exploring more conservative options overland.

Quite apart from the technical and economic feasibility questions, there was also the matter of environmental assessments required for the project to proceed. While considerable work had been happening on the Churchill River itself, in partnership with the Innu Nation, the downstream impacts and those of the transmission lines if the power was to be moved south through Labrador, had yet to be studied.

Over the next two years, the objectives of the project kept shifting. The government said they were open to all options for the development of the Lower Churchill. Redress for the unfairness of the Upper Churchill deal came back on the table, though it was only redress for the province that concerned the government; it was up to the Innu Nation "to go it alone" in seeking compensation.

At the same time, the government knew a deal would have to be reached with the Innu before the Lower Churchill development could proceed. Working with the government on environmental assessments was one thing, but the members of the Innu Nation were determined they would not be ignored in terms of economic benefits and compensation for the infringement of their traditional rights. In that, I was fully on their side, as well as that of the northern Inuit. I was also determined that the southern Inuit and the settler community—both of whom had a long history with the river—would not be forgotten, and I raised the matter with increasing frequency as the government's plans proceeded.

Not that it was easy. While the Premier and his ministers spouted plenty of generalities about the project and its supposed benefits, they were remarkably short on details. Whenever my questions became too pointed, they would hide behind the excuse of not revealing their negotiating position to others—especially Hydro-Québec. When I pointed out that as a one-third owner (with Nalcor holding the other two-thirds) of the Upper Churchill power plant, Hydro-Québec might have plenty of ways to discover what was going on, I was told that was Nalcor's business and that politicians shouldn't meddle in the operations of an arm's-length Crown corporation.

Although the government did have discussions with Hydro-Québec on developing the Lower Churchill and transmitting power through the Quebec and Ontario grids, they were simultaneously pursuing a ruling from the Régie (the Quebec regulatory agency) to ensure that power from the Lower Churchill would have access to the Quebec transmission system without restrictions or conditions.

In November of 2009, the Premier announced that he had instructed the government's lawyers "to undertake an extensive and thorough review of potential legal remedies [in the study]. As a lawyer by profession, I was determined to ensure that no legal stone was left unturned." The Quebec Civil Code required that parties "act in good faith in all legal relationships, including the negotiation and ongoing performance of contracts." After consulting some of the leading legal minds in Quebec, the government informed the CEO of CF(L)Co. (the subsidiary of Nalcor responsible for the Upper Churchill power generation), who in turn wrote Hydro-Québec asking for the contract to be renegotiated.

I had been asking for details about these negotiations throughout 2009 and into 2010. I had also begun to ask questions about all of the matters that had come to concern me. Was there a realistic alternative to transporting power through the Quebec grid? The Maritime route had been studied and it was eventually revealed that extensive pre-engineering and costing had been undertaken, but was it economically viable? What would be the impact on power rates in Newfoundland and Labrador? Were there technical or engineering issues that could delay the project or cause significant cost overruns? How were the rights of all three Indigenous people in Labrador going to be protected?

I had plenty of questions, but I didn't get a lot of answers. The Premier and his ministers didn't take kindly to being pressed on the issue. They particularly didn't like it when I pointed to alternative views that suggested the Maritime route was not only more difficult than described, but was at risk of serious cost overruns. This should have come as no surprise. Megaprojects frequently go over budget, and we didn't have to look much farther than our own offshore. The estimates for the cost of developing the Hebron field had risen by sixty-six per cent in just a couple of years (they would eventually triple); why would the development of the Lower Churchill—then estimated at $6 billion to $12 billion—be any different? Even the size of that price range called into doubt how accurate those estimates could be. Nalcor itself admitted that even a ten per cent increase in costs would lower the profits from the Lower Churchill by thirty-two per cent.

I wasn't the only one to question the viability of the Maritime route. When *The Globe and Mail* ran columns questioning the technical feasibility of the undersea route, the Premier dismissed it, saying they "obviously were following direction from Hydro-Québec." I suppose I shouldn't have been surprised when the same allegations were levelled at me, initially by Premier Williams, who wondered where I was getting my questions and information if not from Hydro-Québec.

Later, his successor was even more pointed, suggesting a previous Liberal administration was prepared to give away the power from Muskrat Falls and that I would do the same if I were Premier. Neither, of course, was remotely true, but for some people in politics, when you don't have evidence on your side, an unfounded accusation will do. In politics, you realize that your opponents don't let facts stand in the way of the message they are sending. That was the case with this government.

By 2010, all talk of shipping power through Quebec came to an end. The Régie dismissed the government's request on "technical" grounds, and Hydro-Québec refused to reopen the hated contract. Subsequent decisions by the highest courts in the land upheld their right to do so, and Newfoundland and Labrador would have to wait until 2041 for things to change.

The Premier's response was telling:

"Mr. Speaker, my preference was always the Maritime route but that was because it was a personal preference. I think it was more to get away from Quebec than anything, but it also has to be a rational decision and an economic decision and based on good financial consideration. So as a result, all the way through what we have done is we have done parallel plans. We have looked at the Quebec route and moving all or most of the power into Ontario but we have also, on a parallel basis, simultaneously looked at the Maritime route, and the Atlantic route."

The Premier went on to assure the House and the people of Newfoundland and Labrador that, while the project would be technically challenging, those challenges could be met and were not an obstacle to the construction of the project; that it was within the financial capacity of the province and would only have a positive impact on the electricity rates consumers would pay.

On November 18, 2010, the government announced a partnership with Emera to construct the first phase of the Lower Churchill, that is, the power plant at Muskrat Falls (saying Gull Island would follow "several years later"), the transmission lines through Labrador, the underwater link at the Strait of Belle Isle, and the further underwater line to the province of Nova Scotia. An agreement with the Innu gave them a quantum of land, first crack at jobs created by the project, and an annual cash benefit of $5 million, rising to $6 million with further increases dependent on the revenue from selling electricity to consumers. Less than a month after signing the deal, Danny Williams announced his return to private life, leaving his successor, Kathy Dunderdale, to actually bring the project to life.

Danny was generally hailed as hero for developing the Lower Churchill without the involvement of Hydro-Québec. Others, including myself, wondered if he was getting out before the hard part began. In any case, he was convinced (as was the general public) that: "The benefits of this project for our province will be enormous, including thousands of jobs and billions of dollars of economic activity. From day one, our government has taken a long-term, strategic approach to developing this project. Our priorities have remained steadfast; that is to achieve maximum benefits for our people, and to secure stable rates and markets with a good return for the people of this province."

I was far from convinced. Muskrat Falls would only generate 824 megawatts of power, yet the stated price tag was $6.2 billion, which was the low end of the original estimate. Gull Island, when (or if) developed would add another 2,250 megawatts, but no price tag was attached to the construction of that power plant. Still, if the Muskrat Falls plant was expected to cost $2.9 billion (with the transmission lines and associated infrastructure making up the rest of the cost), one would presume the much larger Gull Island plant would cost at least $3 billion and probably more.

At best, Muskrat Falls would only stabilize power rates at current levels. Cost overruns would mean higher rates for consumers; delays in completion were also costly. Muskrat Falls was meant to replace power generated at the oil-fired plant at Holyrood by 2015. If the project couldn't come online before then, significant upgrades would be required to that plant to reduce pollution and extend its operating life.

My own predictions were that the project would add billions to the province's public debt and, with the likelihood of cost overruns, substantially increase the cost of power to provincial consumers, while any power sold to Nova Scotia and New England would be priced at local market rates, considerably less than the rates in Newfoundland and Labrador. I was convinced a better deal could be negotiated.

As 2011 wore on, the government continued to evade pointed questions about cost overruns, the impact on local power rates, and environmental issues raised by the Nunatsiavut Government (Northern Labrador Inuit) around mercury contamination of the river downstream. There were days when it seemed the government didn't really understand the agreement they had signed or the project they would construct. I said so on several occasions in the House; you can imagine the response I got.

Although some concessions were made around the provision of power to Southern Labrador for industrial development, the government remained resolute in their arguments that this was the best deal available and would provide massive benefits to the province in the long run. Questions began to arise about when the project would be started, as a federal loan guarantee for both Newfoundland and Labrador and Nova Scotia had not yet been finalized.

As the election approached, I persuaded the party to make the renegotiation of the Lower Churchill deal a key plank of our platform. We developed a website and social media campaign, cleverly entitled "Muskrat Fails." While we would present a broad platform addressing all the issues facing voters, the megaproject would be a major focus for me and the party.

As it turned out, of course, I didn't get to fight the election as Liberal leader, or even participate much beyond my own riding (which I won with seventy-one per cent of the vote). Other issues took precedence, and the PCs under Dunderdale were returned with a somewhat reduced majority. Kathy Dunderdale became the first woman to be elected Premier of Newfoundland and Labrador. She had worked in community development and served on the Burin town council before being elected as an MHA in 2003. A high-profile member of the Williams Cabinet, she held a number of portfolios before becoming Deputy Premier, prior to Danny's retirement.

An agreement on the loan guarantee was finally signed in 2012 (and finalized the following year), the province sanctioned the project, and construction began in 2013. Clearly, power to replace Holyrood would not arrive by 2015. In fact, the first electricity was produced in late 2020 and that was only available in Labrador. Electricity from Muskrat Falls was only integrated into the entire grid in November 2021.

I know it's a bit rude to say I told you so, but the questions I raised were exactly the ones the government needed to hear. Unfortunately, they weren't listening, at least not to me and not to the public, and provided no answers.

Who they were listening to became clear during a public inquiry into the project in 2019. When Nalcor was formed with its multitude of subsidiaries, the team that was gathered to manage the project was heavily weighted with people from the oil and gas industry rather than those with expertise in hydroelectricity. Former Premier Kathy Dunderdale testified that the government trusted what Nalcor told them, but as the CBC summarized it: "Nalcor's team was given an unrestricted leash by its political masters, including what amounts to a blank cheque from the public treasury, to build the generating station at Muskrat and the transmission lines to Churchill Falls and Newfoundland's Avalon Peninsula." Reports were sanitized and note-taking was prohibited during briefings because of the "risk of leaks."

Even before the project started the cost had escalated by $300 million, though few in the government seemed to take note. In any case, the cost estimate failed to take interest on loans into account and officials went to extremes to keep the numbers presented low.

The report of the public inquiry was damning. The government had predetermined that the project would go ahead before studies were complete. Nalcor had mismanaged the project at numerous stages, incurring cost overruns that could have been avoided. Muskrat Falls was, as Nalcor chair Stan Marshall agreed when offered the description in 2016, "a boondoggle." Danny Williams predictably weighed in to defend Nalcor and his own role, promising the CBC that "any public inquiry into what some are now calling a scandal would only restore the reputations of those involved with the project, including his own."

However, at the time of this writing—late 2023—the project is still not fully operational, with final delays caused by failures of software and toppling transmission lines. The cost of the project has ballooned to $13.5 billion and counting. Power rates for consumers were set to double before the Liberal government in

Ottawa provided a $5.2-billion bailout to the province. The Innu Nation is suing both governments as a result because of the lost revenues the higher rates would have delivered. They also swear they will do whatever they can to stop the development of Gull Island—which the Premier of Quebec has mused about developing.

Danny Williams' legacy project has turned into an albatross around the neck of this province, and that will not change until the project begins to bear fruit. As for me, I always wonder if the Opposition at the time had had more resources, could we have asked tougher questions and dug deeper into what was really going on?

Labrador did reap some benefits in terms of jobs and business opportunities and availability of power, and if I contributed to that in any way, it was a job well done.

5 WING GOOSE BAY

The story of 5 Wing Goose Bay is one that places Labrador at the centre of every major military dispute in the world since 1941. Unlike most air bases across Canada, the air field at Goose Bay is used for civilian operations and civilian aircraft, as well as military operations. The airport facilities are classified as an airport of entry by NAV CANADA; they operate commercial and private flights, and they are staffed by the Canadian Border Services Agency. However, the military air fields and facilities are owned and operated by the Royal Canadian Air Force and the Triple 4 Squadron under the Department of National Defence.

The mission of 5 Wing had always been to support the defence of North American airspace since its inception, as well as supporting the RCAF and Allied forces around the world in training. For eighty years this has been a source of pride for Labradorians, knowing that we were contributing to training in the world and defending the safety and security of Canadians and our allies.

There is a tremendous amount of history written about 5 Wing Goose Bay. Briefly, in 1941 Goose Bay was chosen as a site for a Canadian airbase. Canada was under tremendous pressure from Britain and United States to have the work completed so they could use the airbase during the war. By November of that year they had completed three runways, each measuring 7,000 feet long, all gravel and ready for operation. The first aircraft would land there in December of that year, opening the airbase to military operations. In 1942 the base was bustling with air traffic, welcoming aircraft from the United Kingdom and other allies.

Facilities were built up on both sides of the runway. The RCAF built temporary premises on the northeast side of the runway, including hangars and a control tower. The American Air Force built on the south side of the runway, building aprons, hangars, a control tower, and other infrastructure. Goose Bay started to welcome other NATO countries, too, as Germany, Italy, and the Netherlands chose Goose Bay for their operations.

During the Cold War, the Goose Bay airbase was the site of the first nuclear weapons in Canada, brought in by the US military. In 1954 the Americans built the first strategic air command weapons storage area. The facility was protected by high fences topped with barbed wire, and it was said to be the highest-security area at the base. Local people tell stories of the facilities being guarded 24/7, and no one was permitted in the area.

The next chapter for the Goose Bay airbase would be low-level flight training. In the 1980s, it was thought that low-level flights were tougher to detect by the enemy, and there was anticipation there would be a demand for more and more instruction in this technique. Labrador was the ideal location. It had large masses of land and water that were supposedly uninhabited by people, which would allow for training in daylight and darkness so that forces would be able to get the skills they needed to outmanoeuvre the enemy in a time of war. Many NATO countries moved into the area, with a primary focus on low-level flight and tactical training. The population on the base grew to as many as 10,000 soldiers on occasion.

However, the increase in low-level flights by fighter aircraft was not without serious controversy. Sheshatshiu Innu First Nation protested these operations vociferously, stating that the noise from the aircraft flying close to the ground was negatively impacting caribou and other wildlife in the area, and causing upheaval to their way of life on their traditional lands.

Near the end of 1988, when I went to work at *The Labradorian*, Innu protests at 5 Wing Goose Bay were a regular occurrence. They were drawing the attention of people from around the world to the impact of low-level flying on their traditional lands, the animals, and their way of life. I covered many of their stories at that time. Most days, women and children were being dragged off the end of the runway for their safety by military and police officers. David Suzuki, host of the television program *The Nature of Things*, latched onto the story of the Innu of Nitassinan—which means "our land" in Innu-aimun—and came to Happy Valley-Goose Bay to visit with the Innu in order to better understand and tell their story. At that time, I was invited—along with many other journalists—to visit the tent of Elder Elizabeth (Tshaukuesh) Penashue, when she met with Suzuki. Elder Penashue explained in her own language the migration patterns of the Innu of Labrador, straddling the Labrador–Quebec border.

Innu are traditionally nomadic, spending much time living out on the land, hunting but also observing animals and their habits, such as the migration patterns of caribou. They understood the impact low-level flying could have on the environment far better than anyone else. It was their advocacy for, and education about, the natural environment of Labrador that led to the low-level flying monitoring board of experts, who worked in partnership with Innu to ensure the protection of animals and natural habitat. Low-level flying continued in Labrador until 2005.

With the end of the mandate for low-level flying at 5 Wing Goose Bay came a lull in activity. The community had a strong Senator in Bill Rompkey, and he advocated using CFB Goose Bay as a site for a missile defence radar system that was being developed by the United States Department of Defense. MP Lawrence O'Brien lobbied the Liberal government for upgrades at the facilities. When the federal government changed to Conservative, Liberal Todd Russell, as the local MP, had his work cut out for him. Rumours were circulating that top brass at the Canadian Armed Forces were ready to write off 5 Wing Goose Bay and shut down operations. They were unable to get a long-term operational contract for the base, and many of the nearly 500 local jobs were in jeopardy. It was not a pretty picture, and it was causing a tremendous amount of stress in the community. Todd was not giving up, however; he had come from decades of lobbying and fighting for the rights of the people of NunatuKavut, and he knew that it was going to take a strong, aggressive approach to obtain a new mandate at the Wing.

During the 2006 election, Stephen Harper made a full commitment to 5 Wing Goose Bay for a new rapid reaction Army battalion and a new long-range unstaffed aerial vehicle squadron for the base. The battalion was supposed to have consisted of approximately 650 troops, while the drone squadron was to have around 100 personnel. However, none of these commitments materialized. At the time, local MHA John Hickey and Premier Danny Williams went after Prime Minister Harper and Defence Minister Peter MacKay, but to no avail. The relationship between Williams and Harper had been strained, and the gap was widening. The controversy over 5 Wing Goose Bay was just another file left in limbo between the province and the federal government of the day. Other than money invested to do an environmental cleanup of the base after years of Canada and our allies leaving dangerous waste in the area, nothing sustainable materialized.

By 2013, the operational requirement at 5 Wing was being reviewed and rolled over every five years. There was no long-term commitment to Goose Bay operations by the federal government, and they were not carrying out the upgrades that were required. Year over year, more and more barracks and buildings were being dismantled as a part of the environmental cleanup program. Economic fear was a constant in the community.

In the election of 2013, I ran for the federal Liberals in Labrador against Conservative MP Peter Penashue. At every door in Lake Melville, I was confronted with the issue of 5 Wing Goose Bay; I wanted the job of representing the people and they wanted to know that I could deliver. With the Harper government in charge, I knew that what was decided for the base would be done with little or no input from me. I was elected that spring, and it was just a year later when we started to see layoffs at the airbase. My questions to the government fell on deaf ears. I could feel the tension in the community; I knew that people feared the worst.

As a member of the Opposition, I knew the best thing that I could do was continue to lobby within my own party and keep the issue front and centre. I was hopeful that a change in government would bring a change in attitude. But National Defence is not like most government departments; the military has a tremendous amount of control and input into military assets and how they are used. I had to be creative and seek support from outside of government, from those who knew that I understood the strategic importance of 5 Wing Goose Bay, especially when it comes to the Arctic and protecting our safety and sovereignty.

When the Liberal Party won the federal election in 2015, the first task for me as a Member of government was to secure a long-term contract for the operation of 5 Wing Goose Bay. After many discussions and meetings, I discovered that the writing had been on the wall for the base for a long time. It was an asset that was costly and not deemed particularly valuable to the government at the time. This was a narrative that would be hard to change, but I would do everything in my power to change it, and through hard work and the support of colleagues such as Newfoundland and Labrador MHA Perry Trimper, I was able to build a case within government to maintain the base.

After a governmental review, it was decided to extend the Wing's mandate. It would become a strategic post to support Canada in our NATO operations. Training at Goose Bay would resume, and all countries would be welcomed to the region. It was a very happy day for me when we were able to sign a twenty-year contract for the operations of 5 Wing Goose Bay, and it was even more important for me when the Government of Canada solicited the new operational requirements for the Wing. The job was not yet done, though. Infrastructure at the base had not been modernized and updated in many years, and money would have to be spent in those areas.

The new Liberal government almost immediately provided funding for improved infrastructure at northern military bases by including $200 million in the 2016 budget for that purpose. In June 2016, the Minister of Defence announced that $12 million would be used to improve the facilities at 5 Wing, with another $2.3 million provided in 2019 for runway improvements as the first step of a long-term plan to maintain and upgrade facilities. Canada continued to show its commitment to the base in 2021 by announcing a ten-year contract to renew 5 Wing Goose Bay's existing support services and facilities maintenance contract. This ten-year contract is valued at $694 million, and up to $1.5 billion over twenty years if two five-year extension options are exercised.

The most exciting development was yet to come. In June 2022, the government announced a twenty-year plan to modernize Canada's NORAD capabilities. This included nearly $16 billion to upgrade four northern bases, including the one at Happy Valley-Goose Bay. No longer would the facilities simply be maintained or repaired; they would be upgraded and enhanced. As Defence Minister Anita Anand—only the second woman in Canadian history to hold that position—said at the time: "In the years to come, the air operations infrastructure here at Goose Bay will receive significant upgrades, which will enable its continued ability to support NORAD operations and to ensure the defence of North America."

The Russian invasion of Ukraine in 2022 was a game changer for countries surrounding the Arctic circumpolar region, and Canada was no exception. In 2021, the Canadian government announced that it would invest $40 million in its North American operations to modernize the infrastructure across the Arctic and to better prepare Canada against any threats. Once again, 5 Wing Goose Bay would play a strategic role as the most easterly base in North America, with the longest runways and some of the most accessible infrastructure; it was a unique location for NORAD. When these investments were announced, Goose Bay was identified as a forward base for NORAD operations. We had come full circle from 1941. We were once again poised to play a major role in the safety and security of North America, and we would do so with our allies.

BURTON WINTERS

On Sunday, January 29, 2012, Burton Winters, a fourteen-year-old boy from the small village of Makkovik on the central Labrador coast, took a wrong turn on his way home and wound up out on the sea ice. His snow machine got stuck and he was forced to abandon it. The tragic end to his story shone a stark light on the problems with search and rescue services in Labrador.

Burton had taken part in some day exercises organized by the Junior Canadian Rangers that weekend. He had participated for two days and had returned to Makkovik around noon on Sunday with the others, where the group marshalled to return the borrowed equipment provided them by the Canadian Rangers. They were permitted to keep the gasoline they were given for the outing. At about 1:30 that afternoon, Burton dropped off his best friend at their grandparents' house before heading back up the hill toward the trail from Killman Pond, where the exercises had taken place. If he had turned south there, he would have reached home, but he mistakenly turned north and arrived at Perret's Point. Due to the worsening weather, he may have lost sight of the community and focused on the next visible point of land, heading across the ice of Makkovik Bay. He never made it back to the village.

At about 7 p.m. that evening, Burton's father contacted RCMP Cpl. Kimball Vardy to see if Vardy's stepdaughter, who was Burton's friend, knew anything of his whereabouts. Vardy then initiated a "quick search" for Burton using the volunteers of the Newfoundland and Labrador Search and Rescue Association (NLSARA) to cover the five or six kilometres around the community for traces. None were found, and as weather conditions worsened, the search was called off for the day. Just before 11 p.m., Vardy contacted headquarters in St. John's and spoke to Sgt. Lloyd Youden, who was the co-ordinator for RCMP search and rescue operations in Newfoundland. He indicated that they might need air support for the rescue at first light the next day, the weather being too bad that night for helicopters to safely fly. Meanwhile, an experienced hunter reported seeing a fresh track on the ice heading out to sea. Attempts to follow the track had to be called off due to poor visibility and brittle ice.

The following morning, Vardy made a request for air support which was forwarded to Fire and Emergency Services NL (FES-NL) as per the existing protocol. Paul Peddle of FES-NL called Universal Helicopters, the provincial contractor, but was informed that the weather conditions prevented the light-duty copters from flying that day. Peddle then reached out to the Joint Rescue Co-ordination Centre of the Canadian Armed Forces to request humanitarian assistance for the search. However, despite repeated calls that day, the CAF was unwilling to dispatch aircraft (either helicopter or fixed-wing), partly due to local weather conditions but also because one of the aircraft was under repair.

Despite this, the search continued the next day, focusing on an open stretch of water in the sea ice. Snowmobile tracks were seen leading up to the water but not away from it. The searchers now came to believe that the rescue operation had become a recovery one. It was assumed that Burton was dead. A local company, Woodward Group, had a small helicopter in the area and volunteered its use, but it broke down after an hour of searching. In any case, the heavy, overcast sky made it difficult to make out details, such as tracks on ice and in snow. A second helicopter from the provincial contractor arrived that morning, but was hampered by the same poor weather conditions of low cloud and frequent squalls.

On the third day of the search, the focus was on an underwater exploration of the gap in the ice. Cameras were delivered by an RCMP aircraft, which later the same day spotted Burton's snowmobile several kilometres away from where the search was taking place. That night, a Griffon helicopter was able to survey the vehicle and spotted tracks leading away from it. An Aurora aircraft arrived at about midnight but could detect no heat signature in the area.

The next morning dawned bright and clear, and the government helicopter was able to follow Burton's footprints moving away from the snowmobile and, sadly, always away from home. His body was found on February 1, nineteen kilometres away from the stranded snow machine. He had walked that far before lying down to die, overcome by cold and exhaustion. My colleague in the House of Assembly, Randy Edmunds, was part of that search and the one who spotted Burton's body.

We now know how the search for Burton Winters was conducted, who was called, who responded, and why. But at the time, and for years after, Burton's family, the community of Makkovik, and all of Labrador had questions. Why did the CAF not send its helicopter and fixed-wing aircraft on the night Burton went missing or, at the very least, the next morning? Would it have made a difference if they had? Was the search made in the most effective way, or were mistakes made, possibilities left unexplored? Rumours circulated, but facts were few and far between.

The search for Burton Winters so close to home triggered an outcry across the province—and especially in Labrador—when it was revealed how the process was handled and mishandled.

Although Makkovik was not in my district—at the time it was represented by Liberal MHA Randy Edmunds—I had visited the community on a number of occasions and had friends from there. Having lived my entire life on the coast of Labrador, I knew how beautiful and how dangerous the land could be. A single mistake could be fatal; even if you did everything right, the weather or the shifting ice could turn against you. In the low light of winter, ice, rock, and sky could merge, making travel treacherous.

The coast of Labrador was no stranger to calamity, and as an MHA, I had regularly fought for better resources for the area to cope with unexpected disasters. Only the previous year, I had been actively pressing the provincial government to purchase a third plane to use for air ambulance services, especially for the Labrador coast and northern Newfoundland. At the time, air ambulances were stationed in Goose Bay and St. John's, both distant from the communities in those regions. While I had some success during my time as a government MHA and minister, there remained much to be done. It did not take a visionary to know that this casual inattention would inevitably cost lives. The air ambulance debate and government action to strengthen the service out of Goose Bay had only come after two families lost a loved one. The gaps in service were symptomatic of the lack of concern for the communities of coastal Labrador.

The problems with search and rescue were made worse by the fragmentation of jurisdiction. Ground searches were the responsibility of the provincial government, whereas marine searches and responses to aeronautical accidents fell to the federal government. In the province, the Royal Newfoundland Constabulary was tasked with co-ordinating searches on the island and in Southern Labrador. In Northern Labrador, the RCMP was the main contact. Most of the real work of searching for and rescuing lost individuals was actually carried out by volunteers, organized across the province by the Canadian Rangers and the Newfoundland and Labrador Search and Rescue Association. This dedicated but under-resourced group had more than two dozen regional chapters. Most communities, including Makkovik, also had community committees that could be quickly mobilized to hunt for missing people.

The province had limited search and rescue resources, having no dedicated planes or helicopters to conduct aerial reconnaissance. They contracted helicopters from a commercial company, but these were not heavy-duty machines like those used by the federal government for their own search and rescue responsibilities. The federal team would supply those aircraft on "humanitarian grounds" if requested by the co-ordinating organization. However, if there was simultaneously a requirement elsewhere for marine or aeronautical search, the copters would be recalled to meet the federal government's responsibilities.

Few communities on the coast have avoided the pain and suffering of having loved ones lost on land or at sea. Some individuals have had the skills to survive long enough to be rescued. When someone is lost, the reasons for their death are often well understood. Burton's death stood out, however. A boy just beginning to learn about the land, he was without the well-developed survival skills of his elders, or even of some of his peers. It was never clear how he had arrived in the precarious position he was in, or why it took so long to find him. His death united Labrador. Candlelight vigils were held, protests erupted in front of government offices—such as that of the local Conservative MP, Peter Penashue—and a campaign was created called "He Walked This Far," to demand the establishment of a permanent and well-resourced search and rescue base in Goose Bay that could respond to all emergency searches, whether on the ground or the ocean.

More than anything else, people wanted answers to their questions—answers that could only be found through a public inquiry. I had no authority to make this happen, but I knew in my heart I had to try to do more. After I met with Burton's family, I was more determined than ever to get answers. I organized a pan-Labrador rally in Happy Valley-Goose Bay. Every community in Labrador showed up for Burton; he was a son of Labrador and represented all of our children. After many phone calls to Ottawa, I got a meeting with Defence Minister Peter MacKay. He indicated that the federal government would be willing to participate in such an inquiry, but apparently that was never communicated to Premier Kathy Dunderdale. If it was, nothing ever came of it.

It was clear that we needed better resources to deal with future events. Everyone knew what was needed, and had known for a long time, but we could never get a commitment from either the provincial or federal government to create a permanent search and rescue base in Labrador. Indeed, during the same period, the federal government was closing the sub-base for marine searches in Atlantic Canada, reducing resources instead of increasing them. Despite the demands of the people of Labrador, which I regularly communicated to the government in the House of Assembly, no public inquiry was called by the Dunderdale government.

By 2013, I had moved on to federal politics, but the story of Burton Winters still was on my mind:

> "Mr. Speaker, it is important to note that when the announcement was made that there would be a third helicopter added at 5 Wing Goose Bay and that this would be seen as an improvement to responding to search and rescue operations, we learned two things: one was that protocols got changed and there was no longer a requirement to respond, but we also learned that when the next tragic event occurred, the helicopters were not available. They were down for maintenance, or were unable to be used or had been sent out. There was every reason why these helicopters could not respond.

> "When [the loss of Burton Winters] happened, people in Labrador, in Newfoundland, all over the country and in this Legislature asked the government opposite to do an inquiry into the death of Burton Winters to see what went wrong. Where did the protocols go wrong? Why was the response system of search and rescue not adequate to respond at that time? Where do we need to make improvements?

> "We never did get the inquiry. We never did get the investigation. Instead, a government minister, who is no longer in this Legislature, flew into Labrador and made an announcement that a third helicopter would be added

to provide those services in Labrador. We found out a few months later that at the base in Goose Bay there was no longer a requirement to respond to those search and rescue calls. What was the point of adding the helicopter?"

It certainly was not to support civilian search and rescue operations. I did not see this as a partisan issue but a matter of desperate need. It was a clear indication that no matter how many nice words were spoken, public safety for northern residents was never going to be a priority for politicians who didn't live in Labrador or any other northern region. In the 2015 election, the new provincial Liberal government led by Dwight Ball agreed to launch a public inquiry into search and rescue in the province, which finally provided the answers that people had been seeking for over nine years. The full story came out and the inquiry made numerous useful recommendations—including, not surprisingly, better resources in the area and better co-ordination between the federal and provincial governments in the deployment of those resources.

The needs became more evident with further loss of life in Labrador. The disappearance at sea of Marc Russell and Joey Jenkins in a fishing vessel off the coast of Labrador in 2021 prompted yet another call for more effective search and rescue services.

Despite this, a year after the inquiry report was released, the provincial government in November 2022 was still calling on the federal government:

"...to take immediate action to improve federal search and rescue operations in Labrador. The demand for action is shared by stakeholders from the marine and fishing industry, safety advocates and governments, as well as identified as a recommendation from the Public Inquiry Respecting Ground Search and Rescue for Lost and Missing Persons."

I'm pleased to say that a meeting was held in February 2023, which I attended, between provincial and federal ministers, as well as representatives from Labrador communities, to discuss the needed changes. The federal minister, the Honourable Bill Blair, committed to some immediate improvements and promised to work closely with his provincial counterparts to find a long-term solution to the search and rescue needs of Labrador.

We will not give up. We continue to fight for Burton, Joey, Marc, and many others, and we demand that a call for help be answered, no matter where you live in Labrador.

COVID-19

COVID-19, a coronavirus that creates flu-like symptoms and can easily be transmitted between individuals, began to appear in Canada in December 2019 and early January 2020. The virus was making headlines, and while it was not yet identified as COVID, scientists knew it was something different and paid close attention, having learned much from the Toronto severe acute respiratory syndrome (SARS) outbreak in 2003. Doctors were scrambling to find out more about why the coronavirus was so contagious and why it was a growing phenomenon, not just in Canada, but around the world. On March 13, 2020, we were called to a government briefing on the situation; later that day Prime Minister Justin Trudeau would call a news conference to address Canadians and to close the people's House—the Parliament of Canada would shut down for a short period of time. It was necessary in order to get a grasp on what this virus was, how rapidly it could spread, and what was available to neutralize it.

As an MP in Labrador, I began to receive phone calls and messages from people, many alarmed by what they were hearing. Question after question was fired at me; however, I had no answers. Federal, provincial, and territorial governments were depending upon the brightest scientific minds on the planet to determine what we were dealing with, and then came the breakthrough and the precautions needed to immunize the population against COVID-19's deadly spread. On my birthday, March 15, 2020, the country shut down. Businesses, educational facilities, and public services closed their doors one by one, and people started isolating in their own homes.

Across my district, whole communities had gone through two months of really bad flu- and cold-like symptoms, with people running high fevers and being hospitalized—in some cases medevacked to larger hospitals for treatment of severe respiratory issues. Schools had been closed for days due to a lack of students and teachers. Because of Labrador's history with the Spanish flu of 1918 that wiped out whole families and communities, no one was taking chances, and people immediately took COVID-19 seriously.

I went home to Mary's Harbour for the spring to work from there. Thankfully, we had slightly better internet service in the community by then, and I was at least able to set up and work remotely to do meetings online. Parliamentary board meetings became virtual, using platforms like Zoom and Teams; conferences switched from brick-and-mortar centres to online webinars; voting in the House of Commons became computerized and electronically driven. It was a turning point for technology and how we work with it, but it was also an indication of the gaps that existed in our health care structure.

There was no precedent for what the Trudeau administration was about to face, no blueprint for protecting people, and no script to follow in instructing Canadians. In fact, things were now in the hands of Canada's chief medical officers and the leading scientists in the world. I believe health care professionals, governments across Canada, and individuals did a remarkable job of keeping each other safe in what was a supremely difficult period in history.

Businesses were offering online ordering and safe home delivery; people were seeking the services of medical professionals only when they absolutely needed to; and families were having to say farewell to loved ones from a distance, sometimes without ever getting to see them and make that final personal goodbye. It was an incredibly difficult time for many people, putting a strain on relationships, families, and businesses. It pushed health care workers in our medical system to the point of burnout, as they worked to save lives. Canadian Rangers, reserves, and military personnel were available to help and assist in any way they could, supporting people who could not support themselves. When I reflect on it now, it is unbelievable the contributions that some individuals and groups made, and I will always be so very grateful for their efforts.

As a politician, it is never easy to hear about the plight of people who can no longer afford to pay their mortgage, rent, or car payments, or even buy groceries. During the pandemic, even many people with steady jobs were unable to earn a living. The Government of Canada was their only option. I am so proud of the government that I was a part of during COVID, simply because we stepped up to do the very best we could—not just to save the lives of Canadians and their families, but to ensure that they had an income when all else failed—so that they could continue to pay their bills, have a roof over their head, put food on the table, and cope with their day-to-day expenses. Trudeau's Liberal government helped ensure that they got the resources they needed to survive the crisis.

During the height of COVID-19, I saw families relocate to other communities to leave everything they knew behind for a new life. It was a time of trauma for some, a place to start over for others. For me, it was a time to learn good coping skills in order to deal with long days of online meetings and taking constituents' calls, trying to help people navigate through the system that we were still building.

Being in Labrador, I had an advantage over many in this country and around the world: I had access to wide open spaces. I had hills that I could roam, kilometres of terrain to trek across on snowshoes or ride over on snowmobile, and that's exactly what I did. Every day from 5 to 6 p.m. I would get on a snowmobile and take to the trails and the backwoods and just ride, letting my mind clear, feeling the sun and winter breeze on my face. Often I would stop by the water at the edge of the ocean and watch as the tides washed against the sea ice, lifting it up and down. Some days I would ride to the top of the hills where I could gaze out in the distance over the tops of trees, across beautiful mountains and valleys covered in pure white snow.

If I had to live through a pandemic, at least I was doing it at home, in the land I love.

CHAPTER 15

GRIEF, LOSS, AND CANCER AGAIN

The COVID pandemic was the first time in almost twenty-five years that I got to live home for nearly an entire year: to be around my family, to spend time with Mom and my brother Keith, who lived with his family in Lodge Bay, just ten kilometres away. Every day he would come through the "drive-through" as he called it—he'd drive up to my patio with his son Colin, and I would pass out a cup of coffee as they sat in the truck. I would sit in my fur hat and parka on the deck and we would have coffee together. Then in the evening I would go on my therapy snowmobile ride to de-stress after the day and get ready for evening meetings. Some days Keith would come along with me on his snowmobile, and I got to share time with him as I hadn't been able to do in a very long time. As hard as COVID was professionally and personally, those moments with family on the land in Labrador, even at a distance from one another, kept me well and strong.

Under ordinary circumstances I would never have had those experiences, because both of us would've been away working and our time together would have been limited to Easter break and spring snowmobile trips, summer camping and fishing trips, and outdoor boil-ups. During the pandemic we got to spend more time together reliving our childhood, and those were treasured moments. In February 2021, Joseph and I were in Happy Valley-Goose Bay, and Keith and Colin came up for a weekend. We took a snowmobile trip around Lake Melville, did a little partridge hunting, and saw new sights that we hadn't seen before. We also planned a trip from Happy Valley-Goose Bay to Nain for the following year when the lockdown would no longer be in place.

After their visit, Keith packed up his pickup truck and trailer with the snowmobiles and headed out early over the Trans-Labrador Highway to Lodge Bay, some 450 kilometres away. Then he was off on his next adventure in the Big Land. He would wake to another beautiful Sunday morning, enjoy a full home-cooked dinner at noon with his family, and then join his buddies for their winter saltwater eider duck hunt. A group of them did this annually to stock up on wild game for the season. They would tow a speedboat by snowmobile to the edge of the sea ice, then launch it into the water. Two of the guys would take the boat over the water while the others would take the snowmobiles over ice and land to the hunting cottage where they'd meet up with the boys in the boat.

Like my father before him, Keith always skippered the boat, while one guy in the front would keep watch for the ducks flying by. They would hunt from the boat, stock up, and then head to the cabin for a night of cleaning and preparing the meat. These were trips my father, my grandfather, and generations before had done for hundreds of years. My brother was keen to be on the water and a terrific mariner, having worked on the trawler *The Osprey* for nearly 30 years on the high seas. He had often received praise from inshore and offshore fishers for his navigation skills. If you went hunting with him, you knew you were coming home with a bounty after having a wonderful experience on the water.

That same Sunday evening, I left Goose Bay on snowmobile for a three-hour spin over the trails. Missing my family's company and with no destination in mind, I made a number of stops along the way, taking photos and enjoying the beautiful outdoors. I returned home just before dark so that Joseph wouldn't worry about me. When I arrived, I was surprised to see I had messages to call my friend Sandra Pye in Mary's Harbour. Sandra was my cousin Todd's wife; he and my brother Keith had been best friends since the day they were born.

I was not prepared for her news. My brother had drowned while duck hunting.

Keith had been travelling through some heavy wind and rising seas when the boat capsized and he was lost in the cold, dark ocean. His friend's son Robert, who was with him, was fortunate enough to make it to the shoreline and crawl to safety, although he was very cold and in shock. The hunters who had arrived by snowmobile got the young man to safety at the cabin.

My brother had drowned instantly. They could see his body floating toward the shoreline, tangled in the frozen slob along the water's edge. Todd, and Keith's son Colin, were able to hook him with what we call a dapper dog or a hook dog, a device with hook and a rope for hauling ducks out of the water after they are shot. They managed to bring Keith's body to shore, while the angry sea rolled and roared toward them.

The news sent my entire body into spasms of utter devastation. I could not think; tears just kept flowing, and screams ripped out from deep inside my body. I could not believe I would never get to hug him again, to be beside him, to share with him the joy of living. It took me a few hours to calm myself down and to put in perspective what this meant for his wife and for his children, and what it meant for my mother. For all of them, I would have to be strong and prepared for what was to come.

We have always been a very close family, simply because to survive in the early years we had to depend on each other. And it didn't end at childhood; it extended throughout our lives as we supported each other through thick and thin. I cannot imagine what it was like that day for my nephew Colin, who was then twenty-three years old. He had learned the craft of hunting and fishing from his father and was every bit the expert that his father and grandfather had been. I thought of what it must be like for my cousin Todd; he and Keith had been best friends for their entire lives, and Todd was one of the ones to pick him up after the tragedy and bring him back home. What must it have been like for his friends Garland and Bob, who stood there that day at the edge of the ocean and ice, doing all they could to save him, or at least bring him back. And my mother's loss—I knew a little of the pain, having lost my daughter only hours after she was born, but that was much different than losing your son after fifty-one years of loving, caring, and depending on one another. My mother carries the weight of that tragic loss to this very day. Keith's wife was shattered, and their daughter was in shock for days before she could begin to recover from the devastation. To this day, when I look into the eyes of my siblings and say his name, I see the pain of loss in my brother Brad's, and the sadness of what would never be in my sister's.

My grandmother Jean would often say: God will never give you more than you can handle. While those words may have been meant to be comforting and to encourage you to push through when times are tough, in reality many people are overwhelmed by the trials and suffering they face. Some turn to God, the spirits, the universe, hoping to find the way through. Others don't make it that far; they don't see a path forward in the struggle, and they turn to drugs or alcohol to help deaden the pain. Others can't see any end in sight; some, in their most difficult and traumatic times, cannot reconcile their pain and hurt, and sadly it often results in death by suicide. And there are those, of course, who do find it within themselves to keep moving forward, to keep working for a better life, and they find their way around that difficult corner.

Personally, I've learned that through success you build incredible confidence, and through difficulty you build stamina. For me, life has become a journey from which I draw new energy every day. Joseph and I have two rules we live by in our home: the first person awake in the morning makes the coffee, and complaining hour is just that—the first hour in the morning. What we have learned is that by morning, whatever complaint you had the day before is almost always no longer relevant. It works. Most times, coffee is the only wake-up we need.

We adults teach our children so many things. At a young age I learned great card games and how to skate and ski. I was taught how to build a fire, catch a rabbit, and cook it. I learned how to sew and knit. I was taught when to be quiet, when to speak, and when to listen. I would've also loved to have learned to identify signs of inappropriate behaviour, to be taught to tell others when something was wrong. I didn't know how to do that. After nearly fifty years, I think I finally do. I urge parents and teachers to watch for signs of fear, signs that their kids want to talk about something but can't bring themselves to do it. They have to teach their children how to recognize when bad things are happening and to seek help, and encourage them not to feel ashamed or guilty for the things that have been done to them.

I still have inside me the little girl who was victimized and abused, who didn't understand—who still doesn't understand— what was done to her or why. All she knows is that it hurt her and set her apart from everyone around her, made her different and of no worth. There were times when I wondered if I could go on myself, if I could continue to move forward in the face of grief. I suppose, in a way, grief made me who I am today.

I would say to people who have also suffered abuse that you need to care for that little child that lives within you, who will always be with you. Talk to them and help them make it through. Be strong for them; be their comfort and guide. You have to be the one who inspires. That struggle—and believe me, it is often a terrible struggle—is the way to build your self-confidence and your self-esteem, and to discover that you are worthy and that you are loved.

No matter how positive I try to be about my successes in life, I cannot help but relive the setbacks and losses that have weighed me down and made it such an effort to go on at times. They say whatever doesn't stop you makes you stronger; I know this, but sometimes I wonder why I have to be so strong. The loss of my baby daughter, only hours after her premature birth, and the subsequent decline and end of my first marriage were difficult days, but hard work and my determination to make a positive difference to my community pulled me through, as did the great support of my family and closest friends. Now the loss of my brother was another blow that I had to find the strength to deal with.

I learned to put my own sadness into perspective by considering the suffering of others and finding a role in comforting those in need of solace. My best childhood friend was Elaine Rumbolt. She was born a week earlier than me; her mom and my mom were pregnant at the same time, and my dad and her dad had been best friends through their lives. As children we went to school together in the one-room schoolhouse, and they lived right next door to us. We have been the best of friends for fifty-six years, and I always say childhood friends are your best friends in the whole world. She was never just a friend, though; she was my sister. She's still a big part of my life, and so was her daughter, Stacy. Sadly, Elaine's daughter died at the age of twenty-four, a heartbreaking loss that caused a tragic rift in my best friend's life.

The philosophy I have worked hard to embrace over the years is that you never move past tragedy, you just learn to move with it, accepting the reality of what has happened and the gap that's been left in your life. Yet it was a struggle to see how that could be. I watched Elaine go from the happiest moments of her life—being a mom, raising her two kids, celebrating their accomplishments— to mourning the loss of her daughter and being overwhelmed with grief. She almost completely removed herself from everyday life, isolated by her grief. I stood with her even in her darkest times. It was the best I could do. It was all I could do.

Lost opportunities are still losses. In my professional and political life, there were challenges, losses, and setbacks. I was sad when I didn't get the federal nomination in 2006, but I truly grieved when cancer took away my leadership role as an MHA and stole my chance to have the fight of my life in the 2011 provincial election. But each of these setbacks led to new challenges and new victories.

Everyone loses someone they love at some point in their lives. Every loss hurts, but some are part of the normal course of events. The loss of a parent always feels more natural than the loss of a child. Nonetheless, I endured great sorrow when my father died in 2012. We had a difficult relationship at times because of his drinking, but I loved him beyond measure and mourned him deeply. His loss was expected, natural even. It carried none of the shock and pain of my brother Keith's death when he was only fifty-one, leaving behind a wife and two children. I mourn them both still.

Now, cancer has touched my life again, threatening to take even more from me than before. I can only endure. I will find a way to deal with it, as I have with so many things, in a way that allows me to continue to live a full, accomplished life, continuing to contribute to others and to Canada, in the way that I have always done.

When I began writing this book, I was once again in a fight for my life. After twelve years free of it, cancer—breast cancer—had returned. Cancer is a journey no one ever wants to take in life, most especially not a second time. But at fifty-four, I found myself on that journey again. It wouldn't be the same as when I was forty-two, but I can still use the lessons learned then to reflect on the journey that lies ahead and to gather perspective and strength toward the ultimate goal of good health And I guess that's where I am right now.

In September 2022, after two mammograms and a biopsy, it was confirmed that I did indeed have a recurrence of breast cancer in my left breast. It was an in-situ carcinoma, meaning it was not invasive and not hormone positive. Therefore, by having a mastectomy, I could very well be rid of the cancer. After consultation with my surgeon, I decided that I would have a bilateral mastectomy; that is, I would have both my right and left breasts removed. As part of that process in the weeks leading up to the date of my surgery, I underwent a few more tests, including an MRI. During that procedure, it was determined that there was a spot in my right breast as well, but because I had already made the decision to have a double mastectomy and we were getting close to the date of my surgery, a biopsy would not be required.

On November 16, my dear husband Joseph brought me to the hospital to have me checked in. As we walked in together, I knew that this was another one of those moments that would indeed change my life. I sat there holding my husband's hand that early morning as they prepped me for surgery, doing the normal things that they do: take your temperature; take your blood pressure; do a COVID test. Then I was ready in my blue gown and booties, lying on the gurney to be transported to the operating room. I didn't feel afraid going into the surgery, but I did have a swell of anxiety that filled me: what was it going to feel like after? During the same surgery to remove both breasts, they were going to begin the process of reconstruction by inserting expanders in my chest. I wondered how I would feel about having such body augmentations. This was not just physically life-changing; it was mentally life-changing.

I was focused on getting rid of the cancer, and I wanted it removed from my body as quickly as possible. To delay or take half-measures would leave me with both fear and anxiety and the risk of recurrence. There was no other option.

The surgery lasted about five hours, and after Dr. Christopher Cox had performed the bilateral mastectomy, Dr. Joy Cluett came into the OR to begin the process of reconstruction by placing the expanders and closing the incisions. When I woke up, I was groggy and had too much pain to actually care much about anything other than just lying there and getting the "good" medicine. Normally with a procedure like this, I would be kept in overnight and then released. Unfortunately, because I ran a high temperature and had some issues with my breathing, they kept me in the special care unit for about four days. Quite honestly, I think it was probably the best thing that could've happened to me.

It was during my time in the SCU that I met the most remarkable nurse named Marie. She had had a bilateral mastectomy a few years before, and during the night when I couldn't sleep and not even the medication could settle me down, she would stand by the bed and talk me through it. She told me her story and what she had been through, assuring me that the pain I was experiencing was normal, that all of the effects that I was feeling post-surgery were perfectly routine, and that I had nothing to fear. "You are a strong woman," she said. "You can do this, as I have done it." And I knew that she was right. You meet the most inspiring people sometimes in the most unusual circumstances of your life. Through those couple of days in special care, Marie helped me get to a place where I was able to function. I can never thank her enough for her words of encouragement, for sharing her story with me and, of course, for the wonderful care she gave me as a nurse.

Four days later, my husband and my mom came to bring me home. I was pretty excited and ready to go. I had been placed in a ward the day before, which I shared with a darling woman from Petty Harbour, Mrs. Chafe. She had been in hospital for about two months and was longing to go home. She had told me she couldn't walk, but she still was living in hope that she would get out of the hospital and be home before Christmas.

When my mom and my husband picked up my things, I got up and walked out of the hospital. The aide came behind me with a wheelchair, but I was determined. I had no issue with my legs—I had full use of them, unlike my friend Mrs. Chafe—and I thought to myself, I can walk out of here. In that moment, I felt very grateful, and I said to the tiny voice inside of me that would rather sit or lie down: "You can do this! Every small step will make a huge difference for you in recovering your good health."

We drove to the house where I would be staying for the next few months. Kelvin Parsons and Jeanette Fleming welcomed us into their home with such love and kindness. I wasn't going to a stranger's place; I was going to be with family, people who loved me dearly, and who would do anything in the world to get me back to good health. I thank God, the universe, and the Great Spirit for the fact that I have been truly blessed with wonderful people in my life who were always there when I needed them the most.

The first week was very difficult for everyone in the household, even with daily visits by a nurse. I had trouble sleeping, turning in bed, getting up and down, and doing even the simplest of things. After two weeks I started to feel much better and began to be able to do more for myself. The drainage tubes were removed and the bandages came off, and I was ready for my first appointment with the two surgeons and the physiotherapist. After those appointments I was energized, because they were so pleased with the great progress I had made. I went home ready and willing to do more, walking around the house, taking care of myself, and doing my physio exercises—everything needed to keep me moving toward my goal of good health.

As I progressed in my recovery, I continued to have the constant love and care of my family and friends. Mom would come and sit with me and talk when I felt like chatting or sitting up for a while. My husband was a constant support, keeping me filled in on all the news—because he knows how much I love politics—and keeping up on what was happening in provincial industries. Every day he would sit with me to watch Question Period from the House of Commons. Even if I fell asleep after the first couple of questions, I would always make an effort to keep up to date with the goings-on there, even on the worst days of my recovery. Jeanette was there to help me with all the things I needed help with. She kept me well-nourished, and her beautiful smiles made me happy. And, of course, Kelvin was up at 5:30 every morning, so the coffee was on. Sometimes he would bring the breakfast tray or a coffee and stay for a chat.

As the weeks passed, I recovered my strength and could venture out, taking the walking trail along the Waterford River for a kilometre or two. The smell of the trees, the sound of the river rolling over the rocks, the feeling of fresh air on my face were all little things, but they brought me such pleasure. These little things, these small steps that are so important in life—I could not have asked for more. I had such love and support around me, which was exactly what I needed to heal, and heal I did.

When you're hit by any kind of crisis in your life—a challenge to your health, a change in your career, family issues that you're unable to solve but you want to so badly, the loss of someone you love deeply—all of these crises in our lives impact us. Strength and growth can be found in many different ways, but I'm not sure any are as quick, as rude and abrupt, and sometimes as costly, as crisis and challenge.

Being strong is not about physical strength to me; it's more about mental willpower. When I look at the strength of a person, I look at the strength of that person's mind, the strength they have to carry ideas forward and to endure, and to accomplish great things that look to be beyond their reach. I look at strength as endurance in the face of life's challenges, the trials and tribulations we must all experience. I treasure having the mental strength to deal with the situation before me, the stamina to keep going when times are rough. I aspire to share that strength with others and to be their rock to cling to when the moment is beyond enduring. Because it does get better.

Sometimes I think my life is shaped entirely by challenge, but I know I'm not an exception. So many people deal with all the same things that I deal with. They navigate their way through all the same issues at one point or another in their lives. How we deal with crisis, how we find resolution to it, and how we transition to a better place is what matters. Those of you who have known me over the years and have talked to me on a personal level know that I'm willing to share some experiences and some of my thoughts and feelings, if I think it can be helpful or supportive to another person.

It's also true that I like it when other people share their experiences with me, just like Marie did those nights when I was in the special care unit at St. Clare's Mercy Hospital. She taught me things, and I hope that when I share my experiences I'm helping someone else to be stronger and letting them know that they are not alone—because no one ever has to fight alone, no matter what the situation.

Kindness is the highest form of intelligence.
There are strangers out there who still think of you
because you were kind to them when they really
needed it. Never stop being that person.

— Madelyn Kelly,
retired educator

CHAPTER 16

POLITICS IN THE AGE OF SOCIAL MEDIA

I've often heard it said that politics was once more gentle, more collegial. (I should note that most all of the people I've heard say that were white men of a certain age and background.) Certainly, the cut and thrust of political debate included the occasional insult, and tempers sometimes flared, but politicians also had friends across party lines and were generally respected by the public. There were exceptions, of course, but mostly discourse was polite and relations were civil.

But contrary to one of the favourite myths of the old-guard political elite, public life was never sweetness and light for women, or people of colour, or those from the 2SLGBTQ+ community. It is important for people to know that life in the political sphere has always had an element of unpleasantness. And since the advent of social media—which brought with it increased polarization and a culture of permissive nastiness—it has become nearly intolerable.

I experienced more than my share of bullying growing up in Mary's Harbour. My father's alcoholism and the effects of my own private shame as a sexually abused child helped make me a target for those in the community inclined to cruelty. Still, I learned how to handle it through humour and by building a strong circle of close family and friends. I also learned that being useful, through volunteering and public service, was a strong defence against those who tried to drag me down to their level. By the time I went to college and university, I might still have been a frightened child inside, but my exterior shell was pretty tough and my sense of self, fostered in part by my early involvement with the Labrador Métis Association—now the NunatuKavut Community Council (NCC)—was getting stronger.

I expected that when I got to the House of Assembly, I would be treated with respect and as an equal. To be fair, that was how I was treated by the majority—the bare majority—of my fellow MHAs and by most of the press and public. For the rest, it was a lot like being back in grade seven. The bullies were all around me and they were nasty and angry in both their tone and words.

I had been around enough politicians to know that debate in the House—especially during Question Period—could be a bit rough and tumble, and I also knew that I had a few enemies on the Liberal government benches—friends and former caucus colleagues of Danny Dumaresque, who resented me for defeating him. I was frequently heckled while I was speaking, by both Liberals and Conservatives; NDP Leader Jack Harris was unfailingly polite to everyone. I was not even all that surprised that the comments were less about what I was saying as a politician and more about me as a woman—one who, in their opinion, clearly didn't belong in the House.

I was aware of the difficulty women sometimes had in being heard, let alone respected in politics, and I knew I had to be tough and sharp and give as good as I got. I remembered how Sheila Copps had stood up to Newfoundland's own John Crosbie in their epic battles across the aisles of the House of Commons. Like her, I was determined to be "nobody's baby."

I prevailed and never backed down from a fight. Mostly, I won people over through hard work and (usually) gentle humour, winning many friends on all sides of the Legislature and gaining grudging respect from the rest. Still, on more than one occasion, I and other women in the Assembly had to call out particularly nasty misogynistic comments, raising points of privilege that almost always forced apologies and even, in a few cases, changed the old-fashioned attitudes of some of the male MHAs.

Times, we thought, were changing. Newfoundlanders were and are a fair-minded people, who like a good argument no matter who's making it. The public quickly came to accept women and Indigenous MHAs as normal. Even those who were inclined to prejudice learned to keep quiet about it—though there were always a few backsliders. With more intense public scrutiny of what was going on in the House of Assembly after its proceedings began to be broadcast in 2001, Members soon learned the political price of being exposed as bigots, although it still took some a decade to figure it out.

Despite this, I still had to endure a certain degree of public abuse almost from the first day I entered the Assembly. Initially this came in the form of letters, often though not always anonymous, that attacked everything from my weight and hair colour to the ways I expressed myself. They questioned my competency and my right—and by extension those of any woman—to even be an elected official.

One "correspondent" faithfully hand-wrote unsigned letters and dropped them off at the front desk of the Legislature for years. The letters were patronizing in tone and insulting in nature. When they first started to arrive I found them hurtful, but eventually I didn't even bother to open them. I never did find out who my mystery "admirer" was, but the letters did stop coming—after I had been diagnosed with cancer. You will have to take my word for how nasty they were because I won't quote from them here—not to spare sensibilities, but because I won't give my attacker the satisfaction of having their words in print.

Letters were almost always local, and while I did get correspondence from my district and from other parts of Newfoundland and Labrador seeking help with a problem or agreeing or disagreeing politely with some position I'd taken, the hate mail almost always came from the populous parts of the province, particularly St. John's.

While the first versions of email were invented in the early 1970s, it only became available to the public after 1996, the same year I became an MHA. Initially the number of individual users was small, but its use had become widespread by 2005, when more than fifty per cent of Canadians had access to an account. Instead of taking the time to write and send off a letter, almost anyone anywhere in the world could send you an email. As a public official who needed to be in easy contact with a wide range of people, my email address wasn't hard to find. Pretty soon the messages, again mostly anonymous, started flooding in.

Email also made it easy to launch massive communications attacks, which I experienced every time I supported the seal industry in Newfoundland and Labrador or took what some people considered a controversial stand on some other issue. Certainly, over the course of the first decade of the twenty-first century, the number of messages filling my inbox continued to grow. It became time-consuming for my staff to weed out the spam, such as offers from "Nigerian princes" and the hate mail from closer to home, just so I could deal with the legitimate correspondence that remained. Gradually technology to block the first two improved, but plenty of nasty notes still came through, making it pretty tough on my assistants, who were often young and inexperienced.

It was a learning experience for all of us; I remember one day going into my Ottawa office as an MP, only to find my male assistant very upset and distraught. He was a homosexual man who'd had a tough time identifying with his sexuality; he had grown up in Toronto, which might seem more open and progressive, but there was still no escape for him from the stereotyping and the bullying. He was a good person and a hard worker, and I could relate in some ways to the struggle he was dealing with. He was going through my correspondence, and this one letter was lobbying the government to make homosexuality illegal, claiming that "they should be treated for their condition." He knew he was born the way he was and that no amount of suffering or harm was going to remove or change his sexuality. We talked about it and I did my best to comfort him, telling him to believe in himself first and to know that the opinions of others do not define you—only you can define you. What we think of ourselves is important, what others think not so much. I know he stills wrestles with these uncaring opinions; however, now he is strong and supported in his life, married to a beautiful husband and very happy. I might have been able to avoid the worst of it, but I still had to comfort and support those who couldn't, for the words of others can shake the core of the strongest people if they are not taught to guard against the hate.

Facebook and Twitter surfaced in 2004 and 2006, respectively, swiftly followed by the first true smartphones in 2007. Within a few years almost everyone had a smartphone and used it daily or hourly for all sorts of useful purposes—communications, calendars, banking, photography—as well as plenty of nefarious ones. Communication that was previously highly or partially mediated was transformed into the constant ping or buzz of phone notifications. You could avoid your email inbox for an hour or a day, but there was little escaping the constant demands from the devices that we had purchased as tools but that were well on their way to becoming our masters.

Almost twenty years later, refusing to be connected is generally viewed as anti-social and eccentric, although some studies show that time away from devices is vitally important to health and well-being. Nonetheless, connectivity is vital for politicians—to communicate with each other, with journalists, and most importantly with their constituents and the general public. Nothing is quicker than a tweet, and nothing lingers longer than the sour taste of an ill-conceived one.

Of course, the rising polarization of political views and the nastiness that accompanies it both predate the technology that has done so much to facilitate it. Those rifts are being deliberately created by activists on both the far right and the far left, to advance their own agendas—promoting a particular issue, bringing down an effective opponent, or simply selling a product or message.

The advent of (un)social media made it ever harder to bridge the gap between opposing views. The algorithms often made it so that people were only posting or tweeting to like-minded people, building up an ever-increasing storm of righteous anger and uncontrolled outrage that inevitably burst through onto its perceived enemies. No compromise was possible—how could it be, with such horrible people on the other side? Debate and dialogue turned into argument and accusation and before long, the nastiness of the internet spilled out into real-life encounters, where everything, no matter how vile, is fair game. The birth of social media seems to have marked the death of civility. Unfortunately, its force for good is matched in every way by its force for misinformation and hatred.

Nothing and nobody is immune. Recently, I posted a photo on my birthday, along with a brief update on my cancer treatment. The picture was a selfie of me—with a scarf covering my bald head—posing with Prime Minister Trudeau. We were both smiling, and the message was positive and upbeat. Birthday. Cancer update. Smiles. Within a day there were over 600 comments. Many were positive and encouraging, from friends, constituents, or just well-wishers. At least half, though, were nasty, brutish, and short, often just a vomit emoji or a curse word. A few took the time to say they hoped I would die. It is worth noting that most of the positive comments were from people who used their real names on their social media platforms, while the latter came from those who hid behind pseudonyms. I often wonder if they hide because of fear or shame, or just because they know their comments are harmful, hateful, and totally disparaged by most of society.

If a birthday update with good news about my health can generate such vitriol, imagine what a serious political post generates. And what I experience is minor compared to the attacks that other female or BIPOC politicians experience.

Take the example of Catherine McKenna, former federal Environment Minister, who was labelled "Climate Barbie" by Gerry Ritz, a Conservative MP. No male minister was ever called "Climate Ken" by members of the right-wing press. Ritz was forced by his leader to apologize, but that didn't change the effect of those words. The insulting title was posted to Twitter and produced a storm of nasty echoes. In 2019, McKenna was provided with an RCMP security detail over verbal harassment issues. On October 24, 2019, her office was defaced with a misogynistic slur. Both incidents were apparently inspired by social media comments triggering irrational behaviour among men who lacked critical thinking or moral judgment, or both.

In February 2023, Melanie Mark, the first Indigenous woman to serve as an MLA and Cabinet minister in British Columbia, resigned her seat, citing abuse and harassment as the reason. "This place felt like a torture chamber," she said. "I will not miss the character assassination." Cathy Bennett, Finance Minister for Newfoundland and Labrador from 2015 to 2017, was a frequent target of body-shaming and other abuse through social media, with some posts suggesting she kill herself, or that she should have a bounty placed on her head. She left politics in 2018, citing that abuse as well as bullying by her own caucus colleagues as causes. All the battles I thought we had begun to win in the early part of this century seem to have flared up once again.

Politicians are people, and unfortunately the permission to be nasty granted by the frequently anonymous character of social media—undoubtedly magnified by the isolation of the COVID years—seems to have infected them, too. While Canadian politics has not come close to the viciousness seen in the United States and Great Britain, I often fear we are moving down the wrong path here as well. What once was restricted to the cloud has come down to earth in the form of the ugly rhetoric and behaviour of certain members of the so-called "Freedom Convoys," and the willingness of protesters to confront our leaders with hate-filled language and acts of violence. No one is immune from this; politicians of all types have suffered attacks from those who know better but appear to feel that they can bully, mislead, and discriminate on social media without suffering any consequences.

While I have experienced plenty of insults and misogynistic attacks in my life, none hurt me more than comments made by MP Mumilaaq Qaqqaq from Nunavut. Responding to a two-year-old tweet of mine, she attacked my identity, saying: "Jones is not an Inuk." She posted this comment after we had a spirited exchange during Question Period that day. The next day in the House of Commons, I asked for an apology, which she refused to give. Rather, a few days later, she posted a thirty-one-minute video, repeatedly stating that I was not an Inuk and questioning my well-established Indigenous identity. Later the same day, she issued a statement by email saying, "Recently, I made comments on Twitter that personally challenged the identity of MP Yvonne Jones. The way that I handled the situation and the way I commented was aggressive and disrespectful and I'm sorry for making them."

Would she have been, as she said, less "aggressive and disrespectful" if the nature of social media was not encouraging that sort of behaviour and freeing people from consequence? Based on the many people who have seemed genuinely sorry for comments made in haste on those platforms, I have to think that the medium was definitely part of the message.

A few months later, in a Twitter post in the early hours of a Sunday morning, Qaqqaq again questioned my identity and accused me of intimidating her. She also attacked the leadership of her own party for not backing her up in her attacks against me. At about the same time, she also accused the Premier of Nunavut of intimidation tactics, which he strongly denied. As he said in an interview, "I would have welcomed the opportunity to hear from Ms. Qaqqaq about her concerns directly, instead of using social media to spread concerning and incorrect information." This is precisely the problem with social media—comments made in haste and more often than not unverified or simply wrong, suddenly take on the weight of some deeper truth. It's sad, but the old adage that a lie can travel halfway around the world before the truth can get its boots on is certainly supported by social media.

It is unfortunate that this event unfolded as it did. It was not only hurtful to me, but I think it played a role in her later decision not to run for re-election. Perhaps she was a little naive and misinformed about the Inuit of Labrador. If so, it could not be viewed as completely her fault. As I said in an interview a week or so after the initial incident: "I am a descendant of both Inuit and settler in Labrador. My roots go back to the 1800s in identifying my Inuit lineage in Labrador. I grew up in a very traditional culture. I very much practised the traditional way of life."

For decades, confusion about the Inuit in Labrador has persisted because the colonial system of the federal government identified people of mixed Inuit and settler ancestry as Métis—a term traditionally used for people of mixed First Nations and French descent in Western Canada. The term Métis was never meant to describe the descendants of Inuit and settlers; rather, it was applied to us because governments had no "colonial slot" to fit us into. Only when the NunatuKavut Community Council had the strength in 2004 to assert their own identity as descendants of the southern Inuit was the term relegated to history.

Perhaps that's where Qaqqaq became confused. If so, it was brought on by a colonial system that really didn't know where Indigenous people lived in this country. Out of that confusion arose this incident of lateral racism, an attack of one Indigenous person on another.

Can we do better? I certainly hope so. I believe it is possible to improve people's behaviour—including the attitude they bring to many social media platforms. As an individual, I try to think twice and post once when it comes my engagement on X (formerly Twitter) or other platforms. When possible, I don't read the negative, hateful comments, although that sometimes defeats the purpose of the engagement. I regularly take breaks from my device—going out on the land, far from cell towers and free Wi-Fi—in order to regenerate my body and mind. We are in a society of information overload, in which untruths and fake news cloud the real facts, making it difficult to tell truth from fiction.

Government has a role in regulating social media or, at least, insisting that the companies and individuals that own the platforms do a better job of regulating themselves. I also think that collectively, through organizations like Equal Voice—which encourages women to enter politics—and anti-bullying groups, we can join together to make social media truly social in nature. In the end, we all have a responsibility to speak out against hate, to recognize disinformation and propaganda. Most importantly, I believe that engaging directly with others instead of anonymously through social media is the first step toward building civility and respectful dialogue, where we argue about ideas and not identity.

CHAPTER 17

I KNOW WHO I AM

The first treaty with southern Inuit people in Labrador was signed with the British government in 1765 in Southern Labrador in the community of Chateau Bay, and it exists as a legally binding document to this day.

This treaty, ratified by the Privy Council in 1765 and protected under Section 35 of the Canadian Constitution, forms the basis for the claims of the NCC to Indigenous rights. The NCC, once known as the Labrador Métis Association, began organizing in the late 1970s and was formally established as a society in 1981; it incorporated under provincial law in 1985. It was at that time that I served as youth representative on the board. It now represents roughly 6,000 Inuit in southern and central Labrador, and for the last forty years has fought to have their rights as Indigenous people recognized by other levels of government.

My grandmother of Inuit descent on my father's side came from the small community of George's Cove. Her name was Eliza Burden and as a young girl, she came to work as a servant in a merchant's house in Battle Harbour. She and her sister, Clara, came on a fishing boat with the prospect of jobs. They were full of hope, though they knew they had no say in the decision. The family needed them to earn their own way.

The two of them had strong Inuit features and had come from further north, which was pretty common in those days, with young girls and sometimes young boys sent from other villages to work in more affluent white people's homes. They were about fourteen and fifteen when they arrived, and they were treated unkindly. They were called "old Eskimos" and other racial slurs, and although they lived and worked in these houses, it was made very clear they weren't part of the household. If the merchant or fishing captain had guests they were sent outside, even in bad weather, so they wouldn't be seen or noticed.

It was a very hard life for the sisters, living as outsiders and with long working days. Though she was badly treated by the merchant family and much of the settler community there, my grandmother met and married my grandfather, a fisherman from the small community of Indian Cove. Eventually Clara went back to George's Cove, where she married a lovely man and settled in Port Hope Simpson. I met her and other relatives later in life and learned about these experiences. Although my grandmother died before I was born, she certainly was known to me—if only through my father, his brothers and sister, and my great-aunt's stories and memories of her.

My mother was European, though her family had been in Labrador for several generations. By coincidence they had settled in Chateau Bay (also known historically as York Harbour), which was the same place the British—under the authority of Newfoundland Governor Hugh Palliser—had signed a treaty with the Inuit of Southern Labrador in 1765. There had been intermarriage and contact between her family and the local Inuit in the region; at the time she met and married my father, the Inuit culture was even more prevalent in the region, she said.

When I was growing up, I knew of my grandmother's Inuit origins, but I was only vaguely aware of what it meant to me, my family, and the community to which I belonged. Yet there were so many aspects of our culture and daily life that reflected our mixed-race heritage of both Inuit and settler.

Being on the land and water has been a central part of my life since I was a little girl. Every spring we went by boat, while the ice was still in the water, to our summer place at Indian Cove, where my grandfather had lived. We stayed in a small cabin, with two bedrooms—one for my parents and one for us kids. When our chores were done, we were free to roam where we liked and to play with the other kids who were there, and I suppose that was where I gained my confidence being on the land and water.

My father was a fisherman, a hunter, and sometimes worked cutting wood in the winter months—whatever he could do to make a living and feed his family. He would often take me and my siblings, especially my eldest brother, with him on day trips to go fishing, but later also to hunt small game like rabbits and porcupines. I learned how to use a rifle and to kill and clean game. It is something I do to this day, but only for food. When I think of a gun, I don't think of it as a weapon but rather as a tool. As is the case with most Indigenous people and rural Canadians, guns are tools we use to provide sustenance to our families. Sometimes I look out over the House of Commons and wonder if any of the other women there have firearm certificates and the various hunting licences I possess. I'm sure there are some, but I suspect they are few.

We would go out, my father and one or two kids or sometimes the whole family, onto the land with a snow machine—often the smallest and cheapest one you could get, because we never had much money—hauling a komatik, an Inuit sled, behind. My mother would put blankets against the back of the sled where the kids could nestle down and stay warm, and we would camp out, hunt, and gather delicious food from the land.

As I became a teenager, I became increasingly interested in who I was and where I came from. I had light brown hair and blue eyes and spoke English, yet my family and my friends' families engaged in a subsistence lifestyle on the land and sea that was not much different from that practised by Indigenous people across northern Canada.

This growing interest in my origins had led me, when I was about fifteen, to run for and be elected to the position of youth representative on the board of the Labrador Métis Association. I still remember flying into Goose Bay; this was before we had a proper airport in Mary's Harbour, and so the plane was outfitted with skis, and we had to land on the harbour ice. I was met in Goose Bay by one of the members of the board, Ruby Durno, who kind of looked after me, as I was the only youth delegate. I remember going to the first meeting, when they didn't even have an office with furniture. It was just an office someone had said they could use to get the organization started. We all sat around on the floor to discuss where we would go from there.

Did I really understand who I was and what the significance of my work would be? Did I understand our place in the world, being both Indigenous and non-Indigenous? Absolutely not. I was in pursuit of answers about who I was and how I fit into society as an Indigenous person. That was the beginning of my involvement and my long journey—one that is ongoing.

In the early days of organizing, we called ourselves the Labrador Métis Association (or LMA) because this was the name available to us under Canadian law—but it was never the right name; it was a misidentification. In Canada, there are Inuit, First Nations, and Métis. The Métis are a recognized Indigenous people from Western

Canada, descendants of First Nations people and Europeans—mainly French, but also English. They have their own communities, cultural traditions, and dress, and even their own languages, the most common of which is Michif. We were called Métis as well, because it was one of the three categories available to the federal government, but we were not descended from First Nations people but from Inuit and Europeans. It is why we eventually developed our own name that reflected our own reality, and not one imposed on us by colonial institutions.

We had always had our own names for ourselves: livyers, Labradorians—distinct, I assure you, from Newfoundlanders—'breeds, or even Eskimos, the latter a name bestowed on us by the Hudson's Bay Company. Yet none of these were the right name. It took a long time and a lot of careful research to document our history and our distinct way of life, which is similar to that practised by other Inuit people in Canada, but intertwined with what we inherited from settler communities. We are the NunatuKavut Inuit, whose traditional territory spanned from Chateau Bay in the south to Lake Melville in central Labrador.

The organization had to grow and develop, and from those humble roots of a few dozen people sitting on an office floor in Goose Bay, it has expanded and prospered over the years. The president at the time was Reg Michelin, who had long history as an Inuit leader in central Labrador. Like many others who made up that organization, he was an Indigenous person who was very proud of who he was and where he had come from. He had a strong sense of belonging to the Aboriginal movement in Labrador and in Canada at the time. He, like many Elders, never questioned who they really were.

It was a long struggle to get any kind of recognition, and there were many setbacks along the way. Premier Danny Williams had promised, during his first winning campaign in October 2003, that the Newfoundland and Labrador government would recognize southern Inuit and their entitlements. The Powley decision had just come out of the Supreme Court the month before, with a narrow interpretation placed on Métis and their rights. Despite that, Williams and his administration continued to promise the LMA that their rights would be recognized—but that's not what happened after the election.

I laid it out in the House of Assembly in the spring of 2004:

> "[The] Métis people of Labrador believed what the Premier had to say. They believed this government when they were on the election trail, when they wrote them letters and said that they would recognize the Métis people under the Powley decision.

> "Do you know what they did on January 31, Mr. Speaker? They sent the Member for Lake Melville and the Minister of Transportation and Works and Aboriginal Affairs [John Hickey] up to Goose Bay [...] to the Métis Nation office and they said: We are not going to honour that commitment anymore."

The LMA changed its name to Labrador Métis Nation (LMN), and then adopted a new and more accurate name in 2010 as the Inuit of NunatuKavut, and formed the NunatuKavut Community Council in 2012 to represent the 6,000 people of Inuit descent in southern and central Labrador, many of whom were displaced by Nunatsiavut Government. In 2019, the federal government and the NCC signed a memorandum of understanding (MOU) that recognized NunatuKavut Community Council as "an Indigenous collective capable of holding Section 35 Aboriginal rights." Negotiations have since been proceeding slowly on a new process called "recognition of Indigenous rights and self-determination."

Funding for the LMA, and later NunatuKavut Community Council, has been sporadic; continued opposition by others with settled land claims or self-government agreements has made it difficult to move forward. In 2019, the Innu Nation launched an appeal in federal court to squash the MOU, and in the process accused me of being in conflict of interest because of my membership in NunatuKavut Community Council. I was present at the signing of the MOU, and I certainly support the process, but I'm not directly involved. I've also been a strong supporter of all the claimant groups, and of the claims they have settled or agreements they have reached or are negotiating.

Nonetheless, one of the most difficult decisions I ever made as an MHA was to vote against the Nunatsiavut Land Claim Agreement in 2005.

I remember that day so well, as I stood in the House of Assembly in Newfoundland and looked up into the visitor's gallery at familiar faces, faces that were worn and stressed. They looked so proud, dressed in beautiful clothes in patterns handed down over generations, decked out in hide, sealskin, and beading inspired by Inuit history. Other than one specific clause, what they had accomplished would be—for me—one of the most successful and comprehensive land claims of our generation. These people were finally going to take their place in their homeland, and they were going to get the benefits that they deserved.

While I supported the overall agreement, there was this one clause that extinguished the rights of all Labrador Inuit outside of their land claim area; this included all the members of NunatuKavut Community Council. As I said in the House and happily repeat now, "I am in full support of a land claim agreement for the Inuit people of Northern Labrador and have applauded the work that they have done, both their president, their board of directors, the leadership in the organization." However, despite assurances from the provincial government and the minister responsible that there was no intent to deprive the Labrador Métis Nation of an opportunity to pursue a land claim or a self-government agreement based on their Inuit heritage, the bill itself provided no such assurance. The northern Inuit land claim and subsequently the self-government agreement that created Nunatsiavut included language that might do exactly that.

Moreover, when combined with their rules around who was and was not a beneficiary, which was connected to time and place of birth, there was a risk that the children or grandchildren of beneficiaries could lose their rights in the future, and this is exactly what has happened. In fact, many of these Inuit descendants have lost their rights, sometimes because of who they married or in other cases because of where they happened to be born, if it was outside the Nunatsiavut territory. None of this should really matter if someone is of that bloodline—especially where they are born. What matters is the connection to Inuit culture, tradition, way of living, and blood relationships through their parents and grandparents. I did try to amend the legislation to remove that clause, but it was voted down, which was unfortunate given the course of events that followed.

I wonder what they thought of me as I sat alone and took that vote to defeat the claim, the only MHA to do so. I cried over this because it touched me deeply; I was so proud of the northern Inuit. Their resilience and sacrifice through the years of colonialism and their success in overcoming it was unbelievable to imagine in my lifetime. After 30 years of strong negotiations pushing ahead, they were finally getting the recognition they deserved. They were ready to take their place, take their homeland back, affirm who they are as a people and culture—and deep down, I celebrated this wonderful victory with them.

However, I was torn; I knew there was no other option for me, simply because of one line in the agreement, which stated that on the coming into force of this legislation it would eradicate the rights of all other Inuit in Labrador, including the rights of central and Southern Labrador Inuit, and those who descended from Inuit culture. They would be abandoned and no longer recognized for their heritage or for their culture, for who they are as people.

I was one of those southern Inuit and I thought this was wrong, not just for myself but for my ancestors and for those people who lived all around me. I was a descendant of my great-grandmother, whose only identification lay in a church record from 1847 where she was listed as Annie the Eskimo. How do you vote to eradicate yourself and your own Inuit roots? It just doesn't happen.

It probably doesn't mean much today to most people, but it still means a lot to me. I still know that I made the right decision; I had to stand up for other Inuit in Labrador, even those not yet born. One day they, too, might have their status challenged. I had to stand up for my ancestors, for my grandmothers and the grandmothers of others, who spent many years on these lands— thousands of years—and where remnants of their old houses and their tent circles still remain.

There was a community event in Nain months after the vote; I got an invitation to go, and I went. I wanted to show them how proud I was of them, how much I respected them for all their work and for their success. I wanted them to understand that I believe children born of even one Inuit parent in the north or south should not lose their rights, but should count in Canada and in the lands of their ancestors, and that all the Inuit in Labrador should be included. If they are descended from the Inuit of Nunatsiavut, they should have the same rights and recognition as all others. Time has moved on, and the southern and central Inuit have taken a different path, but we are still one people.

The issue of Indigenous identity in Canada is complicated, as seen by the many changes to the Indian Act regarding who has status—particularly in light of the equality rights provisions of the 1982 Constitution—and court cases determining what it means to be Métis. Various treaties, dating back to the eighteenth century or negotiated in later years, most recently in 1921, make it more complex, as do various land claims provisions and self-government agreements, each of which define who is or isn't a beneficiary.

I am a descendant of Inuit ancestors, and I've often had to defend that to others or, indeed, to encourage other people who look like me to understand and embrace their heritage. It is hurtful to be told by others—whether they are European colonists or other Indigenous people—that I am not who I understand myself to be. The Innu Nation leadership has been particularly aggressive, essentially saying that we, the descendants of southern Inuit, are imposters or cheats. Despite that, on one level I have good relations with the Innu, with the communities and individuals.

My first experience with the Innu was when I was working in Happy Valley-Goose Bay as a journalist with *The Labradorian*. At that time, the Innu—who had been a nomadic people following the caribou and the fish from Quebec to the coast of Labrador and back—had been settled into two communities in Labrador: Sheshatshiu, located near Goose Bay, and Davis Inlet, on the northern coast between Hopedale and Nain. Davis Inlet residents were relocated in 2002 to the new community of Natuashish.

In the late 1980s, there were a lot of low-level military training flights out of the base in Goose Bay, and the Innu were protesting them, citing damages to the caribou and to human health. They would protest at the base and on the runways and would be arrested and hauled away. Yet the next day, they would be back: men, women, children, and Elders, to protest. I covered it for *The Labradorian* and for the Canadian Press, and was astounded at the courage and convictions of these people, and the intelligence of their arguments and the evidence they had gathered.

I met a lot of the leaders, like Ben Michel, Daniel Ashini, and Bart Jack, and got to know them for the couple of years I was there. Many of them have passed away now, gone to the spirit world. Others, like Elizabeth Penashue, continue to inspire a strong bid by Innu to take control of their lands and waters. As the MP for the region, I've worked closely and successfully on community problems like the need for better infrastructure, housing, senior care, and addiction issues.

It is hard for me to understand the opposition of other Indigenous groups to the interests of NunatuKavut Community Council. Certainly, there are overlapping claim areas, but these have been negotiated successfully in other places—the Inuit and Cree of Northern Quebec, for example. Some are worried over the allocation of funds for social programs or economic development, but the federal government has shown its willingness to come up with new money, and fighting over money is counterproductive. For example, the development of Mealy Mountains National Park has been delayed for years by these disputes. Much of the proposed park is in Southern Labrador, but both the Innu Nation and Nunatsiavut Government have overlapping claims in the area, and the refusal of the Innu Nation, particularly, to participate in negotiations on the park has delayed it—and the subsequent economic development that would benefit all parties—for years, with no end in sight.

In the meantime, NunatuKavut Community Council continues to grow and develop. Many people who have lost their rights and beneficiary status as an Indigenous person in the north, and whose Inuit family connections move between the north and south coasts of Labrador, are now members of NCC. With more Inuktitut speakers and people wanting to reclaim their ancestral language, we are seeing Inuktitut being taught in schools and a greater emphasis placed on traditional cultural activities and economies.

Labrador is the place where I belong. It is so important to me; it reaches deep into my heart. I don't know if anything touches my soul more intensely than Labrador. It doesn't matter what part of the land I travel over, or what season of the year it is, Labrador is always spectacularly beautiful in my eyes. When I am there, something wells up from deep inside me, a profound sense of belonging and pride in the place I come from.

When I come back from Ottawa and I'm feeling stressed by all the work, I will often head out of town by myself on my snowmobile or bike and spend an afternoon or a day out on the land. It is very relaxing and energizing, and I don't think I could carry on if it weren't for my time out there, appreciating the gifts that were bestowed upon us.

As MP, I continue to fight for more funding, better programs, and increased local control for all three Indigenous groups, and I pray that one day they will see that by joining forces and supporting each other, they can make Labrador stronger, more productive, and successful as a territory for all their people.

In the end, I know who I am because Labrador tells me. I am and always will be from NunatuKavut, descendant of both Inuit and European settlers. I am also, first and foremost, a Labradorian. I know that one day, we will be united by our common experiences, our shared love of this place, and by the pride we feel in meeting the challenges Labrador throws our way.

CHAPTER 18

LABRADOR, UNITED AND STRONG

I love Labrador and the people who live there with all my heart. No matter where I go in this great country or in this wide world, I am only truly at home and at peace when I am back in Labrador. I know the people of Labrador are resilient, hard-working, and smart; they have demonstrated those qualities repeatedly through the years. They are strong and independent, but they also embrace the importance of family and community and of working together for the common good. We have done so much, but there is so much left to do.

Since I first entered politics as mayor of Mary's Harbour, my mantra has always been that the development of the economy of Labrador should, first and foremost, benefit the people who live there. Right from the beginning, the principle of adjacency—that those who live closest to the resource should gain most from its development—has been at the heart of my politics.

To me this seemed utterly logical, and I was often surprised when others thought differently, yet gaining benefits for the people of Labrador from the resources on land or offshore was something I always had to fight for, as did every generation of Labradorians.

My primary focus as a first-time provincial MHA was the construction of the Trans-Labrador Highway. Money had been given by the federal government to the provincial government as part of the transfer of marine ferry services. That money had been designated for the development of transportation infrastructure in Labrador, but as I described earlier, it was sometimes hard going to get that work done in a timely and comprehensive manner. I won a lot of battles, but I still smart over the ones I lost and the damage that was done to several communities as a result. I continue to advocate and negotiate for ongoing improvements of the existing road as well as an extension of highways to northern parts of Labrador—an increasingly important project as climate change wreaks havoc on traditional travel over sea ice and on the land.

The Voisey's Bay agreement, which was negotiated and signed while I was a member of the Tobin/Grimes governments in 2001–2002, enshrined the principle of local benefits and ensured that jobs and business opportunities went first to the Indigenous people on whose traditional lands the development took place, and secondly to other residents of Labrador. While I can claim no direct credit for the contents of that agreement, I know that my continuous advocacy of this approach supported the thinking of those who negotiated the final benefit agreement. To this day, the Voisey's Bay mine continues to deliver significant benefits to the people of Labrador as well as royalty and tax revenues to the Government of Newfoundland and Labrador.

Even the deeply flawed Churchill Falls agreement with Quebec contained opportunities to benefit the local economy, through the reserve power clause that set aside a portion of the generated power for specific use in developing the Labrador economy. This reserve power was never, in my view, exploited effectively for that purpose, but again, it was not from lack of trying on my part or on the part of fellow Labradorians. The same can be said for the ongoing development of the Lower Churchill, including Muskrat Falls. Plans for power production and transmission frequently left Labrador needs by the wayside, including the Voisey's Bay nickel mine (ironically a key ingredient for electric cars), which remains reliant on diesel generation. Recent speculation that ongoing problems with the transmission system might lead to a repurposing of the electricity to power industrial developments in the region is heartening for the people of Labrador, but would be a painful outcome for the taxpayers and power users of the province, as it always calls into question the investment required. However, without clean, stable power, all resource projects in Labrador will be limited in their potential, as will the province's ability to grow and expand future opportunities. In light of that, I was very pleased to announce, in the fall of 2024, the funding for the engineering of the second transmission line between Churchill Falls and Labrador West.

Too many decisions regarding infrastructure and economic development in Labrador have been made by and in the interests of people who don't live there. When locals were able to take control of the process, they had notable successes. I've mentioned the Labrador Fishermen's Union Shrimp Company as a shining example of what can happen when local people are able to exert control over their resources. They have succeeded, when all around them larger corporate entities have failed. Similarly, the increasing number of Indigenous development companies set up and run by local Indigenous governments have provided a great deal of stability to many communities by building a skilled workforce locally and fostering small- and medium-scale businesses. These are designed to take advantage of development opportunities for the benefit of their members—that is, the people who have lived in Labrador for generations.

As I've often said, being in Opposition can be rewarding as a politician, revealing government failures and forcing them to do better. However, there is a real advantage to being in government, too, especially if it is an activist one whose core value is to support and grow the middle class. You don't do that by focusing on corporate interests or by benefiting urban centres while neglecting rural and remote regions. Since October 2015, I've been proud to serve in such a government, playing an active role in caucus advocating for Labrador, while working as a Parliamentary Secretary to deliver the goods to northern territories and peoples.

In the last eight years, more money has been spent by the federal government supporting individuals, businesses, and communities in Labrador than ever before. As well, the federal government and its provincial partners have worked closely with local people and Indigenous organizations to empower them to take their future into their own hands. Especially during the pandemic years of 2020 to 2022, federal funding has been instrumental in keeping families together and businesses open. It also served as a backstop to the long-term approach that had begun in 2015 and will continue.

The future strength of Labrador will be galvanized as we extend the idea of working together beyond the neighbourhood and community to encompass the length and breadth of Labrador. Currently, there is too much dissension among the three Indigenous groups that dwell in Labrador: Nunatsiavut Government, Innu Nation, and NunatuKavut Community Council. The first represents the Inuit of Northern Labrador; the second, the Innu people who mostly reside in the two communities of Sheshatshiu and Natuashish; the last, the descendants of southern and central Inuit and European settlers. The three groups have their own distinct cultures and territories, but have overlapping claims and interests with each of the other two groups.

Of these peoples, only Nunatsiavut Government has a settled land claim and self-government agreement. The negotiation of this settlement was accelerated after it was determined by a joint study that the establishment of a national park was feasible in 1998. The impending development of the Voisey's Bay mine in 2002 added further impetus to the need to create certainty over land ownership and governance rights. The Land Claim Agreement, which is constitutionally protected, was passed into law in June 2005 and Nunatsiavut Government created its own constitution. An overlap agreement was initialled with the Innu Nation that same year.

The Innu Nation land claim was accepted for negotiation by the federal government in 1978, the same year negotiations started with the northern Inuit. However, it has yet to be settled, though significant progress was made in 2008 with the signing of the New Dawn Agreement between the Innu and the Government of Newfoundland and Labrador, which resolved a number of issues between the two parties. An agreement in principle (AIP) was signed by all three governments—federal, provincial, and Innu Nation—in 2012 but has not yet reached final agreement status. At the time of this writing, the Innu Nation is suing the federal and provincial governments for what it believes are violations of the terms of the AIP and other agreements under the umbrella of the New Dawn process.

Meanwhile, the NunatuKavut Community Council followed a different path. They began to come together as an organization a few years after the others. All three Indigenous groups had been encouraged by the Calder decision in 1973, made by the Supreme Court of Canada in a case brought by Frank Calder and other Nisga'a Elders in British Columbia. This decision recognized the existence of Aboriginal title. The settlement two years later of the first land claim in Canada—the James Bay and Northern Quebec

Agreement in 1975—was also encouraging. However, it took until 1981 for a formal structure for southern Inuit to appear in the form of the Labrador Métis Association. In 1991, the LMN filed its statement of intent under the comprehensive land claims process, with subsequent submissions thereafter. In 2010, after extensive research traced the ancestry of southern Inuit—including myself—to those who signed a treaty with the British in 1765, they changed their name to NunatuKavut Community Council and relaunched their claim. In September 2019, the federal government signed a memorandum of understanding with the NCC that recognized them as an Indigenous group as defined by Section 35 of the Constitution. This MOU opened the door for negotiations to proceed.

Unfortunately, both the Innu Nation and Nunatsiavut Government have objected to the MOU. The Innu Nation went to court to try and quash it; they lost the case and were required to pay legal damages. While Nunatsiavut Government acknowledges that NCC members do have Inuit ancestry—it's hard to deny, since family relationships between the two groups is well documented—it maintains they were not historically a collective entitled to claim rights and land. The same might have been said of many Indigenous groups whose communities were fragmented by colonial actions in Canada.

Natan Obed, the head of the Inuit Tapiriit Kanatami (ITK), the national representative organization for Inuit in Canada, also objected, saying there can be no Inuit outside the region covered by existing settlement areas. I think this perspective held by the ITK has instigated lateral violence. Todd Russell, head of the NCC, responded by saying that Obed has no right to define who is or is not Inuit, which is consistent with the provisions of the UN Declaration on the Rights of Indigenous Peoples (UNDRIP), which Canada endorsed in 2010 but only formally adopted and became a signatory to in 2016.

I certainly understand why existing Indigenous organizations might adopt this position. Historically, Canada and the provinces have been reluctant to acknowledge Indigenous rights and are parsimonious in supporting Indigenous communities. Canada went from the White Paper of 1969, which would have revoked all treaties and rights and fully assimilated Indigenous people, to the 1982 Constitution, which enshrined those rights and recognized Indigenous people as a permanent and distinct part of Canada. Given that both documents were authored by governments headed by Pierre Trudeau, it was a tremendous shift in thinking—driven by public protests, high-profile court cases, and vigorous debate.

Despite that significant victory, Indigenous people have had to constantly go to court to make the government abide by the terms of treaties and agreements, which they had willingly signed, but failed repeatedly to implement. In almost every case they won, and gradually the entrenched colonial mentality of governments began to shift. This movement reached its pinnacle in 2015 with the release of the Truth and Reconciliation Commission Reports and the adoption of reconciliation as a central component of the new government headed by Justin Trudeau.

Still, most Indigenous groups in Canada have a long memory. For years their communities, schools, and health care systems have been underfunded by the federal government, their land claims agreements have been ignored, and they have been pitted one against the other with the mantra of "there is only so much to go around." For the Innu Nation in particular, whose land claim has been stalled at the AIP stage for over a decade, it must be concerning to see another claimant group on their borders, claiming benefits and control over the same land they have traditionally occupied.

Indigenous people have always had conflicts over land and resources, dating from long before the Europeans arrived. The vast majority of these were settled peacefully, creating the central

Indigenous value of sharing, which greeted and benefited the new arrivals from across the ocean. But what they were willing to share, the settlers decided to take entirely for their own. It has been a long struggle to right that wrong, one which continues to this day.

That history of sharing is reflected in the many overlap agreements signed by neighbouring Indigenous nations through the modern treaty-making process. These agreements were demanded by successive governments—perhaps as a further roadblock to settlement—but were negotiated solely by the affected nations. They proved to be much quicker and less confrontational in reaching settlements than their settler government counterparts.

I believe that there is more than enough to go around. Recent settlements by the federal Liberal government related to the foster care system and other historic inequities have shown their willingness to fix what was broken in the past. When previous settlements have proved inadequate, they have been willing to sit down and negotiate to reach a mutually acceptable solution. The process is far from seamless, but we are all still on a learning curve.

Labrador is a vast land and the people who live on it have a long history of sharing resources. While there have been notable conflicts in the past, especially between Indigenous groups and settlers, solutions have frequently been found that were amicable, if not perfect. It is my sincere hope that that the Innu Nation and the NCC are able to negotiate successfully to achieve their goals with both federal and provincial governments, and in the process can sit down together, as the Innu did with the northern Inuit, to share the bounty of our land and sea so that both benefit from the vast natural resources they contain.

I have always tried to work with everyone in Labrador—even in the face of slurs and accusations of bias—and will continue to do so. I may be a member of the NCC and deeply proud of both my Inuit and settler heritage, but I am a Labradorian first and I have learned over my career that what benefits one part of Labrador inevitably benefits all parts of Labrador.

Still, it is disheartening to live in a society where some people want to ridicule one another and direct violence and racism toward their neighbours. Leaders of Indigenous governments have shown anything but leadership when it comes to forging relationships in which all Indigenous people in Labrador can take part. There is room for all Indigenous people in the Big Land. It is a not a matter of who has the *most* blood ties but a simple question of ancestry, heritage, culture, and the understanding of who we are that grant people inherent Indigenous rights.

I always hoped and believed that all Indigenous groups would come together to make Labrador stronger, but as time goes by, even my eternal optimism starts to fade. As the MP for all of Labrador, this often puts me in a difficult position. Because I identify as southern and central Inuit, I've been asked by some Indigenous leaders in the Innu Nation to leave meetings or had them walk out of meetings because of my heritage, not because of the work I've done or the issues I've supported unconditionally—often issues that were central to their own objectives. Recently, I arranged a tour by charter plane to Voisey's Bay and invited representatives from all three Indigenous groups to take part. The Innu Nation and Nunatsiavut Government refused to put representatives on the plane because, in their view, members of the NCC had no right to go to Voisey's Bay. I let the invitation stand and they refused to go.

I am not alone in facing this kind of bitterness and animosity. Recent calls for the resignation of Lisa Dempster as Minister of Indigenous Affairs in the Newfoundland and Labrador government by Nunatsiavut Government came because of her membership in the NCC and her heritage as a southern and central Inuit, not for anything she said or did wrong as Minister. This is a dangerous precedent and one that can only sow dissent and bitterness when we desperately need to come together to build a better Labrador. Leaders are pitting one group against another, neighbours against neighbours, brothers and sisters against brothers and sisters. It is wrong, it is hateful, and it has no place in our society. It is not for me to determine who is Indigenous in Labrador and who isn't, nor is it the role of Nunatsiavut Government, Innu Nation, or the NCC. It is the role of the *people* who occupied this land to make their case for their inherent rights. We know that southern and central Inuit have rights in Canada. They know who they are. The Government of Canada knows who they are. Whether they have a collective right (which I believe they do) may be at the centre of this debate, but there is no reason to dismiss the harm that they have suffered or to diminish the impact the residential school system had on many of them.

What right does a leader or government of an Indigenous body in Labrador have to diminish the suffering of residential school survivors simply because of their heritage and lineage? We all know the atrocities that were committed. They may not all have been committed equally, thankfully, but we do know that harm came to many. They were innocent children and did not ask for these punishments and did not ask to be removed from their homes and their culture and the people they loved. What I'm seeing today is a further assimilation of those people who were survivors, further denial of who they are and where they come from, further attempts to deny or destroy their Indigenous identity.

We must all have confidence and faith in each other. There has to be a level of trust amongst Labradorians, or nothing can succeed, and without success, we all fail. Labradorians—even all of us taken together—are such a small number of people and will always be a small number of people. Unless we get ourselves together collectively as a passionate group of people that wants to put Labrador first, we will not move the dial. If everyone continues to just want to work in silos, in hatred across the kilometres of mountains and bogs and rivers in Labrador, we are never going to bridge the way to a better future for all of our children and that, to me, is very sad.

Let's imagine a different future.

Let's suppose, for a minute, that all three claims are settled and agreements are forged between the three nations. I think there is another step that could then be taken. My work with the Combined Councils of Labrador—formed in 1972 to address issues common to all municipalities in the Northern region, and eventually including all Labrador communities—showed me that we can come together on a regional basis and across ethnic lines to co-operate and forge solutions that benefit us all. In recent years, I've spent a great deal of time travelling across the Canadian North, looking at how the Northwest Territories has dealt with similar governance issues. As an MP, I took the lead for my party in debating the act that devolved the final federal powers to the government of the Northwest Territories. I have to say I was envious of their new-found autonomy, and I admire the way they and a half a dozen Indigenous nations, some with settled claims, others still in negotiation, could work out shared governance systems.

I have sometimes felt Labrador might be better off on its own, perhaps as a separate territory, or at least as a semi-autonomous region. After all, it has a history of moving around from jurisdiction to jurisdiction since 1763, with both Newfoundland and Quebec having control of all or part from time to time; the question of who it belonged to was only settled in 1927 by the British Privy Council, which granted the current territory to Newfoundland. An interesting footnote to that settlement was that two years earlier, the Government of Newfoundland offered to sell Labrador to Quebec, but was turned down by the then-Premier of Quebec.

It is, of course, unlikely that the current or any future government of Newfoundland and Labrador would agree to secession, given the vast resources known to exist or yet to be discovered in the region. Nor do I think that most Labradorians want to completely cut their ties to the island of Newfoundland—there are many family ties and a shared history that is important. Still, if the three Indigenous groups can have their own governments within a united province, perhaps there is room for a pan-Labrador assembly with representatives from the three Indigenous governments and the significant settler communities. The province could delegate or devolve powers and responsibilities to this regional body. I've always thought such an arrangement would be more flexible and responsive to local needs than the government bureaucracy that is located largely in St. John's. It is certainly a concept to which I'd be happy to devote my energies in the future. Strengthening local relationships between Indigenous governments is key to Labrador's progress.

Regardless of whether such a semi-autonomous region might be created, Labrador and Newfoundland are, as I've said, inextricably linked by bonds of family, culture, and history. We are both stronger together than we are apart, in terms of wealth and political power within Confederation. I always believed that those bonds could be made even stronger through the construction of a fixed link joining the two parts. For more than twenty years, I've argued for the building of a tunnel connecting us under the Strait of Belle Isle. After decades of being largely ignored, I was gratified when the pre-feasibility study of 2004 was expanded and updated in 2018, and even happier when a memorandum of understanding was made between the provincial government and the Canada Infrastructure Bank to look at a fixed link. "The MOU will allow the Canada Infrastructure Bank (CIB) to explore the technical and financial requirements of such a project and move forward to the next step," I said after the announcement. "This is not a study in any way, shape, or form. I don't particularly see a need for another study. What I do see a need for is for them to look at all the research that's been done and move forward with construction."

This would be a major endeavour, costing between $2 billion and $3 billion and taking up to fifteen years to complete. However, the social and economic benefits would be enormous, and the fixed link would eventually pay for itself, increasing provincial and federal revenues. I hope to be around for the ribbon-cutting ceremony.

No place can really call itself a place unless it remembers and celebrates its history. I began my working life in the early 1990s helping to restore the historic site of Battle Harbour. Today it is a major tourist attraction, and more importantly, a centre to celebrate our history as coastal fishers. There are other equally important historic sites at Red Bay and Hopedale.

Remembering Indigenous history is also vitally important, though it is seldom tied to particular communities or old buildings. Rather, it is mapped on the land itself, in the traditional trails and in the way of life on the land or on the coast. The right to hunt, fish, and trap and to maintain a traditional lifestyle is how we remember and preserve this history. This is why settling land rights and gaining official recognition are critically important.

Settling claims and self-government agreements and establishing national parks provide a way to preserve and protect culturally important places—rivers, forests, mountains—for future generations. This has already happened in the Torngat Mountains, with the full co-operation and participation of the northern Inuit. Work began on creating a national park in the Mealy Mountains many years ago, and a park reserve was created in 2015. However, progress on the finalization of the Mealy Mountains National Park has stalled, in part because of disputes between the three Indigenous governments of Innu Nation, Nunatsiavut Government, and NCC, all of whom claim portions of this area as part of their traditional territory. As with their other disagreements, I sincerely hope this one can be resolved so that this beautiful area gets the full protection it deserves and Labradorians get to share with the world our proud culture and legacy in Canada.

Equally important is the preservation and, in some cases, restoration of Indigenous languages and culture. I grew up living a traditional Indigenous lifestyle, but cannot speak the language other than a few dozen common words. They say you can't miss what you've never had, but in the case of language that simply isn't true. I deeply wish I had been able to learn Inuktitut when I was growing up; it is never too late to learn it, of course, but it requires time and access to do so. It is not too late for the next generation. The federal Liberal government has committed significant funds for language recovery and teaching, and I was thrilled when I witnessed the first Inuit language classes being offered in more schools across Labrador. I was also troubled at the opposition to such classes; they were called cultural appropriation by Nunatsiavut Government, even when they acknowledge the Inuit ancestry of many of the children enrolled. Surely, the preservation of language among the southern Inuit has to strengthen and encourage language learning in their own communities. Again, the motive seems to be a fight over limited resources; I believe the fight should be for more resources instead. I'd happily pitch in for that.

Our history gives us the foundation for building a strong future. The resources of Labrador are virtually limitless. In addition to the abundance of game—and despite the loss of the cod—fish and other marine resources provide a living for the people who harvest them, provided we learn from the lessons of the past and create a sustainable harvest. Our tourism industry has not yet reached its potential and can only grow as transportation improves and community infrastructure expands. The addition of broadband internet will also be a boost to tourism throughout the region—the first question a prospective tourist asks is "Do you have Wi-Fi?"

The commissioning of the Muskrat Falls hydro-generation project is, despite the difficulties experienced, an important milestone in making Labrador a major contributor to green energy in the province and North America. Further development of the Churchill River and other smaller rivers is inevitable, and hopefully the lessons learned from Muskrat Falls will ensure they are better conceived and developed. In the meantime, a number of wind energy projects have reduced our reliance on dirty diesel generators, and the potential for wind, solar, and even wave generation has not yet been fully tapped. A northern highway may also unlock the potential of natural gas off the Labrador coast and the potential for a stable economy—especially in a future impacted heavily by climate change.

Minerals, too, are found in abundance in Labrador, with rich deposits of iron ore and nickel already being exploited. Better roads and cheaper, greener power can only enhance those operations and make other developments, like the rare earth deposits around St. Lewis, manganese in Wabush, and uranium in Northern Labrador more economically viable. Improved mining technology, much of it developed using grants from the federal building back green program will inevitably lead to more minerals being discovered and extracted for generations to come.

The biggest challenge facing the world today is a rapidly changing climate. It poses an existential risk to us all but is particularly hard on northern regions that, as predicted by science, have already experienced massive changes. Thinner and more unpredictable sea ice and snow cover have interfered with, and in some cases destroyed, traditional ways of travelling on the sea and land. This has caused communities to be more isolated, impacting the ability of hunters, trappers, and fishers to pursue a subsistence economy. Food security has been threatened and the mental health of residents is at greater risk.

In Labrador, we watch the stories of out-of-control wildfires in BC and the western Arctic and look to the mass of old trees and bush that surround some of our communities and wonder if we'll be next. In 2024, we *were* next. Labrador City and Churchill Falls were both evacuated and fire suppression support was called in from across the country to combat unprecedented wildfires near the two communities. It is incumbent on governments to support a small forest industry—with subsidies if need be—in order to mitigate the risk to life and property of future fires. All our communities are threatened by climate change, and therefore will require proactive solutions to diminish its impact.

Climate change is not something the people of Labrador can solve on our own; we will always be the victims of it more than the perpetrators. Canada is limited as to what it can do by itself—although we are quickly dropping from being one of the highest per capita emitters of greenhouse gases in the world, we must still do whatever we can—but moving away from fossil fuels to greener sources of energy is essential. Where we do still have to use oil and gas, we need to make it net-zero, both in production and end use, through better technology and carbon offsets. Progress is being made and we are establishing ourselves as a world leader in the race to slow and stop climate change. However, the demands of the economy make it difficult, and are made infinitely harder by those who profit from the carbon economy while paying mere lip service to the dangers of climate change. They have to stop their outright denial of climate impacts and be a part of a progressive solution.

As I've learned through my life so far, every challenge is also an opportunity; the one thing I know about the people of Labrador is that they will seize every opportunity given to them to sustain strong and vibrant communities.

Finally, what does it mean to be a Labradorian?

Many people have asked me that question. It is a difficult one to answer, but I think what defines me as a Labradorian, and most of the people that I have met in my lifetime, is our sense of resilience, our love for the North, and how we embrace the culture of Indigenous and European lifestyles.

To be a Labradorian, you have to feel it in your heart. You have to feel the ground under your feet. You have to be able to envision embracing the vastness of the mountains and straddling the rivers, because nothing in Labrador is easy—but it's all worth the work.

I can close my eyes and imagine myself as I walk across the land. I can hear the scrunch of the frost in the caribou moss under my feet and know that winter is coming. I can smell the scent of black spruce trees and the freshness of vapour rising from the morning dew. I can hear the animals as they gather food and make their homes for winter, because that's the environment I have lived in and experienced. I can feel the fresh, pristine water from the waterfall as it rolls down the mountain crevices and sprays across my face.

I'm awake to the potential of each drop of water, each stretch of bog and forest, each rocky coastline; I open my eyes to see a huge land filled with opportunity, people that are motivated and inspired, and I wonder what direction I will take next, what direction Labradorians will take next.

Because as you know, a new day is just around the corner.

My sincere thanks to Breakwater Books for all their hard work and support. Many thanks to my editor, Jocelyne Thomas, for making my words flow more smoothly and clearly. I thank all the people who have supported and helped me along the way to getting my story out into the world.

I also want to acknowledge the women and girls who continue to forge ahead in the world, opening doors, raising roofs, building bridges, and changing the nasty out there!
#Peace #Unity #respect #equality #YouHaveWhatItTakes

This year, we celebrate the 100th anniversary of the women's suffrage movement in Newfoundland and Labrador. On April 3, 1925, all women aged twenty-five and up—with the exception of those of Asian or Indigenous descent—were granted the right to vote. Later, in 1946, all people over the age of twenty-one were granted that right. My grandparents got to vote for the first time in 1949—in the vote for Confederation with Canada.
#Resilience #WomenRiseUp

Yvonne Jean Rumbolt-Jones was born and raised and has spent her life in Labrador. Of Indigenous descent, she grew up in the isolated Indigenous-settler community of Mary's Harbour in Labrador in the '70s and '80s. Leaving home for college at seventeen, she worked as a journalist for the Robinson-Blackmore chain of weekly papers and later the *Evening Telegram*. Jones has been the mayor of Mary's Harbour, an MHA and party leader in the provincial House of Assembly, and the first MP elected under Justin Trudeau's leadership for the Liberal Party of Canada. She has won nine elections in the past thirty years and is the longest-serving woman from Newfoundland and Labrador in both provincial and federal politics.

If you looked up 'perseverance,'
Yvonne's name would be part of the definition.

The constant sacrifice of one's self can weaken and
shatter faith in society or it can make them stronger, more
determined individuals. Yvonne's commitment to public
service, her patience and ability to move forward has
made her stronger, and NL stronger.

On the night of the 1996 provincial election,
I broke the news to Yvonne Jones live on CBC Radio that she'd
been elected as an Independent Member of the Newfoundland
and Labrador House of Assembly. Not getting the Liberal
nomination didn't hold her back. Nothing has ever held her
back. When she entered the Liberal caucus Jones was relentless
Opposition, holding the government's feet to the fire on issues
ranging from fisheries to child protection. Yvonne Jones
is and has always been a force of nature!

To witness every day your passion, commitment, and
dedication to our beautiful, magnificent Labrador and its
people; to see it never waver even through your own personal
suffering and tragedy amidst an environment where the
ugliness and negativity can consume your soul, has not only
been a sometimes-baffling journey to take with you,
but also a fulfilling and awe-inspiring one.